THE
UINTAH RAILWAY

R. SCHLECHTER '70

THE
UINTAH
RAILWAY
The Gilsonite Route
by Henry E. Bender Jr.

Printed and bound in the United States of America
Library of Congress Control Number 74-135999
Former ISBN: 0-8310-7080-3;
new ISBN: 0-911581-36-7
Revised Edition, 2003

Endpapers: A Uintah Railway train climbs the 7.5% grade on a 65°
curve at Moro Castle heading from Atchee for Baxter Pass. *F.A. Kennedy
photo. Print from glass negative in the collection of V.L. "Roy" McCoy*

Title page: Engine #21, a Baldwin 0-6-2T, rounds a 65° hairpin curve
eastbound between Lookout Point and Windy Point. *F.A. Kennedy
photo, collection of Mallory Hope Ferrell*

Heimburger House Publishing Company
7236 West Madison Street
Forest Park, Illinois 60130

Preface

Narrow gauge fever! Starting with General William Jackson Palmer's Denver & Rio Grande in 1871, the baby railroads spread like wildfire into and over the Rocky Mountains. Within just fifteen years there were more than 1,600 miles of three-foot gauge trackage in the new state of Colorado alone. The advantages of the slim gauge were obvious — with its narrower roadbed and sharper curves the railway could follow the contours and snake its way up the tortuous canyons and over the high passes. Construction costs in the mountains were generally less than half what they would have been for a standard-gauge line. Indeed, in some of the places where the little trains ran, a standard-gauge railroad would have been out of the question!

But the three-foot gauge had its disadvantages, too — chiefly the expense of transferring freight at points of interchange with the nation's system of standard-gauge roads. As quickly as it had come the narrow gauge fever passed. By 1890 the Rio Grande's main line between Denver and Ogden had been widened to four feet eight and a half inches, and the remaining slim gauge lines were reduced to the status of feeders. After that date only a handful of new three-foot lines were built and practically all of these were strictly local lines, usually through rugged and uncompromising terrain. This book is the story of one of the last to be built, The Uintah Railway.

Besides being one of the last, the Uintah Railway was out of the ordinary for at least three other reasons. First was the unusual mineral it was built to carry, a glossy black asphalt-like substanced called gilsonite. Then there was the railway's wholly-owned subsidiary, The Uintah Toll Road Company, operating its wagons and stages over one of the last toll roads in the West. And last, but certainly not least, there was the fantastic grade climbing Baxter Pass — that five long miles of unremitting 7.5 per cent with its many sharp curves which came to be the best known feature of the Gilsonite Route. Though perhaps the Uintah was better known for its two Articulateds, the only narrow-gauge ones in the country, which were built to conquer Baxter Pass.

My work on this book started over five years ago when I was enrolled at the University of Denver. One of the requirements for my M.A. in Librarianship was that I write a research paper or thesis. I had become fascinated with the narrow gauge railroads more than fifteen years earlier when I was not yet in high school. Since no comprehensive study of the line had previously been published, my choice was the Uintah Railway, and the professor, William Stokes, gave his encouragement and approval of the choice. Being from Michigan, as was Ephraim Shay, Professor Stokes was already familiar with Mr. Shay's unique locomotive.

Probably the most pleasant thing for me, as I started digging out the history of the Uintah Railway, was the chance to meet quite a number of the men who made that history. In more ways than one, this book owes its existence to them. I hope they will find it does justice to the story of The Uintah Railway Company.

To Barbara, and for Phillip

Acknowledgments

Many people over the past five years have given freely of their time and have supplied the photographs, information, maps and drawings which have become part of this book. For their invaluable assistance, I am deeply grateful.

First and foremost were the many Uintah railroaders whom I had the pleasure of meeting. Without exception they were enthusiastic about my efforts to put the story of their railway into print, and they generously made available anything and everything they had which would help. More than the hundreds of photographs and many pleasant hours of reminiscing and tape recording, though, these men provided the inspiration. Without them, this book would not have been written. To each of them I express my thanks and the hope that the book lives up to their expectations. They include Bruce Angus who drove teams and trucks for The Uintah Toll Road Company as well as working for the railway; and W. A. Banks who was a member of the original survey party at Baxter Pass in 1903 and later was agent at Watson for many years. J. L. "Jim" Booth was chief dispatcher for years, and E. V. "Vic" Earp fired and ran the engines before being promoted to superintendent in the 1930s. Roy E. Eno and Sam A. High were also enginemen — Eno pulled the throttle of "Mallet" No. 50 when the last train traveled the line in May of 1939. Walt Hyrup fired on the Uintah for just six months or so, while William F. Karr served many years in engine and train service and in the shops at Atchee. Bill Karr also worked for Meyer Goodstein in charge of the dismantling operations after the Uintah was abandoned. George Komatas and Vernon L. "Roy" McCoy were also long-time employees of the Uintah Railway and both were most helpful. Mr. Komatas served as section foreman at Carbonera for most of the life of the Gilsonite Route. Roy McCoy's jobs on the road were many and varied. Last alphabetically, and least in terms of his service on the Uintah Railway, is Eugene Perry, who spent three days in 1928 as a relief section foreman on loan to the Uintah from the D.&R.G.W. Because of deep snow the night he arrived, Mr. Perry never did complete his assigned job of lining track, but years later he started the ball rolling for me. He was the first railroader I met who had worked on the Gilsonite Route and he gave me the names of one or two others who, in turn, led me to still more.

Relatives and friends of these and other former Uintah men were also of considerable help. My thanks to Mrs. Angus, Mrs. Banks and Mrs. Earp, and also to Mr. and Mrs. Charles W. Baxter, W. E. Booth, Frank "Red" Davies, Mr. and Mrs. Robert O. Perkins, Mrs. Margaret Shafer Romager and Mrs. Beverly G. Whyler. Many of the excellent photographs on these pages are from their collections. In many cases two or more prints of the same picture were available from different sources. This happened frequently with some of the fine work from F. A. "Judge" Kennedy's 5x7 camera, enabling the publisher to choose the print which would make the best reproduction.

Other residents of western Colorado and northeastern Utah who helped in my research were Mrs. W. E. Bowen of Mack, Mrs. Carl Frey, Frank Jonick, Kent J. Jorgensen of American Gilsonite Company, former Atchee Postmistress Ruby Luton, Carl F. Schubert, L. C. Thorne, Mr. and Mrs. Reinhold F. Uhleman, Mr. and Mrs. G. E. Untermann of the Utah Field House of Natural History in Vernal, and Mrs. Sue Watson of the

Daughters of the Utah Pioneers. Thanks, too, to J. V. Kelly of Kelly's Rock Shop which occupies what remains of the old Uintah Railway Hotel in Mack. He had the foresight to save a number of the Kennedy glass-plate negatives.

My special thanks goes to two men from this area. Roy F. Blackburn not only loaned his own fine Uintah Railway negatives for printing but then did considerable last-minute leg work for me. In response to my frantic letters, Roy measured an old passenger car body, contacted other railroaders to get questions answered, and spent many hours going through the dusty back files and microfilm of the Grand Junction *Daily Sentinel*. Charles J. Neal of Vernal, who knows much of the history of the gilsonite industry from personal experience, supplied many photos of the gilsonite mines and the railway and toll road operations as well as such gems as the original final survey maps of the Uintah Railway's Baxter Pass route.

To many of my fellow librarians goes my appreciation for their professional help. The Western History Department of the Denver Public Library has an excellent collection and librarians to match — Jim Davis, Mrs. Alys Freeze and Mrs. Opal Harber. The same goes for the Colorado State Historical Society Library; my thanks to Mrs. Enid T. Thompson, Mrs. Laura A. Ekstrom and Miss Susan A. Nieminen there. The University of Utah Libraries loaned Newell Remington's thesis, *A History of the Gilsonite Industry*, and the many reels of microfilm of The Vernal *Express*. Also of assistance were Mrs. Renze and Mrs. Churchill of the Colorado Division of State Archives and Public Records; Lorena Jones of the Denver *Post*; Jan Cumbie, Dennis North and Mrs. Julie Todd of the University of Denver Libraries; A. L. Mueller of the Colorado Public Utilities Commission; Mrs. Linda Kelley of IBM Corporation; Mrs. Alley of the U. S. Geological Survey Library; and the staffs of the University of California Libraries at Berkeley, the Grand Junction Public Library, the Grand Junction *Daily Sentinel* and the Stanford University Libraries.

Messrs. Roy E. Nelson, president, and Earl H. Owen, secretary and treasurer, of American Gilsonite Company kindly furnished the photographs and information on the present-day operations of their firm, and gave permission to use copyrighted material from the *Gilsonite Guidebook*.

Then there were the many railroad historians, photographers, and ferroequinologists — students of the iron horse. The excellent cartographic work and painstakingly detailed passenger and freight car drawings are from the pen of David W. Braun of Sacramento. Two other experts at the fine art of making accurate scale drawings, Ken Pruitt and Robert Schlechter, provided the beautiful plans of Mallet No. 51 and Shay No. 1. Mr. Schlechter also did the dust jacket and frontispiece water color of the Articulated at Moro Castle. The remainder of the list is long and includes many of the deans of the hobby. For their photographic skill or those bits of knowledge needed to fill the gaps, my sincere thanks to Frank Barry, Gerald M. Best, Stanley T. Borden, James E. Boynton, Herbert L. Broadbelt, Lawrie Brown, Robert W. Brown of *Finelines* magazine, Ray W. Buhrmaster, Jr., Everett L. DeGolyer, Jr., Donald Duke, Guy Dunscomb, Charles T. Felstead, Howard Fogg, Paul Garde, Del H. Gerbaz, W. Oliver Gibson, Leonard N. Gilliland, Vernon J. Glover, Jr., Clifford D. Grant, Robert C. Gray, Hank Griffiths, Robert M. Hanft, Cornelius W. Hauck of the Colorado Railroad Museum, Joseph P. Hereford, Jr., Jack M. Holst, Paul D. Howard of Freight-Master Division of Halliburton Services, R. B. Jackson, Richard H. Kindig, Michael Koch, Robert LeMassena, Edward Mahoney, Terry Mangan, James Ozment, P. E. Percy of Lima, Ohio, formerly with Baldwin-Lima-Hamilton Corporation, Otto C. Perry, Dirk Ramsey, R. D. "Dan" Ranger, Jr., Bill Reynolds, Robert W. Richardson of the Colorado Railroad Museum, Doug S. Richter, Ernest W. Robart, Richard A. Ronzio, Charles S. Ryland, Kent Stephens, Steve G. Swanson, Jackson C. Thode, F. Hol Wagner, Jr., Dr. S. R. Wood and Ted G. Wurm.

And finally thanks to my wife Barbara, who was left in a museum on our honeymoon while I went looking for more Uintah Railway photos and who sent me back to the typewriter on numerous occasions since then when I was procrastinating.

HENRY E. BENDER JR.

San Jose, California
May 1970

Contents

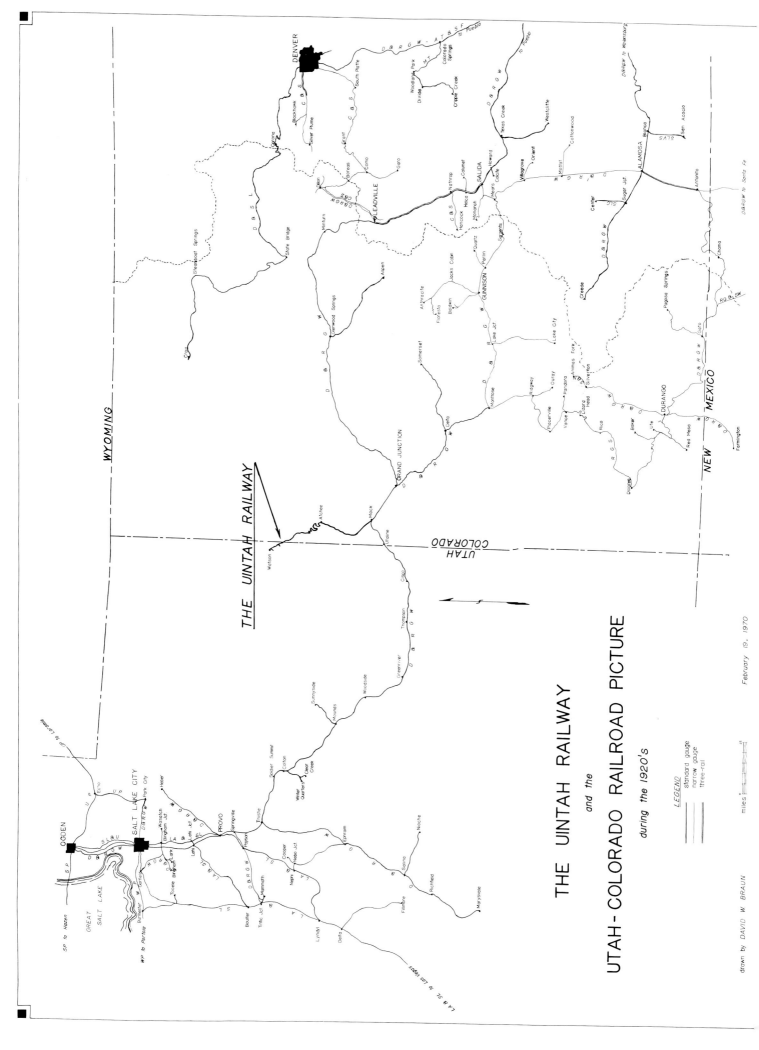

THE UINTAH RAILWAY

and the

UTAH-COLORADO RAILROAD PICTURE

during the 1920's

THE UINTAH RAILWAY

drawn by DAVID W BRAUN

February 19, 1970

LEGEND

standard gauge
narrow gauge
three-rail

miles 0 25

WYOMING

UTAH | COLORADO

NEW MEXICO

DENVER

SALT LAKE CITY

OGDEN

PROVO

GRAND JUNCTION

LEADVILLE

SALIDA

GUNNISON

ALAMOSA

DURANGO

GREAT SALT LAKE

Chapter One

Gilsonite — The Reason for a Railroad

In the northeastern part of Utah and across the border into Colorado, at an elevation of 5,000 to 6,000 feet, lies a great natural valley. It is sparsely settled and rather arid, except where irrigation water from the neighboring mountains has made it green and productive. From the western part of Colorado, this basin runs to the west one hundred and seventy miles to the rugged profile of the Wasatch Range in Utah, with a breadth of almost one hundred miles for most of this distance. The northern rim is formed by the snow-capped Uintas, which include the highest point in the state of Utah, 13,498 foot Kings Peak. And the southern extent of the basin is bounded by the Book Cliffs (or the Roan Plateau) which for two hundred miles present a line of almost unbroken cliffs rising over two thousand feet in height above the valley floor.

A railroad map shows this large basin to be situated about halfway between the Union Pacific on the north and the Denver and Rio Grande Western on the south. It is separated from the former by the Uintas and from the latter by the Book Cliffs, at a distance of over one hundred miles in either direction. The western end of David Moffat's Denver, Northwestern and Pacific Railway, which later became the Denver and Salt Lake and is now a part of the Rio Grande, points toward the basin. But nearly three hundred miles still separate these rails from Utah's capital city — the length of the basin and then some.

Only one railroad ever penetrated the mountain ramparts which surround the Uintah Basin

and cut it off from the rest of the world. And even this narrow-gauge line, which took the Basin's name for its own, never got more than a few miles into the southeastern corner of the Basin.

The word *Uintah* or *Uinta* comes from the language of the Utes, who roamed this land many years before the white man first trod here. And it has been applied to a number of natural features and political divisions throughout the region. The word Uintah is reported to be derived from the Ute word *Uimpahugump*, meaning: the stream of water at the edge of the pine, or the place where two mountain streams come together making a point of land between the streams where the long-needled pine grows. It is said to refer to such a place on the south slopes of the Uinta Mountains north of the present town of Whiterocks. The band of Utes who lived at this place came to be known to the other Utes and then to the white man as Uintahs. The river draining the area took the same name and was at first known as Winty or Tewinty, and later as Uintah or Uinta (with the same pronunciation) by the whites.[1] The National Board of Geographic Names applies the spelling *Uinta* to the mountain range, river and other geographic features, and the spelling *Uintah* to political subdivisions such as the county, Indian reservation and national forest.[2] Despite this ruling, the spelling with the final "h" is more common for the basin itself. Both words are pronounced, *Yew-in-tah.*

Cut off as it was by mountain ranges and high mesas with few practical passes through them, the

11

Uintah Basin remained in the backwashes and eddies of the advancing tide of westward movement. None of the important trade routes or the trails to California and the Pacific Coast passed through the Basin. Most of the Forty-niners, Mormons and other cross-country travelers of the mid-Nineteenth Century preferred the easier route up the North Platte and the Sweetwater and over South Pass, well to the north of the Uinta Range. Or they travelled hundreds of miles to the south of the Basin to pass through New Mexico and Arizona and south of the impassible Grand Canyon of the Colorado. It was not, indeed, until a few months after the Declaration of Independence was signed in Philadelphia that any white men even entered the Uintah Basin.

These first explorers were two Franciscan friars, Fathers Silvestre Vélez de Escalante and Francisco Domínguez, who set out boldly to the northwest from Santa Fé on July 29, 1776. They were accompanied by a map-maker and two other Spaniards, supported by four half-breeds or Indians, and supplied by the governor of New Mexico. They were engaged in an attempt to find an overland route to the newly-founded settlement of Monterey in California. Failing magnificently, they made their way back to Santa Fé on the 2nd of January, 1777, after an almost continuous journey covering fifteen hundred miles in a great circuit through the present states of New Mexico, Colorado, Utah and Arizona. But they did explore and map a large portion of the Intermountain West while looking for the route to Alta California.[3] Traversing the rugged San Juans of southwestern Colorado after leaving Santa Fé, Escalante and his party made their way to the junction of the Gunnison and the Uncompahgre rivers, presently the location of Delta, Colorado, then looped east and north and west around and across Grand Mesa, crossing the Colorado near the present town of DeBeque. From there they journeyed northwest and north across the Roan Plateau, turning west near the present site of Rangely and traveling the entire length of the Uintah Basin westward toward Utah Lake. They first crossed the Green River near what is now the town of Jensen on September 13, 1776.[4]

After Father Escalante's party passed that way, nearly a half century elapsed before another white man set foot in the vastness of the Uintah Basin.

Then, in the 1820s and 1830s various fur trappers and traders, including some of the better-known "mountain men" of the West, penetrated the region. General William Henry Ashley of the Rocky Mountain Fur Company brought a group of trappers into the Basin in 1825 and established a trading post along the White River. His name remains inscribed on maps of the area. The Frenchman Antoine Robidoux also established a trading post and gathering place for the trappers and explorers near the Basin's present village of Whiterocks. Well-known frontiersman Kit Carson wintered in the Basin in 1837, and in 1844 Captain John C. Fremont crossed the Basin on the return trip of his second great expedition. But like Escalante these men, too, were to be only temporary residents of this formidable land. The Indians eventually destroyed the few trading posts, and for another three or four decades few white men ventured into the valley to disturb them.

Brigham Young's famous trek with his pioneering band of Mormons from Nauvoo, Illinois, to the shores of Great Salt Lake has been chronicled by many historians. He and his followers were notably successful in irrigating the desert and establishing their farms and cities. They were followed by numerous additional groups of Mormon immigrants, many of them pushing two-wheeled hand carts loaded with their belongings across the plains. In time the Utah Territory grew and prospered. But even this great immigration starting in the late 1840s was to have no significant effect on the Uintah Basin until decades afterward. Brigham Young's early plans for a State of Deseret in the West envisioned a great self-sufficient empire for his people, and he viewed an outlet to the ocean at San Diego as a part of his plan. For this reason a chain of Mormon settlements stretching south and southwest from Salt Lake toward southern California was established. And the vast Basin to the east across the rugged Wasatch was ignored and left to the Indians. It is estimated that as late as 1878, the year after Brigham Young's death, there were only about 100 white persons in the Uintah Basin. Most of these early white settlers were cattlemen, with a handful of Indian Service employees.

In the early 1860s President Lincoln signed bills setting aside two large areas, comprising practically all of the Uintah Basin, "in perpetuity" for the Utes. The Uintah Utes were given one of these reservations, while the other was for the Uncompahgre Utes, who were moved bag and baggage from their former lands in southwestern Colorado to the new reservation. Then in 1868 Pardon Dodds established the Whiterocks Indian Agency and thus became one of the pioneers of the Basin. It was near this Agency, the following year, that one of the earliest discoveries of the asphaltum which came to be called gilsonite had been reported.

The history of the Uintah Railway, and to a large extent that of the Uintah Basin, is the history of this unusual mineral known as gilsonite. It is a history which begins many millions of years earlier, when the great dinosaurs roamed the then verdant valley. Gilsonite occurs in vertical veins or fissures in the Uinta Formation and occasionally in adjacent formations. These veins run for miles across the Basin in a generally northwest to southeast direction and vary in width from a fraction of an inch to 22 feet. The veins, however, are quite uniform in width over rather long distances. The Uinta Formation is a sandstone and averages about two hundred feet in depth. In deep washes the Formation is comparatively shallow, but measured from high elevations it goes to a depth of more than four hundred feet. The Uinta Formation overlies the Green River shales, one of the richest oil shale beds known. Below the Green River Formation is the Wasatch, which is a hard sandstone, somewhat similar to the Uinta sandstone above.[5] These successive layers were deposited over eons of geological time in the bottom of a very old lake or sea which once covered this area. First the sand on top of the harder bedrock of the Laramie and Montana Formations, then the shale in the form of mud, then more thick deposits of sand on top of the mud. In the course of time the vast area of water disappeared, and the bottom of the lake or sea became elevated and bent into the saucer-like shape of the Basin and the protuberances of the Book Cliff and Uinta Mountains on both sides. In the meantime, with the aid of the tremendous pressures which were causing these land movements, the mud changed to shale and the sand to sandstone. The land movement caused tremendous stresses in the rocks, and the sandstones, being less flexible than the adjacent shale, fractured in many places leaving the north-west-southeast fissures.

According to geologists, the oil or oil-like material in the Green River shale was forced into the widening fissures in the Uinta strata where all but one vein of gilsonite is located. This latter is the Dragon Vein, which exists in a similar fissure in the lower lying Wasatch rock. Evidently the more volatile parts of the oil evaporated at the surface. This evaporation continued until only the asphaltic base remained to harden and form the gilsonite which may be seen today.[6] The exact nature of the process by which the gilsonite was formed is still not entirely clear to geologists. But it is obvious that the parent material was the Green River oil shales, and that large amounts of heat and pressure were present during the transformation.

So we have gilsonite — a lustrous black, solid, asphalt-like hydrocarbon that looks somewhat like anthracite coal, except for the definitely brown dust which it forms. Geologically, it is a rather rare substance, being found in commercial quantities in only one place in the world — the Uintah Basin. Workable veins lie in Duchesne and Uintah Counties in Utah and in adjacent portions of Rio Blanco County, Colorado. Minor deposits of gilsonite-like hydrocarbons have been located in Oregon, Vera Cruz State in Mexico, and Archangel Province in Russia.[7]

Technically, gilsonite is a bitumen, a generic term which includes the petroleums, native asphalts, mineral waxes and asphaltites. More specifically, it is an asphaltite. Abraham, in his comprehensive *Asphalts and Allied Substances*, defines the term *asphaltite* as follows:

A species of bitumen, including dark-colored, comparatively hard and non-volatile solids; composed principally of hydrocarbons, substantially free from oxygenated bodies and crystallizable paraffins; sometimes associated with mineral matter, the non-mineral constituents being difficultly fusible, and largely soluble in carbon disulfide, yielding water-soluble sulfonation products.[8]

This definition of an asphaltite includes the substances gilsonite, glance pitch and grahamite. Gilsonite is differentiated from the latter two by leaving a brown, rather than black, streak; having a specific gravity of 1.03 to 1.10, somewhat lighter than the other two and only slightly heavier than water; and having a softening point between 230° and 350°F., lower than that of grahamite.[9]

The uses for gilsonite have been many and varied down through the years. At the time the Uintah Railway was built in 1904, one of the major commercial uses for gilsonite was in paints, varnishes and japans, to give them a hard, durable, lustrous surface. Henry Ford's "Model T" came in any color you wanted, so long as it was black! For many years gilsonite was a component of the shiny black finish on the "Model T" and other automobiles, and the surreys which preceded them. The advent of multi-colored, quick-drying lacquers largely replaced gilsonite for this use, but the automobile industry still finds it useful for sound proofing and insulating compounds, sealers, battery boxes and brake and clutch linings. Among its many other uses gilsonite has proven valuable in the manufacture of asphalt floor tiles, coated building papers, roofing materials, electrical insulating varnish, acid and alkali resisting paints, oil well cement and drilling muds, printing and rotogravure inks, rope and cable lubricants, fingerprint powders and as a corrosion-resistant thermal insulation for underground steam and hot water pipes.[10] Since 1957, when the production of this mineral increased markedly over what it had ever been previously, a large percentage of all that is mined has been piped, in a water slurry, seventy-three miles across the Book Cliffs to American Gilsonite Company's refinery at Gilsonite, Colorado, west of Grand Junction. There it is refined into high-octane gasoline, a high-grade metallurgical coke and smaller quantities of other petroleum products such as diesel fuel, road oils and paving asphalts.[11]

Despite this potential for so many varied applications, gilsonite was not actually put to commercial use until the late 1880s. Even then it was available only in small quantities and at a rather high cost, primarily because of the expense of the long wagon-haul from the mines to the nearest railroad at Price, Utah. Although gilsonite is reported to have been discovered as much as twenty years earlier, it was not until 1885 that a man came along who suspected that it might have com-

mercial value and started experimenting with it and promoting it. That man was Samuel Henry Gilson.

Although the mineral came to be named for him, Sam Gilson was not its discoverer. Actually, the discovery of gilsonite cannot be credited to any single man with any degree of confidence. Numerous conflicting claims of original or important discoveries of the ore have been made. And it appears that a number of such claims were made in honesty and good faith, but usually in ignorance of other claimants.

One of the earliest discoveries is reported to have been made in the year 1869 at the Whiterocks Indian Agency. It was in 1869 that Major J. W. Powell, a director of one of the United States Geological Surveys of the Territories, first visited this agency.

> It is related[12] that the agency blacksmith, John Kelly, asked the Indians if they knew where any "coal" was located. They replied that they knew where to find "coal" as described by Kelly, whereupon they brought him a quantity of gilsonite from the Carbon Vein south of the agency. The results of Kelly's use of this new "coal" were memorable because the ore burned at a high temperature, giving off a heavy, black smoke and a strong, petroleum-like odor as it melted and ran flaming from the forge, nearly burning down the blacksmith shop. It is further reported that samples of this strange ore were given to Major Powell, though he never mentioned this in his journals. The agency employees wasted no time in being escorted to the ore vein; and soon after, George Basor "located" the vein, posting his location notices, but doing no assessment work and making no recording of his claim, since the vein was within the Uinta Indian Reservation and there was no local land office in which to make the recording.

Another instance of gilsonite being mistaken for coal was reported in a 1907 issue of *The Vernal Express*. Referring to the "early days" in the Uintah Basin, the paper noted that cowboys T. C. McNeil, Jesse Hainline, L. H. Woodward and the Burton boys while camping in the badlands had gathered together a small amount of the mineral to build a campfire. "When they attempted to burn the stuff it melted like rubber and spread over the ground."[13] The date of this incident was not remembered by the cowboys.

14

Among the earliest documented discoveries of what later became known as gilsonite were two independent discoveries of the same vein made by government geologists in 1876. Reporting in the *United States Geological and Geographical Survey of the Territories, 10th Annual Report,* F. M. Endlich tells of his find of "approximately vertical veins" of asphalt on Two-Water Creek, a southern tributary of the White River lying between the Colorado state line and the Green River. He noted that the veins varied in width from a quarter of an inch to several feet. Chittenden, of the same White River expedition, found "springs of this mineral" at the head of Sweet Water Creek "where the asphalt slowly oozed out of the sandstones similar to petroleum in certain regions."[14] These same asphaltum springs between Sweet Water Creek and Willow Creek were observed the same year by Dr. A. C. Peale, geologist of the Grand River District of the same Hayden Survey. He visited them "early on a cool morning and no flow was noticed. Near the crevice, however, the tar was soft."[15]

Other discoveries of gilsonite were made in the 1870s and on into the 1880s, but generally the material was not recognized as a new substance. It was usually referred to as "asphalt" or "asphaltum." Then, too, the prospectors or cattlemen who did notice the stuff ordinarily paid little attention to it. They were more interested in gold or silver. Asphalt just wasn't inviting enough there in the heart of Indian country and at such a great distance from a railroad.

It was Professor William P. Blake of New Haven, Connecticut, and later of Provo, Utah, who apparently first recognized the mineral as a new substance. Writing in 1885 for *The Engineering and Mining Journal,* he described "Uintahite — A New Variety of Asphaltum from the Uintah Mountains, Utah."[16] Thus "uintahite" is the original scientific name for this asphaltite, and it is occasionally seen spelled "uintaite."[17] But gilsonite is now by far the most commonly used and therefore the accepted name. Certainly gilsonite is not as hard to pronounce!

But who was this Sam Gilson who left his name affixed to the mineral briefly called "uintahite?" He was not one of its discoverers, but was instead one of the most enthusiastic of its early promoters and one of the first to recognize the vast possibilities for its use in industry. He has been called "an ambitious and imaginative man with extremely varied interests and activities. His energy and creativity left its mark wherever he went."[18] Moving from Plainfield, Illinois, at the age of fifteen, he settled in Austin, Nevada, and there married Alice Larkin Richardson. They soon moved to Gilson Valley, Nevada, to develop their interests in cattle. From Nevada the Gilsons moved to Utah, first to Juab County, then to Price and eventually to Salt Lake City.

Sam Gilson supplied horses to the Pony Express during the year and a half that it operated, in 1860 and 1861, and is reported to have ridden for them for a time. Years later, he made a business of rounding up wild horses near his home in Juab County and trailing them across the Wasatch Plateau, the Book Cliffs, the Uinta Basin and the Uinta Mountains into Wyoming to the Union Pacific Railroad. He is reported to have been making this long drive, traversing the Uintah Indian Reservation and the gilsonite fields as early as 1878, as evidenced by the inscription, "Sam Gilson, June 1878, by God," found on a cedar tree in Horse Canyon.[19] At other times Gilson served as a U. S. Marshal and was the discoverer and promoter of many mining properties. He was also the inventor of several successful machines, including a hydraulic ore concentrator or separator.[20]

There are many stories concerning the manner in which the unusual asphaltite which was later named for him was first brought to Gilson's attention. Kretchman, for instance, in his *The Story of Gilsonite* tells of Gilson observing an anthill and becoming curious about the shiny black material that the ants were carrying. He followed the ants' trail and discovered a vein buried under a few inches of wind-blown sand.[21] In fact, however, Gilson received samples of the ore in 1885 from cattlemen who had found it by some means near Fort Duchesne. Gilson took several sacks of it home with him where his ever-curious mind went to work. Mrs. Gilson later reported that she "was not exactly overjoyed with her husband's discovery, since he filled practically every pot and pan in the house with the 'messy stuff' in order to carry out his experiments."[22] Gilson's efforts during 1885 and 1886 bore fruit, though, as docu-

On an inspection tour of one of the new gilsonite mines, C. O. Baxter stands, right arm raised, indicating the extent of the vein stretching toward the horizon. The gentleman at Baxter's left with the walrus mustache is Bert Seaboldt. *(Charles W. Baxter Collection)*

mented by at least four United States patents.[23] Among other things, he developed a sort of "chewing gum and an insulation for wires, and paint for the piles at Saltair . . . with the tar-like substance."[24]

Sam Gilson made another visit to the Uintah Reservation in 1886 and was shown the Carbon Vein. Upon his return to Salt Lake City he met and joined forces with Bert Seaboldt, who became an equally-determined promoter of gilsonite. Seaboldt was assistant to the chief engineer and was manager of construction for the Denver & Rio Grande Western Railway between 1882 and 1890, and he saw their line from Salt Lake completed to a connection with the Denver & Rio Grande which built west from Grand Junction. It was through Seaboldt's arrangements that the first recorded locations of gilsonite claims, the Carbon #1 through Carbon #7 Claims, were made at the United States Land Office in Salt Lake City on January 9, 1886. These seven claims were recorded in the names of six men other than Seaboldt and Gilson, primarily mining men and associates of Seaboldt's. Seaboldt himself had previously been introduced to the mineral on a trip into the Uintah Basin when he stopped at Pardon Dodds' Ashley home, where he had met George Basor. Both Dodds and Basor had learned of the substance in the late 1860s from Indians in the vicinity of the Whiterocks Indian Agency. Basor showed Seaboldt several pieces of the black stuff and then took him to the Carbon Vein, which may have been a mistake on Basor's part. Seaboldt learned that Basor had done no assessment work on his claim and had not recorded it, since it was on the Uintah Reservation, so he jumped the claim and posted his own notices.[25]

Between Sam Gilson's experimenting with the stuff and Bert Seaboldt's promotional activities, such as carrying samples of the ore to some of his associates, considerable interest was generated. Seaboldt brought out a thousand pounds of sample ore and then built a wagon road from Price to the Carbon Vein, after which he "set up a tent town" at the Vein and began experimenting with the ore. He found that "the stuff was absolutely impervious to acids of any kind and of course to moisture," and his experiments resulted in a high-quality varnish and an insulation. During the time that Seaboldt was doing this, his associates sent Sam Gilson to the Smithsonian Institution in Washington to determine just what this new material was. The Smithsonian people declared it to be a hydrocarbon or bitumen which was 99.6 per cent pure.[26]

While Seaboldt was engaged in his experimentation on the Carbon Vein, Indian Agent T. A. Byrnes notified him that his tents were on the reservation and that he was trespassing. This was very likely not news to Seaboldt, but the Indians had been acting very surly and hostile about the mineral explorations and trespassing on their reservation, and a warning was not out of order. Not long before, a number of Utah Utes had been ambushed and killed in Colorado, and as a result federal troops were rushed in to establish Fort Duchesne during the summer of 1886. Settlers in the Basin were not happy with the resulting war-like activities around the Ute camps. Memories of the infamous Meeker Massacre of a few years previous still haunted their minds.

This left Seaboldt with a dilemma. He checked surveyor general records, talked with former Indian agents and even made his own surveys, but no matter how he figured it, the Carbon Vein was within the Uintah Reservation. He and his partners had two choices as he saw it: either "to abandon the whole thing or attempt the impossible by getting a piece cut out of the reservation."[27] Knowing the political situation in Washington, the group attempted the impossible. Two of his associates provided $25,000, and Seaboldt went to Washington to persuade Congress to remove the area in question from the reservation. Although Congress adjourned in 1887 without taking any favorable action, Seaboldt was successful the following year in getting them to remove a triangular "Strip" of about 7,000 acres from the eastern end of the Uintah Reservation. The act provided a payment of $20 per acre to the Indians and required the Indians' approval, which was obtained in September, 1888, through "much proselyting," as Seaboldt put it.[28]

With the Carbon #1 through Carbon #7 Claims off the reservation, the Gilsonite Manufacturing Company was organized in Salt Lake City by Bert Seaboldt, Sam Gilson and others, and the company actively commenced mining activity. It is reasonable to assume that some mining had been going on before the claims were legally removed from the reservation. During that year of 1888 it is reported that 3,000 tons of gilsonite were shipped to the railroad at Price. At the time the gilsonite was selling for $80 a ton loaded on the cars at Price.[29] Even with the expense of hauling the ore nearly 100 miles from the mines to Price by horse-drawn wagon, the new company was making a healthy profit.

As a result of Sam Gilson's tireless efforts to develop uses for the mineral, settlers in the Basin had dubbed the hydrocarbon with the name "gilsonite" in the mid-1880s, and by 1888 the name was pretty well established. Calling the original mining concern the Gilsonite Manufacturing Company helped to clinch the matter. The name *uintahite* had never really had a chance to catch on and be accepted in common usage. The following year when the Gilsonite Manufacturing Company was bought out by a group of St. Louis businessmen, an incident occurred which added further permanence to the name *gilsonite*. Charles O. Baxter, the first president and chief organizer of the new company, later related that when the St. Louis men held their initial board meeting in Price to organize and name the successor company, Sam Gilson jokingly offered one silver dollar to have

Formal portrait of Charles O. Baxter and beard. (*C. R. Savage photo from Charles W. Baxter Collection*)

it named after him.[30] The joke carried, and the new firm was incorporated as the Gilson Asphaltum Company of Missouri, and their patented trade mark became "Gilsonite."

Starting with the first mining activity by the Gilsonite Manufacturing Company on the Carbon Vein in 1888, the gilsonite industry was on its way. Over the next fifteen years numerous other mines were started, and claims were staked on nearly all the available gilsonite in the Uintah Basin, although many of these claims were still on Indian land at the time. The Gilsonite Manufacturing Company, as mentioned, sold out to the Gilson Asphaltum Company of Missouri in September of 1889, for a price variously reported as $150,000 or $185,000.[31] This latter firm went on to acquire title to a large percentage of all the gilsonite land in the Basin. And it was, in turn, bought out in 1900 by a New Jersey corporation formed for the purpose, also named The Gilson Asphaltum Com-

Flesh and blood horses supplied most of the horsepower required by the gilsonite industry during its early years. On the left (above) a single white horse is hitched to the whim ready to hoist another sack of ore from the depths of the Thimble Rock mine, while at the right in the same picture a team stands ready to depart with a wagonload of the bulging sacks. In the photo below another team is practically lost in the shadows of one of the wider veins. *(Top and bottom photos: Frank A. Kennedy; top: Charles J. Neal Collection; bottom: D. H. Gerbaz Collection)*

Pictured (opposite) just a few months before the Uintah Railway was built is a four-horse team with two wagonloads of gilsonite. Tom Taylor is the teamster astride the wheel horse. *(Charles W. Baxter Collection)*

pany. Bert Seaboldt and several other employees of the original Gilsonite Manufacturing Company were retained by the Missouri corporation in 1889, with Seaboldt serving as their superintendent of mines. And, in turn, many employees of the Missouri firm continued on eleven years later to hold responsible positions with The Gilson Asphaltum Company of New Jersey. Among the latter, Charles O. Baxter especially deserves mention.

Seaboldt, years later, related the rather involved chain of events which brought C. O. Baxter into the gilsonite business.[32] It seems that Seaboldt had given a few pounds of gilsonite and a bottle of his gilsonite varnish to C. E. Soest, a long-time friend and the vice-president of the Anheuser-Busch Brewing Company of St. Louis. When Soest returned home from Salt Lake City he varnished a big safe in the treasurer's office at the brewery. Adolphus Busch became interested in the varnish and immediately sent for a Mrs. Murphy, a widow and varnish company owner whose late husband had been a close friend of Busch. Busch had bought a part interest in Mrs. Murphy's varnish company as a means of subsidizing her, and he showed her Seaboldt's so-called "first perfect varnish." She tried it out on her own safe, and while she was so engaged C. O. Baxter, who was in the picture frame business, came into her store to make his usual purchase of varnish. Baxter, too, was a close friend of Busch, or at least their wives were close friends, and Busch sent Baxter to Utah to investigate more thoroughly the source of the varnish. After inspecting the Carbon Vein with Seaboldt, and seeing the process for manufacturing the varnish,

Baxter hurried back to St. Louis, only to return to Utah accompanied by Busch's counsel Charles Nagel (who later became secretary of commerce). Negotiations with Seaboldt's associates, R. C. Chambers and Richard McIntosh, resulted in the quick purchase of the Carbon claims, as noted above.

As the president of Gilson Asphaltum Company, C. O. Baxter was a promoter and salesman who kept a keen eye to the future. Ore was "furnished consumers free of charge in order to introduce it and establish it in the market as a commercial article."[33] Adolphus Busch himself wasted little time in experimenting with gilsonite as a replacement for an asphaltic product which he had been importing from Sicily to line his beer barrels. The experiment was a costly and disappointing failure, however, for the gilsonite coating flaked off and ruined the beer.[34]

Despite a few failures, though, Baxter's energetic promotional activities greatly expanded the market for gilsonite during the 1890s. Before long a major bottleneck was found to be the long wagon-haul from the mines, wherever in the Basin they were located, to the railroad. The round trips for the horse-drawn wagons took around ten or eleven days, and the cost of hauling the gilsonite to the railroad ran in the neighborhood of $10 to $12 per ton. The miners could never realize the economies of large scale operation in the mines. Nor could they continue to supply the increasing demand for their product until they had a more efficient means for transporting their ore out of the Basin. It was for this reason that the Uintah Railway was built.

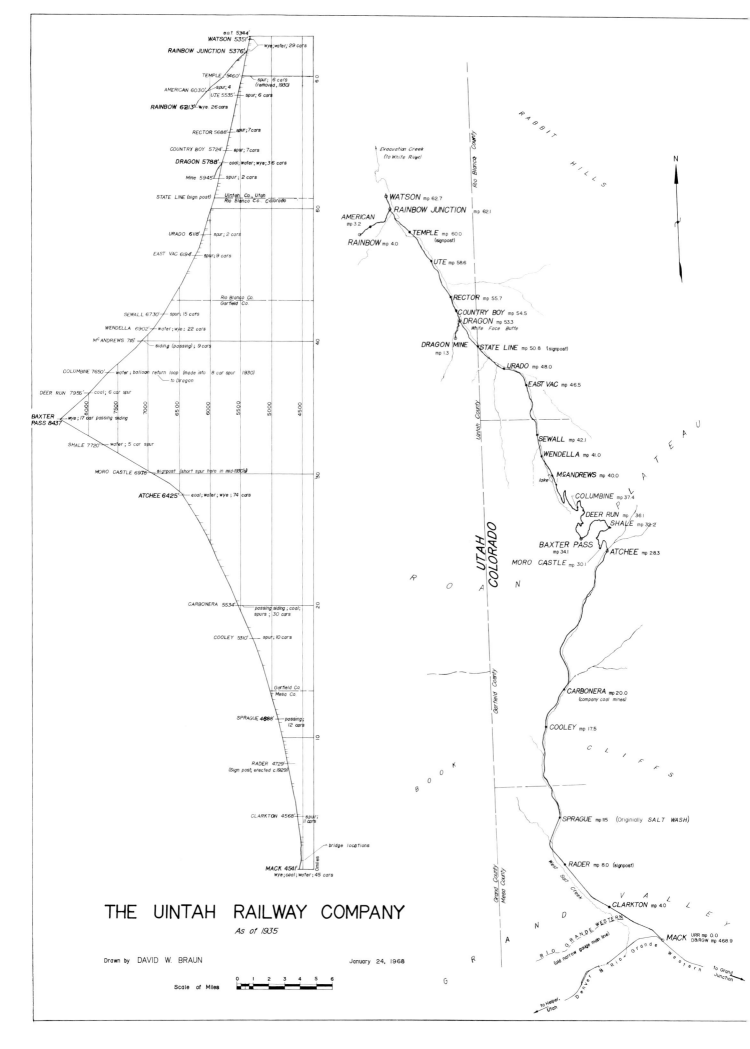

e.o.t. 5344'
WATSON 5351'
RAINBOW JUNCTION 5376'
wye; water, 29 cars

TEMPLE 5460'
spur; 6 cars
AMERICAN 6030' spur; 4 (removed, 1930)
UTE 5535' spur; 6 cars
RAINBOW 6213' wye. 26 cars

RECTOR 5688' spur; 7 cars

COUNTRY BOY 5724' spur; 7 cars

DRAGON 5788' coal; water; wye; 36 cars

Mine 5945' spur; 2 cars

STATE LINE (sign post) Uintah Co., Utah
Rio Blanco Co. Colorado

URADO 6118' spur; 2 cars

EAST VAC 6194' spur; 9 cars

Rio Blanco Co.
Garfield Co.

SEWALL 6730' spur; 15 cars
WENDELLA 6902' water; wye; 22 cars
McANDREWS 785' siding (passing); 9 cars

COLUMBINE 7650' water; balloon return loop (made into 8 car spur 1930)
to Dragon

DEER RUN 7956' coal; 6 car spur

8000 7500 7000 6500 6000 5500 5000 4500

BAXTER
PASS 8437 wye; 17 car passing siding

SHALE 7720' water; 5 car spur

MORO CASTLE 6978 signpost (short spur here in mid-1930's)

ATCHEE 6425' coal; water; wye; 74 cars

CARBONERA 5534' passing siding; coal; spurs; 30 cars

COOLEY 5310' spur; 10 cars

Garfield Co.
Mesa Co.

SPRAGUE 4688' passing 12 cars

RADER 4729' (Sign post; erected c.1929)

CLARKTON 4568' spur; 11 cars

bridge locations

0 miles

MACK 4541' wye; coal; water; 45 cars

THE UINTAH RAILWAY COMPANY
As of 1935

Drawn by DAVID W. BRAUN

January 24, 1968

Scale of Miles
0 1 2 3 4 5 6

Evacuation Creek
(to White River)

RABBIT HILLS

Rio Blanco County

N

WATSON mp 62.7
AMERICAN mp 3.2 RAINBOW JUNCTION mp 62.1
RAINBOW mp 4.0 TEMPLE mp 60.0 (signpost)

UTE mp 58.6

RECTOR mp 55.7
COUNTRY BOY mp 54.5
DRAGON mp 53.3 White Face Butte
DRAGON MINE mp 1.3 STATE LINE mp 50.8 (signpost)
URADO mp 48.0

EAST VAC mp 46.5

Uintah County

SEWALL mp 42.1
WENDELLA mp 41.0
McANDREWS mp 40.0
lake COLUMBINE mp 37.4
DEER RUN mp 36.1
SHALE mp 32.2
BAXTER PASS mp 34.1 ATCHEE mp 28.3
MORO CASTLE mp 30.1

UTAH
COLORADO

ROAN PLATEAU

CARBONERA mp 20.0
(company coal mines)

COOLEY mp 17.5

CLIFFS

Garfield County

BOOK

Grand County
Mesa County

SPRAGUE mp 11.5 (Originally SALT WASH)

West Salt Creek

RADER mp 8.0 (signpost)

VALLEY

GRAND VALLEY

CLARKTON mp 4.0

RIO GRANDE WESTERN

MACK URR mp 0.0
D&RGW mp 468.9
(old narrow gauge main line)

Denver & Rio Grande Western

to Helper, Utah

to Grand Junction

Chapter Two

The Coming of the Railway

A few railroads such as the Duluth, Missabe & Iron Range or The Virginian have become well-known for transporting a single commodity almost to the exclusion of all other traffic. But most common carriers make their money hauling a large variety of products. The Uintah Railway was in the former category. To a greater extent than most lines, it was built for a single purpose: to serve the gilsonite mines of the Uintah Basin.

To set the stage it is necessary to outline the rather involved corporate structure into which The Uintah Railway Company was born late in 1903. Substantially all the stock of the Uintah Railway Company was owned by the Barber Asphalt Paving Company, which furnished the money for the construction of the railway and superintended the construction in the name of the Uintah Railway Company. In turn, substantially all the capital stock of the Barber Asphalt Paving Company was owned by the General Asphalt Company, which also owned the Gilson Asphaltum Company of New Jersey.

The General Asphalt Company was in reality a holding company which became known, in the asphalt industry, as "The Trust." Amzi Lorenzo Barber, who had become involved in the paving industry as early as 1878, had acquired large asphalt holdings on the islands of Trinidad and Cuba and in the United States. By 1896, although thirty companies were active in the industry, Barber had laid over half of all the pavement in the United States. Early in 1901 Barber disposed of his personal holdings and allowed two great com-

bines, the Asphalt Company of America and the National Asphalt Company, to go into receivership. There were at the time charges and recriminations as to the profits made by the transfer of various stocks involved.[2] Barber himself retired, and the General Asphalt Company was formed to serve as the holding company for the numerous companies which had been part of his empire, including the Barber Asphalt Paving Company. Some of the other subsidiaries of General Asphalt were: The Bermudez Company; Bertrin Petroleum Company; Iroquois Electric Refrigeration Company; The Petroleum Development Company; Trinidad Lake Asphalt, Ltd.; The Trinidad Lake Petroleum Company; and Venezuela Royalty Contract Company.[3] The Gilson Asphaltum Company which had been incorporated in New Jersey in 1900, and which was a successor to the Gilson Asphaltum Company incorporated in Missouri in 1888, became a subsidiary of General Asphalt Company in 1903.

The pyramiding structure of companies controlled by The Trust never seemed to be very clear to people in the gilsonite country, and thus newspaper editors and others commonly referred to the holding company, General Asphalt Company, as well as various of its subsidiaries as the "Barber Company."

By 1903 the Gilson Asphaltum Company had acquired a sizable percentage of all the gilsonite claims in the Uintah Basin and, with the backing of the General Asphalt combine, was ready to expand its activities. Also in 1903, the odd-num-

The year is 1904 and the newly-finished grade (top) not far above Moro Castle is ready for the crossties and steel. A group of engineers, surveyors and bridge and building carpenters (center) who worked on the railroad and later on stage road construction pose for their portrait in front of the contractor's tents. Crossties, telephone poles and bridge timbers (bottom) are piled alongside the recently completed track at Baxter Pass awaiting loading and shipment to the railhead farther up the line. *(Top and bottom: photos by construction engineer Wm. H. Wear from W. A. Banks Collection; center: Frank A. Kennedy photo from Denver Public Library Western Collection)*

bered sections of land on the former Uncompahgre Indian Reservation, a vast area to the east and south of the Uintah Reservation, were opened to mining activity, with recognition of those claims located prior to 1891. Gilson Asphaltum Company held claim to far more gilsonite in this area than all other claimants together. When the Uncompahgre Reservation was opened in 1903, The Trust was ready to go into action with a rather ambitious plan.

The key to their plan was transportation and communication. The mining and marketing of gilsonite on the scale envisioned by the Barber people would have been practically impossible without rail transportation. It was evident that the long wagon-haul from the mines to the Rio Grande Western Railway at Price, which had been a major factor in the cost of marketing gilsonite since mining began in the late 1880s, would discourage further profitable increases in the mining activity. Thus it was resolved that a railroad should be built. The only questions remaining were what route it should take and how the construction was to be financed.

Since the Gilson Asphaltum Company controlled most of the major gilsonite veins, they selected the one nearest an existing rail line for immediate development. This was the Black Dragon Vein in the southeastern part of the Uintah Basin, which was part of the biggest gilsonite vein system south of the White River. It was located approximately eighteen miles south of the river and just west of the Utah-Colorado line. This vein was visible on the surface for some four miles, and while it varied considerably in width it averaged six feet wide for over two miles of this length.[4] Most of the ore was of a high quality, known as "selects" in the industry, and in 1907 the Vernal *Express* reported an estimate of 2,086,479 tons available in the vein.[5] The proposed railroad was to connect the Black Dragon Vein with the main line of the Rio Grande Western Railway at Crevasse, Colorado.

Prior to making a choice of gauge and building their own railroad, the General Asphalt interests had approached the Denver & Rio Grande Railroad to try to interest them in building the line. The D.&R.G. declined to consider the idea on the grounds that a branch from their main line to Dragon would, when built, be available for the single purpose of carrying gilsonite to market and would become worthless if for any reason gilsonite were no longer used in large quantities. The Barber Asphalt Paving Company, conducting the negotiations, then offered to guarantee the Rio Grande the shipment of a certain number of tons for a given period of time, but the D.&R.G. still refused to entertain the proposition.[6]

The Barber Company then chose to consider constructing the railroad as an independent proposition. And because of the rugged nature of the Book Cliff range which lay between the Black Dragon Vein and the valley of the Grand River (later the Colorado) it was decided that the new railroad be of narrow gauge. This was despite the fact that the connecting Rio Grande Western had widened its line from three-foot to standard gauge some thirteen years earlier in 1890. It was to be financed by the sale of stocks and bonds on the open market. But difficulty developed here, as well. Financial interests advised that so long as the railroad was capable of being used for only one purpose and was dependent for its income upon that one source, it would be impossible to sell bonds or stocks for anything like their face value. Thus this scheme, too, was abandoned.[7]

Still convinced that a railroad would be the best way to move the gilsonite from the Black Dragon mine to market, the Barber Company started making plans to build its own railroad, as a wholly-owned subsidiary. In actuality, miners already had been put to work on the Black Beauty claim, situated on the southeastern end of the Black Dragon Vein, in the spring of 1903. This was almost immediately after the United States Congress, as a part of their Indian Department appropriation act of March 3, 1903, had declared that mining claims located on the Uncompahgre Indian Reservation prior to January 1, 1891, were valid. But it was still some months prior to the start of actual construction work on the railroad to Dragon. During 1903 and 1904 ore from the Black Dragon Mine was not only stockpiled while awaiting the arrival of the railroad, but much of it was carted over the Book Cliffs in freight wagons to be loaded on the Rio Grande's cars at Fruita and Crevasse, Colorado.[8] Years later Uintah railroaders would still point out traces of the

23

old wagon road where it came down the east side of Baxter Pass, at a steeper angle than the railway itself. Many early photos of railway operations on the Pass show the road quite clearly.

So the Barber people went ahead with plans to build their own railroad, and The Uintah Railway Company was incorporated as a Colorado corporation on November 4, 1903, to build a narrow gauge railway from a connection with the Rio Grande Western Railway "about two (2) miles west of Crevasse station . . . in the County of Mesa, in the State of Colorado; running thence by the most feasible route in a Northerly direction up along West Salt Wash Creek to a point near its source in the County of Garfield . . . ; thence by the most feasible route over Book Cliffs to a point on the west fork of Evacuation Creek; thence down said Evacuation Creek . . . to the west line of the State of Colorado in the County of Rio Blanco . . ."[9] The incorporators were Charles O. Baxter, Colin A. Chisholm, William W. Field, Elroy N. Clark and Herman H. Dunham.

Most of the surveying for the new line had already been completed prior to incorporation, and the initial contract for grading was awarded almost immediately. In its "Railroad Construction. New Incorporations, Surveys, Etc." column, *The Railroad Gazette* for Friday, November 13, 1903, reported that ". . . the Utah Construction Company of Salt Lake City, has received a contract for building a narrow gage railroad from Crevasse, on the Rio Grande Western, in a southerly [sic] direction, 40 miles, to some large mines owned by the General Asphalt Company." Since this news dispatch did not include the Uintah Railway name, it is likely that it was actually submitted to *The Railroad Gazette* prior to incorporation. Two months later, in their January 15, 1904, issue, *The Railroad Gazette* furnished additional and more accurate information, which is quoted here:

UINTAH. — The proposed route of this road is from Mile Post 470, on the Rio Grande Western in Colorado, to the State line between Colorado and Utah, near Evacuation Creek, 52 miles. Surveys have been completed and grading has been begun on the first 11 miles of the line. The Utah Construction Company are the contractors. The road will be narrow gage. A. M. Johnson, Trenton, Colo., is Chief Engineer; C. O. Baxter, Denver, is General Manager.

The next report, in the March 4, 1904, issue of *The Railroad Gazette,* said that grading was in progress on the first 11 miles of the line and that contracts for grading the remainder would be let in the near future.

Meanwhile the Uintah's first two new locomotives, two-truck Shay No. 1 and Consolidation No. 10, had been ordered from Lima and Baldwin, respectively. Both were completed and rolled from the builders' erecting floors during the month of May, 1904, and were loaded on flat cars for the trip west. Prior to their arrival on the site where the town of Mack was rising, the Uintah management purchased another locomotive — a twenty-four year old Baldwin Consolidation. This 2-8-0, previously Denver & Rio Grande No. 55, named the TOMICHI, was sold to the Uintah Railway on May 23, 1904, and promptly put to work hauling construction trains as the steel was spiked down. It retained its D.&R.G. number for a short time before being renumbered No. 11 by the Uintah and was scrapped in 1911 when a brand new Consolidation arrived from the Baldwin works to become the second No. 11.

Construction of the new railroad proceeded rapidly during the summer of 1904, and by October the tracklayers had reached Dragon, Utah, 53.3 miles from their starting place at Mack. A 1.3 mile branch was spiked down from the town of Dragon up Camp Gulch to Dragon Mine, and until 1911 that was to be the full extent of the Uintah Railway. Even before the track reached Dragon, though, there was considerable talk about building on to Vernal and other towns in the Uintah Basin, and this talk was to continue for many years. In their report of the completion of the railway from Mack to Dragon, *The Railroad Gazette* for October 21, 1904, noted that surveys were then "in progress for a proposed extension from Dragon to Vernal, Utah." It was stated that work would "be begun on the extension as soon as the surveys are completed."

The citizens of Vernal and neighboring towns in the Ashley Valley and elsewhere in the Uintah Basin had been hoping for railroad connection with the outside world for many years prior to 1904. In an article reprinted from the Salt Lake *Tribune,* a January, 1896, issue of the weekly Vernal *Express* noted that "Vernal lies almost due

The brilliant afternoon sunlight reflects from the flanks of Shay No. 1 as she churns up the five per cent grade with three loads of gilsonite and two cabooses. The first, more a boxcar with a cupola than a true caboose, was used for l.c.l. freight and saw infrequent use in later years. Baldwin-built No. 10 poses (below) with her crew at Mack just before leaving for Atchee with the one-car train. The engineer, on the ground with his oilcan, is George Lyman and the fireman is Vic Earp. *(Top: Charles W. Baxter Collection; bottom: Frank A. Kennedy photo from V. L. McCoy Collection)*

Eight railroaders and one potential railroader gather around Uintah Railway first No. 11 at Mack. At the time this photograph was taken, about 1910 or 1911, the 1880 Baldwin Consolidation had been extensively rebuilt by the Uintah's shopmen. (Below) the engineer is oiling around Shay No. 2 while another Shay, three cars back, is positioned under the Columbine waterspout. Soon they will resume their climb towards Baxter Pass, up the five per cent grade traversing the mountainside in the distance. *(Both: Frank A. Kennedy photos; top: D. H. Gerbaz Collection; bottom: V. L. McCoy Collection)*

east of Salt Lake City and is 126 miles distant, but at present the easiest route is via Price on the Rio Grande Western, 122 miles from this city, and then 128 miles by wagon road, a total of 250 miles." Engineer Harry Josephs, who had just returned to Salt Lake after surveying gilsonite properties in the Ashley Fork district near Vernal, stated that "the residents in the region around Ashley Fork are looking eagerly for a railroad through their section, and the prevailing opinion in that section is that one is soon to be built, but by whom or from what direction they do not know." The correspondent observed "that the extension of the Utah Central Railway [from the Salt Lake area] would be the better method of putting [Uintah County] in communication with the outside world," but that local residents also had some hopes that a railroad would be built from northwestern Colorado into their county.[10]

It is easy to understand the eagerness with which these pioneers of northeastern Utah awaited the arrival of steel rails into their valley. The wagon road through Nine Mile Canyon to Price was often blocked by snow for weeks at a time during the winter, or was a quagmire of mud in the spring or following a summer rainstorm. During the 1890s this Vernal-Fort Duchesne-Price road carried four times as much traffic as any other route entering the Uintah Basin, but the rain, snow or mud made the journey a hard one. Freighters, generally driving a six-horse team which pulled two tarpaulin-covered wagons, would be away from home for two to three weeks at a time making the round trip from Vernal to Price. Their wagons were usually loaded with gilsonite on the trip to Price, and most of the time they could count on a load of merchandise as cargo for the return haul. If traveling either direction without a load, the freighter would haul feed to be used by his horses on the return trip and would cache it enroute, thus enabling him to haul more paying cargo on the return journey. It was this expensive and inefficient form of transportation which made the need for rail service to their mines obvious to the General Asphalt interests.

Although the residents of Vernal and neighboring towns hoped to have a mainline railroad built through the Basin, even the narrow-gauge shortline planned by the Uintah Railway Company would be welcome. But when the rails reached Dragon, still some sixty miles distant from Vernal, during the fall of 1904, they were to get no closer for another seven years. Even when the extension to Watson was completed in November, 1911, placing Vernal as close to a railroad line as it would ever be, roughly fifty miles of dusty road still separated the county seat from the railhead.

Rumors that any of more than a half dozen railroads would extend their routes into the fertile, irrigated valleys around Vernal were to command front-page space in the Vernal *Express* for the better part of another two decades. And mention of an anticipated Uintah Railway extension further north and west was not uncommon among them. All this talk, however, was to prove to be just that — *so much talk.*

In October of 1904, it appears, the building of a rail line to Vernal was a very minor concern to the Uintah Railway management. Even the organization of the Uintah Toll Road Company and the operation of stages and freight wagons beyond Dragon was then more than a year in the future. Since Gilson Asphaltum Company had begun mining operations on the Black Dragon Vein in the spring of 1903, only a fraction of the ore had been freighted over Baxter Pass by wagon. A sizable stockpile remained at the Dragon mine to be hauled out when the railway arrived. However, when the rails were in place and Shay No. 1 began churning up the five per cent grade trailing loads of gilsonite, a couple of problems were discovered. And the arrival of Shay No. 2, which was shipped from Lima on October 26, 1904, only served to confirm them. It was found that the original, hastily-laid rail for a part of the way where the grades were the heaviest over Baxter Pass was too light, and this portion of the line had to be relaid with heavier steel. It was also found that some of the curves were too sharp, and at considerable expense the curvature was reduced to a maximum of about 65 degrees.[11] In some instances, such as at Moro Castle, the original curvature had been 75 degrees! To put that in more familiar terms, a complete circle of 75 degrees curvature is little more than 150 feet across. At least one reference[12] states that the curve at Moro Castle had been no less than 80 degrees as it was originally built.

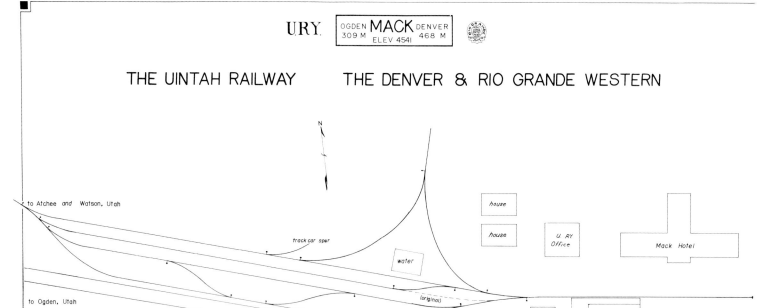

U.RY.

OGDEN	MACK	DENVER
309 M	ELEV 4541	468 M

THE UINTAH RAILWAY   THE DENVER & RIO GRANDE WESTERN

N

to Atchee and Watson, Utah

track car spur

house

house

U. RY Office

Mack Hotel

water

(original)

to Ogden, Utah

platform

D&RGW depot

to Denver

NO SCALE

During the early years on the Uintah, section gangs were based at Mack, Carbonera, Atchee, Baxter Pass, McAndrews and Dragon. Many of the men were Greek by birth. Here three of the sectionmen pose with their families on the front porch of their house at Mack. To the southeast, partially visible under the overhang of the porch roof, is the company's large water tank which stored all of the household and drinking water for the town, as well as that needed by the locomotives. This water was hauled the twenty-eight miles from Atchee in tank cars and then pumped up into the tank. *(Map drawn by David W. Braun; photo by Frank A. Kennedy, from J. L. Booth Collection)*

It is interesting to note that construction was undertaken and completed on the Uintah Railway with a noticeable lack of publicity. Since it was built for a single purpose, the transportation of gilsonite, and was located in a very sparsely settled region, there was no particular reason for the Barber Asphalt people to inform the local newspaper editors of their activities. Some five years after the fact in February, 1909, the Grand Junction *Daily Sentinel's* scribe looked over his files of back issues and found "that an announcement was made of the proposed building of the road." He observed that "we hardly think that much attention was paid to the matter, as there had been conflicting rumors of such a road being built many times before, but nothing tangible had been done and very little thought was given to the matter." In another paragraph he noted, "The truth of the whole matter is that the road built into Mack almost before the people of this city knew that there was a road building from the gilsonite properties to connect with the Rio Grande Western railway. To have permitted that road to build into Mack instead of Grand Junction was one of the most egregious blunders ever permitted by the citizens of Grand Junction."[13]

The editor of a rival paper, the weekly Grand Junction *News,* was also apparently ignorant during the summer of 1904 of the railroad construction commencing only nineteen miles west of his city. But he woke up about the time the line was being completed and in his October 8th issue printed the following article, which also shows a degree of local prejudice towards Grand Junction. It seems interesting, however, that he published this article on page two rather than the front page.

THE UINTAH RAILWAY
Opens Up Rich Territory Tributary to Grand Junction.

The Uintah railroad, which is being constructed along the Book Cliffs from Mack, Colo., a station on the Rio Grande railroad, to tap the extensive gilsonite deposits of the White river country, will have for its terminus at present a station called Dragon at the head of Evacuation creek. Dragon is fifty-five miles southeast of Vernal and a first class wagon road will be constructed between these two points. Within the past few days amended articles of incorporation of the Uintah Railway company, have been filed with the county clerk, which broadens the scope and the territory of this line which was at first simply intended to tap the great gilsonite beds in the Uintah Indian reservation, but its scope of usefulness will now have to be enlarged and it will become an important feeder to the Rio Grande system, and incidentally open up a vast territory, which is now partially settled, to the merchants of Grand Junction.

The purpose of the amended articles of incorporation is to extend this railroad to Vernal and Fort Duchesne and thus give these towns immediate railroad connections and rapid transit for their people and products for which they must find a market. Only fifty miles more of this road to reach Vernal and Ft. Duchesne and then the traffic which has been going on between Price, Utah, and these points over 150 [sic] miles of stage road will be transferred to the Uintah railroad. Steps have already been taken to change the mail route to go via this road.

It is needless to say that this tapping of that rich and practically virgin territory with a railroad will mean much to Grand Junction. A large amount of this trade must necessarily come to our young city, if our merchants are wise enough to prepare to meet that people in the spirit of fairness and cordiality. Only a few months ago our Chamber of Commerce was speculating upon the feasibility of an extended line of railway to the north and reaching the new Moffatt [sic] road on its way westward. Now behold the railroad is already built and what are we going to do with it? Make the very most we can out of it [this paper hopes].

The completion or opening of this road at this time is most opportune indeed for Grand Junction. March 10, 1905 the Uintah Indian reservation will be thrown open for settlement and thousands of people will come to this point to outfit for that country.

The Chamber of Commerce is taking steps to make Grand Junction a point of entry for registration or land filings for that country and it is sincerely hoped that success will attend its efforts. It is the nearest and most practical point on the line of railroad, besides a good wagon road will be completed all the way to the reservation by the time it is thrown open for settlement. It is proposed that we shall lose none of the advantages these points afford us.

Obviously the promoters and brass hats of the Uintah Railway paid lip service to the idea of extending their line on into the hub of the Basin. And they would continue to do so until well into

29

All there was to the new town of Mack, Colorado, can be seen in the panorama (above). The Uintah Railway Hotel, shown in more detail (center), is to the right of the depot and behind the row of poplars. (Below) from the vantage point of the water tank, two houses, the Uintah Railway office building and the hotel are grouped to the left of the cottonwoods. A plume of smoke on the horizon heralds the imminent arrival of a west-bound Rio Grande Western train at the depot. *(Top: J. L. Booth Collection; middle: F. A. Kennedy photo from J. V. Kelly Collection; bottom: F. A. Kennedy photo from D. H. Gerbaz Collection)*

the early 1920s. They were not about to alienate the citizens and potential travelers and shippers of that region. But the sacks of glossy black gilsonite would always constitute more than two-thirds of the annual tonnage for them, and moving this tonnage over the mountain and down to the Rio Grande at Mack was to be the railroaders' major concern. On a railroad such as the Uintah, this would be concern enough for the best of men!

The five miles of steady 7.5 per cent grade snaking its way up the east side of Baxter Pass was the feature that made the Uintah famous, or perhaps it is better said, *notorious*. An examination of the railway's profile, however, reveals that there was hardly a level spot on the entire line. Trains leaving the depot at Mack had the advantage of a descending grade for the first three-quarters of a mile, and then for almost four and a half miles the grade was as nearly level as it was anywhere on the line, ranging between 0.16 and 0.86 per cent. After that there was not a spot on the line, except for a few yards at the summit of Baxter Pass, where the rails climbed less than a foot in every hundred, a one per cent gradient.

For the first two or three miles out of Mack, Colorado, the Uintah's builders utilized the narrow-gauge roadbed which had been abandoned fourteen years earlier by the Rio Grande Western as they widened their main line from Grand Junction to Salt Lake City and Ogden. From Crevasse, Colorado, at milepost 470.5, to Cisco, Utah, at milepost 504.4 from Denver, the Rio Grande Western's locating engineers had chosen an entirely new route through Ruby Canyon of the Grand River (renamed the Colorado in the 1920s) for their standard-gauge route. Upon its completion

in 1890, the rails had been removed from the undulating narrow-gauge grade crossing the deserts to the north of the river.

Mack, which was not in existence prior to the building of the Uintah Railway in 1904, was located at mile 468.9 on the Rio Grande System.[14] The town was named for John M. Mack, who was not only the first president of the General Asphalt Company, but also the first president of its subsidiary Barber Asphalt Paving Company and, in turn, of The Uintah Railway Company. Mr. Mack was also instrumental in founding the Mack Brothers Motor Company, the major forerunner of today's Mack Trucks, Incorporated. It was this latter connection, rather than any strong faith in the future of gasoline-powered rail vehicles, that prompted the Uintah Railway to purchase in 1905 the very first Mack rail motor car.[15]

During the decade or two prior to 1905, irrigation had transformed the arid expanses of the Grand River valley into a verdant checkerboard of farms and orchards. From Fruita, eight miles east of Mack, past Grand Junction to Palisade, some 23 miles further east, an uninterrupted series of prosperous farms had been established. With the completion of the "High Line" ditch by the U. S. Government soon after the Uintah was built, the life-giving water was brought to the vicinity of Mack, and the farms extended two or three miles past Mack to the north and west.

Leaving Mack, the Uintah's trains followed the old R.G.W. grade alongside these green fields until they reached the arroyo known as Salt Wash Creek, which was spanned by a timber trestle, Bridge 2A. This was only one of 37 trestles of various sizes between Mack and the foot of the

The prominent rock formation which became known to the railroaders as "Crow's Nest" is the backdrop for Mack rail motor car No. 50 (above). A few miles farther up the canyon, in the direction the car is headed, was the coal mine at Carbonera. The lower photo shows the tipple, with a number of skip loads of coal ready for dumping into the gondolas below. The mine itself was up the hill to the left, out of the picture. (*Top: Frank A. Kennedy photo, Charles J. Neal Collection; bottom: Roy F. Blackburn photo from V. L. McCoy Collection*)

heavy climb just beyond Atchee. Crossing Salt Wash the track followed the gully of West Salt Wash as far as Atchee, 28.3 miles from Mack. For the first 12 miles or so the country was open, stretching away dry and unproductive toward the Book Cliffs to the north. Except for the numerous trestles and culverts, construction work was light along this portion of the line. For one stretch beginning five miles from Mack the track was tangent for more than three and a half miles. There was a short blind siding at milepost 4.2, named Clarkton, and a longer through siding at milepost 11.5, which went by the name Salt Wash for two decades. In the 1920s Salt Wash was renamed Sprague in honor of the then General Manager. As the foothills of the Book Cliffs grew nearer, the steepness of the grade increased gradually and almost imperceptibly, and soon after leaving Salt Wash, or Sprague, the line entered a canyon in these foothills. Eroded pinnacles and spires and jagged rock outcroppings such as the one called "Crow's Nest" characterized the entrance into West Salt Wash Canyon. For 16 miles on a steadily ascending grade amid strikingly picturesque scenery, the track meandered up the canyon toward Atchee.

The only settlement between the farms just beyond Mack and the company town of Atchee at milepost 28.3 was Carbonera, just beyond milepost 20. In Spanish, *carbonera* means coal mine, and this town, which had a population of 24 in the 1930s, supplied all the fuel to move the Uintah's trains. It was a rather low grade coal, though, and none was ever transshipped beyond Mack. Not less than 480 acres of coal lands in Colorado, together with sufficient machinery for conducting mining operations, had been provided the Uintah Railway under the construction contract by The Barber Asphalt Paving Company. The latter company had received payment of the Railway's capital stock for same.[16] The mines were located up a short incline to the west of town, and the tramloads of coal were let down by cable onto a trestle and dumped down chutes into the Uintah's gondolas, or often directly into the tanks of the locomotives.

The West Salt Wash canyon floor gradually narrows and becomes more twisting past Carbonera until, rounding a curve, a broader valley

Chief Atchee of the Utes. (*F. E. Dean photo from Uintah Railway "Official Folder" in Collection of D. H. Gerbaz*)

at the juncture of two small generally-dry creeks comes into view. Here the railway's locomotive and car shops were erected, along with a two-stall enginehouse, coaling and water facilities, a wye and yards, a small hotel and homes for the engine and train crews, section men, shop men and their families. Within a few years a school was built at the mouth of "Schoolhouse Canyon" behind the town, and a saloon appeared across the tracks on the other side of West Salt Wash. Founded in 1904, the town was named for the Ute chieftain Sam Atchee, who was 44 at the time and a brother-in-law of Ouray, famed leader and peacemaker of the Ute tribe.[17]

Atchee served essentially as a division point for the Uintah Railway, although the entire road was shorter than most mainline divisions. During the line's entire history, very few trains ever operated through Atchee without a change of motive power and engine crews. Even the little 0-6-2 Tankers which hauled the one-car passenger train over the hill to Dragon, and later to Watson, generally exchanged their coach with a Consolidation

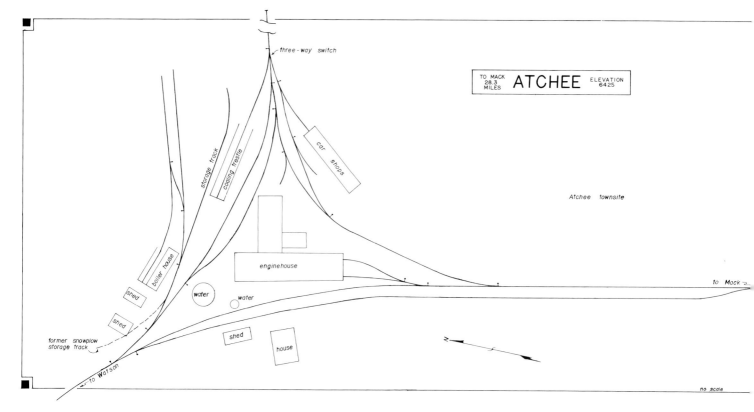

three-way switch

Atchee townsite

storage track

cooling trestle

car shops

to Mack

enginehouse

boiler house

water

water

shed

shed

shed

house

former snowplow
storage track

to Watson

no scale

The town of Atchee and the railroad were both new when "Judge" Kennedy recorded
this scene with his "5x7" glass-plate camera in 1905. The canyon behind town would
later be known as "Schoolhouse Canyon," but the schoolhouse had not yet been built.
The major elements of the railroad facilities were already in place in 1905, but the
coming years would bring additions, such as the car shop building shown in the map
(above). *(Map drawn by David W. Braun; bottom: E. Victor Earp Collection)*

Better than average maintenance of the all-important locomotives and rolling stock became a way of life on the Uintah. Here the men leave their work to gather around the front of No. 10.

The scene below, taken during the winter of 1904-05, even before the concrete-walled machine shop was erected perpendicular to the enginehouse, is the earliest known picture of Atchee. Everything is new. Shay No. 1, ready to depart with the officials' inspection train, and Consolidation No. 10 sitting on the West Salt Wash trestle were both just a few months old. *(Top: F. A. Kennedy photo from V. L. McCoy Collection; bottom: W. A. Banks Collection)*

Some idea of the spectacular nature of railroading on the 7.5 per cent of Baxter Pass may be gained from these photographs. (Above) a Shay works its way up the hill near Shale with a two-car train. (Below) another of the geared locomotives, pushing the snowplow, heads back home to Atchee after clearing the line. *(Both: Frank A. Kennedy photos; top: Charles W. Baxter Collection; bottom: E. Victor Earp Collection)*

at Atchee for the run between there and Mack. All freight moved over the Pass behind Shays, usually two of them, and the Shays seldom ever ran south of Atchee. And of course the Consolidations, and later Mikado No. 40, which handled trains from Atchee to Mack and return, could not operate beyond Atchee because of the extreme curvature at many points between there and Wendella. Thus, for a small town Atchee was a pretty busy place around 7:00 each morning, as three or four engines were taking on coal and water and being oiled and greased for the day's assignments.

Leaving Atchee for Baxter Pass, the Shays had a tonnage rating of sixty tons, while the Baldwin 0-6-2T passenger engines were rated at 35 tons, equivalent to the one combination car which made up the daily passenger train. For the better part of a mile out of town the track angled up the bottom of the valley reaching west from Atchee towards the backbone of the range, and the short trains climbed up a grade just barely exceeding five per cent. Then, reversing direction on a horseshoe curve, the climb up the slopes of the Book Cliffs started in earnest. The remaining five miles to the crest of the Pass were on a steady 7.5 per cent grade! In the 5.8 track miles between Atchee and the top the trains gained 2,012 feet in elevation. And with the unbroken grade there was no lack of curves either. Between mileposts 28, near Atchee, and 40, just past McAndrews on the opposite side of the Pass, there were no less than 233 curves, ranging from four to 66 degrees. This is an average of nearly twenty curves per mile. A 66-degree curve is one with a radius of 87 feet! It's easy to see why this was Shay territory.

Various of the photographs in this book illustrate better than words possibly could the spectacular nature of railroading on Baxter Pass and the magnificence of the views seen from the trains. This is a country that inspired writers to express themselves in superlatives. The author of practically the only booklet the Uintah Railway ever published for "the tourist, hunter, student and health-seeker," used the following glowing phrases:

The Book Cliffs . . . provide an unobstructed view on either side of hundreds of miles.
There are no other nearby mountains to shut off the view, as on other mountain railroads.

Rising steadily up the face of this great range, there is never a moment when the eye of the passenger may not rest with perfect delight and wonderment upon a gorgeous panorama of slopes below, of valleys and deserts beyond, and of snow-clad mountain ranges in the far-off horizon. To the eastward, the great Continental Divide and the Grand Mesa; to the southeast, the precipitous San Juan mountains of Colorado, one hundred and fifty miles away; to the south, the Sierra La Sal in southern Utah, one hundred and sixty-five miles distant, rising in indescribable grandeur on the hither side of the valleys that lead to the Grand Canyon of the Colorado.

These views from the train windows are best appreciated when the summit is reached at Baxter Pass. Here, simultaneously, another panorama is unfolded on the north, as from the narrow summit the traveler sees the valley of Evacuation Creek stretching out to the Grand Canyon of White River, and, over the old Uncompahgre reservation to Raven Ridge and Blue Mountain on the north, eighty miles away, to Rabbit Mountain and the White River plateau many miles further distant in the northeast in Colorado; over the Uintah reservation and beyond to the Uintah mountains in the northwest, one hundred and fifty miles; the breezes flinging through the pines and aspens on the neighboring summits, the blue vault above and eternal peace in all the atmosphere.

Everywhere there is grandeur, accentuated lights and shadows, marvellous combinations of color. It is soul-stirring, poetic, stimulating, satisfying and a never-ending appeal to the artistic sense.[18]

Even today, more than sixty years after the above lines were written, one may drive — at least in the summer months — on the old grade ascending Baxter Pass and marvel at the spectacular views which greeted the Uintah's passengers.

Only two names appeared on the railway's timetables between Atchee and Baxter Pass, although a third location, approximately halfway from Shale to the Pass and one of the more frequently photographed spots on the route, was fittingly known as "Lone Tree Curve." Just 1.8 miles up from Atchee was Moro Castle. It received its name because of a fancied resemblance of the adjacent rock formation to one of the three fortresses named Morro Castle in the Caribbean, most likely the 16th-century fort guarding the entrance to Havana Harbor. (The Uintah was built

The 66-degree curve at Moro Castle (above). With the grade climbing nearly eight feet for every one hundred feet of forward travel, this Shay had its work cut out for it, lifting four cars and the section gang's pushcar up around the curve. The grade is not so evident in the photo below of Mack Rail car No. 50 at Shale Tank, but it's still a steady 7.5 per cent. *(Top: F. A. Kennedy photo from Charles W. Baxter Collection; bottom: Mrs. Ruby Luton Collection)*

One of Claim Agent Kennedy's favorite spots for photographing the trains was Lone Tree Curve (above), about halfway between Shale and Baxter Pass. Another popular spot was the pass itself, where all trains stopped for a few minutes for inspection before starting downgrade. The crowd gathered around combination car No. 52 (below) at Baxter Pass is on its way to Columbine for an Independence Day picnic. (*Top: F. A. Kennedy photo from V. L. McCoy Collection; bottom: Robert O. Perkins Collection*)

Baxter Pass was definitely the *high point* of the Gilsonite Route. In the spectacular view (center) "Judge" Kennedy has aimed his camera in an easterly direction to catch a Shay, train and alpine panorama. From "Lookout Point" (bottom) the regular daily passenger train can be seen rounding "Windy Point." To the left side of the picture are the track and water tank at Columbine. *(Left and bottom: E. V. Earp Collection; center: D. H. Gerbaz Collection)*

Views on the north side of the pass were as scenic as those on the Atchee side, although the railroad's grade was not as severe. No doubt the passengers on the holiday excursion train (above) were enjoying themselves as they rolled around "Windy Point" toward the valley of Evacuation Creek. (Below) the short spur and the mainline at Deer Run. This is the only known picture taken at that location. *(Both photos: F. A. Kennedy; top: D. H. Gerbaz Collection; bottom: Denver Public Library Western Collection)*

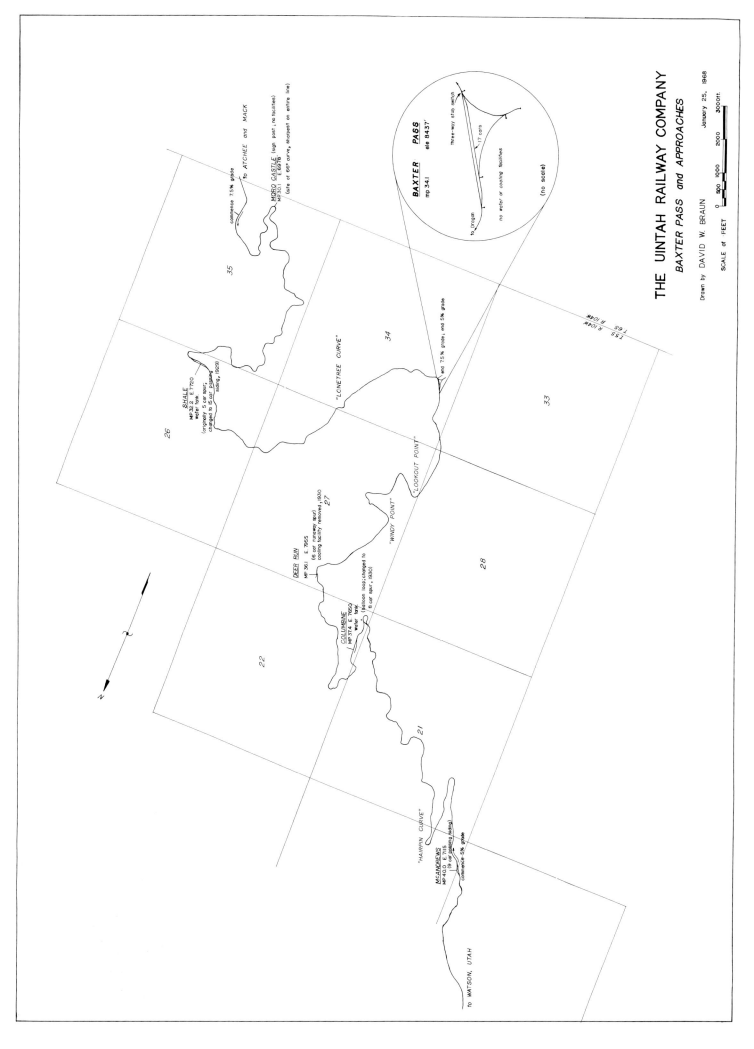

THE UINTAH RAILWAY COMPANY

BAXTER PASS and APPROACHES

Drawn by DAVID W. BRAUN   January 25, 1968

SCALE of FEET

0 500 1000   2000   3000 ft.

BAXTER PASS
ele 8437'
mp 34.1

three-way stub switch

17 cars

to Dragon

no water or cooling facilities

(no scale)

to ATCHEE and MACK

commence 7.5% grade

MORO CASTLE (sign post; no facilities)
MP 30.1   E. 6978
(site of 66° curve; sharpest on entire line)

35

34

"LONETREE CURVE"

end 7.5% grade; end 5% grade

SHALE
MP 32.2   E. 7720
water tank
(originally 5 car spur;
changed to 15 car passing
siding, 1929)

26

33

"LOOKOUT POINT"

"WINDY POINT"

DEER RUN
MP 36.1   E. 7955
(6 car runway spur)
cooling facility removed, 1930

27

28

COLUMBINE
MP 37.4   E. 7650
water tank
(balloon loop; changed to
8 car spur, 1930)

22

21

N

"HAIRPIN CURVE"

McANDREWS
MP 40.0   E. 7115
(9 car passing siding)
commence 5% grade

to WATSON, UTAH

T5S R104W
T6S R104W

just six years after the sinking of the *Maine* in Havana Harbor.) Although there was no siding or any other facilities at Moro Castle, the curve itself was deserving of a name. It was, after all, the sharpest curve on the railroad! Further up the hill at Shale there was a short siding and a water tank, since there were no provisions for taking water or fuel at the top of the Pass (except occasionally in the winter when a gondola of coal was spotted on the siding there for emergency use by the snow-fighting crews).

The summit was the location of a 17-car-length siding, a wye, a section house, and a sign reading "Baxter Pass Elev. 8437." The name honored two brothers — Charles O. Baxter and Frank E. Baxter. One of Frank's sons, Charles W. Baxter, recalls, "Uncle Charlie used to say the Pass was named for Dad, and Dad said it was named for Uncle Charlie." Besides being one of the early promoters of the gilsonite industry, Charles O. Baxter was, more than perhaps any other man, the moving force behind the building of the Uintah Railway. His brother Frank held a high position on the engineering staff of the Denver & Rio Grande, and was "borrowed," during his vacation, to make the preliminary surveys for the Uintah.

The spectacular panoramas visible from the Pass have already been described. From an operating standpoint, Baxter Pass was just as spectacular. The "Special Rules and Instructions" in the Employees' Time Table were quite specific regarding the operation of trains. It was stated that "Trainmen must inspect and see that all retainers are turned up before starting down grade and they must assist when necessary with hand brake to insure safety of the train." Further, all trains were to "be thoroughly inspected and air-tested by car men and trainmen jointly at Atchee before leaving. On all trains at Baxter Pass, train and enginemen must inspect train and test air; while the air is applied trainmen must turn up retainers on each car to ascertain their working condition; examine all hand brakes and confer with engineer and know that everything is in working order and in safe condition before starting their train down the heavy grade." And so the rules continued. Special attention was given to guarding against the parting of trains on heavy grades, handling of cars placarded EXPLOSIVES or INFLAMMABLE, running

Frank E. Baxter was to have graduated in the class of 1881 from Cornell University. A few months before graduation he became ill and, when he recovered, took a job as a chainman with a surveying party to earn the money to complete his schooling. Within weeks he was chief of the party. One position led to another, and Frank Baxter never did get his college degree. He went on after the Uintah was built to become a principal in one of the construction companies that built the Western Pacific. (*Charles W. Baxter Collection*)

over track or bridges covered by slow orders, having a trainman constantly on the rear car of every train when both ascending and descending grades, guarding against flat wheels, and so on. Speed restrictions were imposed requiring all trains to use fifty minutes descending the heavy grade between Baxter Pass and Atchee, and 55 minutes between Baxter Pass and Wendella, although in the 1930s this latter minimum running time down the five per cent to Wendella was reduced to forty minutes and finally to 35 minutes. One of the articulateds with a short train could safely travel this distance, less than seven miles, in 35 minutes, but the Shays they replaced just couldn't be hurried, uphill or down!

Trains drifting downhill from the pass, with their brake shoes smoking, rounded two spectacular overlook curves that soon became known as

A railroad without passenger service would have been practically unthinkable in the early years of this century. Even in a region with few potential passengers, the Uintah ran a regular train. It wasn't long, however, before they discovered the need for more suitable motive power — something more economical and a bit faster than the slow-moving Shays. Early in 1905 Baldwin built a pair of 0-6-2 tank engines to pull the passenger train. They hardly looked like passenger engines. Most railroads would have assigned them to switching duties. But they *could* go over Baxter Pass. Here's one of them doing the job — pulling one car up the pass! Below is the water tank, telephone booth, 60-degree mainline curve, and the reversing track at Columbine. *(Both: F. A. Kennedy photos; top: V. L. McCoy Collection; bottom: D. H. Gerbaz Collection)*

On the occasion of a picnic at Columbine (above) photographer Kennedy has persuaded some of the area's earlier residents to pose before his camera. The Ute gentleman seated with his squaws behind the ice cream freezer was known as Cap'n. Jinks. The Uintah conductor at the right, with his wife and daughter and a young friend, is Henry "Soapy" Smith. *(V. L. McCoy Collection)*

The first 60-degree reverse curve (below) below Columbine was at milepost 39, and it soon became known as "Hairpin Curve." Here two Shay-geared engines pause with their train on the five per cent just above the curve to be recorded on another of "Judge" Kennedy's glass plates. *(Denver Public Library Western Collection)*

Below the "Hairpin Curve" at milepost 39 there was one more 60-degree curve and it, too, was frequently called "Hairpin Curve" or, to keep things straight, "Muleshoe Curve." It was *too* sharp, the men claimed, to deserve the name "Horseshoe." The same Independence Day excursion train is featured in both photos; below, photographer Kennedy has pointed his lens more to the north to include Lake McAndrews in the scene. *(Top: Del H. Gerbaz Collection; bottom: V. L. McCoy Collection)*

"Lookout Point" and, below it, "Windy Point." The views of the valley below and the canyons and mesas to the north and west were truly breathtaking.

Next was a short siding at Deer Run. This spur branched off from the descending five per cent grade of the main line to angle slightly upward onto the adjacent hillside, somewhat resembling a runaway track. During the railway's early years it was reserved for just this purpose, and a switch-tender was stationed there when westbound trains were due. The switch remained set for the siding until the engineer of the downward-bound train whistled for the main, at which time the switch would be realigned. After a few years this practice was discontinued and the spur was used only rarely thereafter as an auxiliary coaling station. A gondola of coal left spotted on the siding would be sufficiently higher than the adjacent main line so that the fuel could easily be shoveled into the tender of an engine stopped next to the gondola. But this still was not as easy as coaling from the tipples at Atchee or Carbonera, and there were fuel facilities at Wendella and Dragon, too, so Deer Run was seldom used.

On past Deer Run there was a sweeping reverse curve near milepost 37 and then a tightening of the brake shoes on the wheels approaching the water stop at Columbine. Named for the state flower which peeked out from the tall grass under the aspen and pines there, Columbine was a popular summertime picnic spot for the railway employees and gilsonite miners and their families. There was the water tank at the upper end of a sharp horseshoe curve, a telephone shack part way around the curve and a track cutting across from near the tank to the lower end of the curve forming a reversing loop. With the wyes at Wendella and Baxter Pass, this loop at Columbine was seldom used, and it was removed in the 1930s.

Downhill from Columbine the trains meandered through the scrub oak for about a mile and a half, steadily losing altitude on the five per cent grade. Then at milepost 39 they reversed direction on another sixty-degree turn, this one appropriately called "Hairpin Curve," overlooking Lake McAndrews and continued on down a short ways to the final sixty-degree "Hairpin" or "Muleshoe" which turned the track back toward the lake. Pass-

ing a couple of corrals, a section house and the large icehouse on the shore of the lake, the grade lessened for a while skirting Lake McAndrews and then resumed its five per cent drop for the last mile into Wendella. Backed up behind a small rock and earth-fill dam built when the railroad was constructed, the lake fed the water tank at Wendella. It was named for John McAndrews, who had been born at Madison, Indiana, on the last day of 1855. He had come to the Uintah Basin in 1884 to accept a position with the Indian Service as chief herder of cattle on the Ouray Reservation. He had possibly been in the Basin earlier, though, in connection with his service since he was 17 in the quartermaster's department of the Army.[19] He had become active in the gilsonite developments in the late 1880s and the 1890s, becoming a friend and associate of C. O. Baxter. He was appointed a superintendent of the Uintah Railway and the connecting Uintah Toll Road Company when they were built.

At Wendella the gradient decreased to a rather modest 3.34 per cent for the little more than a mile to Sewall, then became less than three per cent for the remaining 11.2 miles to Dragon. Wendella was established, with a wye, coaling facilities and a water tank, as the helper station on the north (or west, according to the timetable) side of Baxter Pass. The Shay which had been a helper for a train from Atchee to Baxter Pass would usually run light down to Wendella and wait there to help boost the next eastbound freight up the five per cent. After the railroad was extended past Dragon to Watson and Rainbow in 1911, the Shays seldom ran past Wendella. A brand-new Mikado, the No. 30, which was a large and powerful engine for a three-foot gauger of that date, was purchased from Baldwin late in the year for use on the portion of the Uintah beyond Wendella. Except for a single Shay, most frequently the No. 1, which often worked as mine switcher on the steep Rainbow branch, and the little 0-6-2T's which handled the passenger run, the Mike did most of the work on "the north end" until the articulateds arrived in 1926 and 1928. Even then, in the late 1920s, articulateds Nos. 50 and 51 often were worked only between Atchee and Wendella, turning on the wye at the latter point and coupling onto loads of gilsonite left there by the No. 30.

Most of the town of Dragon, or Dragon Junction, can be seen above. The Uintah Railway depot is to the left and the freight warehouse toward the right, with stables and freight wagons behind it, back near Evacuation Creek. In the right foreground building materials for the railway's hotel are stacked, and the narrow-gauge Pullman nearby is apparently serving as an interim hotel while the permanent one is under construction just out of the picture to the left of the freshly graded area. Below is Dragon Camp. (*Both: F. A. Kennedy photos; top: Charles J. Neal Collection; bottom: V. L. McCoy Collection*)

The photo below shows the open cut of the Black Dragon Vein and the loading trestle extending out from the mine over the railway's siding. At the right is a view looking in the opposite direction from that same loading trestle. Due to a horizontal faulting and shifting, the vein was discontinuous at this level — it extended vertically downward from the small portal seen at the left edge of the picture. *(Right: H. S. Gale, U. S. Geological Survey; below: F. A. Kennedy photo from C. J. Neal Collection)*

The miners of Dragon Camp, Utah, pose like black-faced minstrels at the mine entrance. In picking the brittle gilsonite from the vein, quantities of fine chocolate-colored dust filled the air to coat any and everything within range. The dust was entirely insoluble in water, but did mix to some extent with the body oils and worked its way deep into the pores of the skin. It was impossible to wash off in cold water, and the addition of heat and soap didn't help much. (*F. A. Kennedy photo from E. V. Earp Collection*)

The Baldwin side-tanker No. 20 (below) makes a near-perfect portrait of the Uintah's unique passenger power. Her twin, No. 21 (opposite page) on the trestle at Rainbow Junction has her usual lone combine. Both 0-6-2Ts had 34-inch drivers and 13 x 18-inch cylinders and weighed a bit over 34 tons in working order. Nice compact little packages. Their over-all length was 28 feet, 9 inches — less than that of any Uintah boxcar or flat! (*Bottom: Gerald M. Best Collection, courtesy of D. S. Richter; opposite: F. A. Kennedy photo from Denver Public Western Collection*)

From Wendella the valley of Evacuation Creek descended rather easily between the rolling hills and high mesas on both sides, and the track followed the often-dry creekbed amid the sagebrush, scrub oak and juniper to Dragon. There were short sidings at Sewall and East Vac and an even shorter stub, adequate for only two cars, at Urado. The latter name is a combination of the words Utah and Colorado, though the track, angling gradually toward the state line, did not actually cross into Utah until it was 2.8 miles past Urado. Sewall was named in honor of Arthur W. Sewall, another of the early promoters of the gilsonite industry and the railroad, who served during the first decade of the century with Avery D. Andrews and C. O. Baxter as one of the vice presidents of not only the Uintah Railway but also of the parent Barber Asphalt Paving Company and General Asphalt Company. When John M. Mack retired as president of General Asphalt and its subsidiaries in March, 1912, Sewall was elected president, and he continued to fill that position until well into the 1930s.

Early timetables, incidentally, show two other names, both of which disappeared within five years, between Sewall and Dragon Junction. Davis Canyon was at milepost 49.2 where the canyon of that name joined Evacuation Creek. A second spot 50.9 miles along the line from Mack and approximately at the state line was designated Coluta, another combination of Colorado and Utah. The Davis Canyon name was still familiar

to train crews in later years, once especially when it was the scene of a near-serious washout, although not being a station or a siding it did not show on timetables.

And so the trains reached Dragon, or Dragon Junction as it was called until 1912. This was the end of the line for passengers, 53.3 miles from Mack, but freight crews hauled much of their consist an additional mile and a quarter up the narrow defile of Camp Gulch to the mines. A small community had also grown up there in the bottom of the Gulch adjacent to the Black Dragon gilsonite vein, and it was called Dragon Camp, or sometimes Dragon Mines. The claim, from which both communities derived their names, had been located November 12, 1888, and was called the Black Dragon because the float on the surface of the ground at that point formed a perfect black dragon.[20] When the railway was completed into Dragon Junction in September, 1904, a depot, warehouse, hotel, store and several dwellings were erected there, and it became a bigger town than the mining camp. The "Junction" portion of the name was significant, for it was there that passengers and freight destined for Vernal, Fort Duchesne and other Basin points were transferred from the trains to stage coaches, buckboards, freight wagons and, somewhat later, Buick automobiles. But the story of the toll road and the stage and wagon operations beyond Dragon Junction is a story in itself.

Uintah Railway and CONNECTIONS

Map published by Uintah Railway about 1905, from I. L. Booth Collection)

Chapter Three

Stage Road Operations and Storms on the Pass

The original incorporation papers for The Uintah Railway Company which were filed with the Secretary of State of Colorado on the 4th day of November, 1903, did not, for some unknown reason, include any mention of the State of Utah. The Railway's proposed route, as noted therein, was to begin "at the most convenient point on the main line of The Rio Grande Western Railway Company's railroad about two (2) miles west of Crevasse station . . ." and to continue north "up along West Salt Wash Creek to a point near its source . . . , thence by the most feasible route over Book Cliffs to a point on the west fork of Evacuation Creek; thence down said Evacuation Creek, by the most feasible route to a point on the west line of the State of Colorado in the County of Rio Blanco in said State, together also with such spurs and branches . . . as may be found expedient and useful . . ."[1] The incorporators must have known that their rails would continue across the border into Utah, but they did not say so. It may just have been politics, but whatever the reason for this omission it was remedied at a special meeting of the stockholders, all five of them, held in Denver on June 23, 1904. Even as the construction contractor was getting a good start on the grading, the Articles of Incorporation were amended to include the phrase, "states of Colorado and Utah" in a number of places.

The management had more in mind than just acknowledging the existence of Utah, however. They added three full paragraphs to the description of the proposed route of their railroad, which had been essentially as summarized in the preceding paragraph. Their rather ambitious plans spoke of extending the Uintah Railway past the state line along Evacuation Creek to the White River, then west and northwest to Fort Duchesne in Uintah County, crossing the Green River at the town of Ouray. Connecting with this line at a point in Coyote Basin east of Ouray, another line would be built north to cross the Green River at or below Jensen, then northwest up along Ashley Fork to Vernal, continuing southwest from there to Fort Duchesne. The third additional paragraph mentioned the short branch up Camp Gulch to the mines at Dragon, "together also with such spurs and branches . . . as may be found expedient and useful in the development and prosecution of the business of said Company as a railroad corporation."[2] It seemed logical at the time that the railroad would be built to Fort Duchesne and Vernal. However, such an extension definitely took second place to the branch up Camp Gulch in the minds of the management, since gilsonite was the primary interest. The large bridges which would have been required to cross the White and the Green Rivers caused them second thoughts, as well.

An argument in favor of extending the railway on to Vernal and Fort Duchesne was that a majority of the traffic over such an extension would be destined for points in the Basin. This would provide a revenue backhaul for the trains which had hauled gilsonite down to Mack. The gilsonite traffic was entirely one way, and the empty cars going

The Kennedy photos on these pages show the Uintah Railway stage line between Dragon and Vernal. (Above) the road is high on the mesa overlooking Evacuation Canyon. (Below) the road is farther north in a gulch near White River. (Above, opposite) the team and stage have a little mud to contend with crossing the badlands or "Devil's Playground" north of Kennedy station, between the White and the Green, and (below, opposite) some more mud along the Green River near Alhandra. *(Above: J. L. Booth Collection; below: D. H. Gerbaz Collection; above, opposite page: W. A. Banks Collection; below, opposite page: Charles W. Baxter Collection)*

114

For stage road passengers traveling to Vernal, the Green River ferry at Alhandra was a welcome sign that they were nearing the end of their journey. Barring any mishaps, another hour on the road would see them at their destination. The center photo is of Fort Duchesne — a rather typical Western Army post. Travelers outbound from the Basin looked forward to their arrival at the Uintah Railway Hotel at Dragon (bottom). After the jouncing, dusty eight or nine-hour stage ride, a cooling shower, a hearty meal and the crisp, clean bed were appreciated. *(Top: W. A. Banks Collection; center: courtesy of Mr. and Mrs. G. E. Untermann, Utah Field House of Natural History; bottom: James Ozment Collection)*

back to the mines did not furnish any revenue for the company. Thus any merchandise or manufactured goods billed for Basin destinations could be transported over the railway as far as Dragon Junction at an almost negligible additional cost. But no matter what arguments were presented in favor of extension, it still appeared to the Uintah's builders that the sparsely settled Basin would not generate enough traffic to justify the cost of more than a hundred miles of additional railroad construction. Nevertheless, any traffic that might be developed would be welcome.

Faced with this dilemma, the Barber Asphalt people came up with a logical compromise. They would build toll roads, rather than a railroad, beyond Dragon Junction and would operate a stage and wagon service in connection with the railroad. Soon after the railway was completed to the Junction and Dragon Camp, the grading and bridge crews were put to work to the north and northwest of Dragon building 112 miles of toll roads connecting that point with Vernal and Fort Duchesne. Most of the road construction took place during the spring and summer of 1905.[3] The commissioner of Indian Affairs in his 1905 report to the secretary of the Interior noted that "Permission was granted [The Uintah Railway] company on June 1, June 5, and June 11, 1905, to survey and locate a line of railroad, to construct a toll road, and to operate a ferry in the Uintah Reservation in Utah. The authority was granted in deference to the wishes of the War Department, since the immediate construction of the toll road and operation of the ferry would greatly facilitate the handling of supplies for that Department. The company's employees were permitted to enter the reservation under restrictions intended to safeguard the interests of the Indians, and the War Department will cooperate with the Indian agent to prevent any illegitimate use being made of the authority granted."[4]

As previously noted, Fort Duchesne had been established rather hastily in the summer of 1886 to quiet settlers' fears of possible Ute hostilities in the area. As such it was one of the last, if not the last, Army post established anywhere in the West primarily for protection against Indian uprisings. Troops from the Fort had since that date helped build and maintain some of the roads into the Uintah Basin, especially the road from Price, and the Army was interested in any means of shortening its supply lines to these troops. So the railway company's decision to build the toll roads was encouraged and welcomed by the Army as well as the pioneering settlers in the Basin, although both groups were still eager for actual rail service to reach them. The toll roads were less than they had hoped for, but were an improvement on anything they had previously had.

When construction work on the roads and bridges was complete late in 1905, the railway company secured a United States mail contract to serve the Vernal and Fort Duchesne areas, and they started daily passenger, freight and mail service over the roads to those points. Rather than bridging the wide Green River, the company in a characteristic spirit of frugality installed ferries at Ouray on the Bonanza-Fort Duchesne road and at Alhandra, about twelve miles downstream from Jensen on the Dragon-Bonanza-Vernal road. This move was to cause problems in later years, especially in the fall and spring when the ice forming or breaking up on the river prevented easy movement of the ferries. During the coldest winter months the ice was sufficiently thick to support the teams and the freight wagons or stages they pulled. The company acquired their own teams and wagons for the service and by the end of 1906 owned over 160 head of horses, most of them large freight horses. The Vernal *Express* reported that the feed bill alone was coming to $25,000 per year. The allowance for a freight horse was 25 pounds of hay and twenty pounds of oats per day, while the stage horses got only 18 pounds of oats with their daily 25 pounds of hay.[5]

About a year after the roads were completed, and when the teams were moving the passenger and freight traffic to Vernal and Fort Duchesne on daily schedules, a new subsidiary company was created to continue these operations and maintain the roads. The Uintah Toll Road Company was incorporated November 5, 1906, in New Jersey, with a capitalization of $25,000. Except for five qualifying shares held by its directors, all its stock was held by The Uintah Railway Company. You will recall that all except five shares of the Railway's stock were owned by Barber Asphalt Paving Company, which was in turn a wholly-owned

Wool was second only to gilsonite — though a distant second — as a source of freight revenue for the Uintah Railway. Above, a six-horse team is ready to leave the Bonanza shearing plant with a consignment of the 1912 clip on the first lap of its long trip to Boston. The shearing plant (below) was located about four miles north of Bonanza, Utah. *(Both photos: Charles J. Neal Collection)*

subsidiary of General Asphalt Company. So it is not surprising to find that the directors of the newly-formed Uintah Toll Road Company were John M. Mack, A. W. Sewall, Avery D. Andrews and Clyde Browne of Philadelphia and George H. B. Martin of Camden, New Jersey.[6] All of these men were also officers of the parent companies.

And so for the next two decades, the stage and wagon operations were an integral part of the picture of Uintah Railway operations. They were never successful, in and of themselves, in making any money for the company, but did funnel traffic down from the Basin to the railway. Gradually, as motor vehicles came into more common use and cross-country roads were built, the toll roads fell into disuse and service was abandoned. But during its first years the road system was quite important to the company, and even more important to the economy of the Basin.

It should be noted that the major source of information on both rail and road operations for the following chapters has been the pages of the weekly Vernal *Express*. And, since Vernal was more than fifty miles from the end of the railroad, the stage and wagon operations frequently were given more extensive coverage by the *Express*.

For a number of years weekly advertisements in the *Express* gave readers and travelers the schedules for both the stages and the connecting trains at Dragon. A stage left Vernal for Dragon at 7:00 a.m. daily, while another had departed Fort Duchesne for Dragon an hour earlier. On arrival at Dragon, passengers stayed overnight at the Uintah Railway Hotel there and left at 7:00 the following morning for Mack, with arrival there scheduled for 12:00 noon. Returning, the train puffed out of Mack at 2:00 p.m. daily and pulled into Dragon that evening at 7:00. After another restful night at the hotel, the travelers boarded their stages the next morning and departed for either Vernal or Fort Duchesne at 7:00. These advertisements also affirmed that "all stages carry United States mail and express," and that the trains connected with the Rio Grande Western Railway at Mack, Colorado. The name of the company's Vernal agent, J. Q. Logan, supplied a final official touch at the bottom of each week's ad.[7]

Besides these advertisements, there was some mention of the Uintah Railway or its toll road operation in practically every issue of the *Express* during the early years. Lists of passengers arriving and departing Vernal on the stages were common — generally twenty to thirty people in each direction would be an average week's business over the line. In January of 1906 the *Express* reported that the Uintah County commissioners, meeting in Vernal, had passed by unanimous vote an ordinance "granting C. O. Baxter, his heirs and assigns, the right to construct, maintain and operate a public toll road from a point on Green River at Ouray . . . to Fort DuChesne."[8] Three weeks later the paper noted that the Government telephone and telegraph line between Price and Fort Duchesne had been abandoned, since the Fort had established connections with Dragon. People living along the old line were very anxious that it be allowed to remain in place and had offered to purchase it from the Government.[9] Elsewhere in the same issue the *Express's* scribe reported the Vernal post office had received word of the letting of a new mail contract — henceforth the mail would come from Dragon to Vernal via Bonanza, and from Dragon to Fort Duchesne via Bonanza. John McAndrews as agent for The Uintah Railway Company had received the contract. And so the news continued. Week by week the story unfolded. Brief sentences and paragraphs accumulated over the months in the pages of the *Express* and chronicled the life and times of the Uintah Railway and Toll Road.

The first full year of stage road operations was 1906, and in that year alone there was a great variety of news dealing with the roads, as well as the railway. In mid-February the railway company commenced building shearing pens along the Dragon road just north of the Green River ferry to take care of the wool clip from the region's sheep. A month later the company's bridge across the White River was washed out when a large ice jam upstream broke loose and carried a span of the bridge with it. The railway company had anticipated the loss of the bridge and had strung a cable to carry the mail across the stream, so there was no delay in the mail service.[10] Within a week after the washout the company was again "delivering large quantities of freight at the Vernal depot," although repair work on the White River bridge was not entirely completed until

It's an ordinary day in Dragon as two "trains" of wagons (left) prepare to leave for the Basin. Below, the cargo is more unusual — a boiler destined for the oil fields at Rangely, Colorado. Its water tank is coming along on the trailer behind. The bottom photo shows the White River station, also known as Ignatio. *(Left: W. A. Banks Collection; center: C. J. Neal photo; bottom: F. A. Kennedy photo from Charles W. Baxter Collection)*

early in April. It was reported that the wide wagon wheels were "smoothing the road up nicely and making it an ideal Automobile road." The company had put on eight extra teams and expected to move the 200 tons of freight then waiting at Dragon and deliver it at Vernal within a few days.[11]

Early in April C. O. Baxter spent a week in Vernal looking after the business of the Uintah Railway. He placed an order with the Ashley Lumber Company for lumber with which to build barns where the roads crossed the Green and White Rivers and at Kennedy's Hole, roughly halfway between the two rivers on the Bonanza-Vernal road. Always the promoter, Baxter let it be known the railway would soon speed up the freight service, keeping the loaded wagons moving day and night from Dragon until they reached Vernal. Fresh horses would be kept at each way station so that as soon as an outfit arrived there they could be hitched to the wagons and pull out for the next station without delay. Twenty-two new broad-tired wagons had been ordered and eight six-horse teams were being purchased[12] to add to the ones already on the road. Obviously Baxter and McAndrews were serious about securing and developing the potential traffic of the Uintah Basin.

Besides being a promoter, Charles O. Baxter was also an enterprising businessman not afraid to try out the latest technological developments. In the same April 14, 1906, issue that told of Baxter's visit, the editor of the Vernal Express observed that some people feared Baxter was wasting the Uintah Railway's money by experimenting with automobiles there in the Uintah country. Editor Dan Hillman proceeded to calm those fears with "a little inside information on the subject." He disclosed that "This company established an automobile factory of its own to experiment with large cars for rough road work. When they perfected the large forty-five horsepower car, like the one that has made several trips to Vernal and over the reservation country, and put them on exhibition at the New York automobile show, they took orders for twenty-five of the machines. Probably there was some profit in this deal alone to offset a few dollars of the expenditures in the

Uintah country, as the selling price of such a machine is $7,000."[13] No doubt the editor was referring to the Mack Brothers and their new factory in Allentown, Pennsylvania, which despite his statement was not *directly* connected with the General Asphalt Company. As noted, though, John M. Mack for whom the town of Mack, Colorado, was named was the first president of General Asphalt Company as well as most of its subsidiaries, including The Uintah Railway Company.

But about the stage roads, the Express's writer seldom missed an opportunity to extoll their advantages. "Although the country in general is rougher between Vernal and Dragon than between here and Price," he wrote, "the road is a boulevard compared with the Price road. A force of men with road grader and scrapers are kept at work on the road all the time, by the Uintah Railway people. There are culverts and bridges by the score and all washes are graded in from both sides and made so smooth that it is a pleasure to drive over the road."[14] Later he noted, "Traveling men and others who have occasion to visit every village and town of the state, do not hesitate in saying that the stage road from Dragon to Vernal is by far the best in the state. They also say that the horses and rigs and service in general are better. The Uintah Railway company is giving us good service, putting the mail in here between five and six o'clock every day when the roads are passable."[15] But despite the efforts of the company, traffic volume remained rather low and expenses high. In July, 1906, the freight rate from Dragon to Vernal was advanced from 45 cents per hundred pounds to sixty cents per hundred in an attempt to cut the losses. This was a change that had been expected, as the company had not hesitated to make known that the wagon end of its line was a losing proposition. Although an already high freight rate was thus made even higher, it was argued that no one could expect the company to lose money to accommodate the people.[16]

Early in November, less than four months after the rate increase, the company advised that owing to a lack of freight they were "forced to temporarily abandon the relay system of moving freight from Dragon to Vernal." They promised, however, to resume the relay system at the earliest date

Motor vehicles traveled the stage road at an early date, as illustrated by these two parked in front of the station at Dragon. The larger one at the right is a "Manhattan" omnibus manufactured by the Mack Brothers Motor Company. The year is 1906. The photo below shows a portion of the stage road known as "Boulevard Canyon," probably named by a driver or teamster who wished all the road could have been like that. *(Above: photo by Bessie Dean, now Mrs. Bessie Hunter, from Collection of Mrs. Carl Frey; below: F. A. Kennedy photo from J. L. Booth Collection)*

that increasing freight shipments would warrant its resumption. Putting in his usual plug for the company, Editor Hillman of the *Express* observed, "The system has given general satisfaction among the business people here and is by far the best freight service this remote county has ever known." He urged, "All who have freight shipped to Vernal should have it sent via Mack and Dragon, in order that the enterprise of the Uintah Railway people may be upheld and a return to the relay system hastened."[17]

Meanwhile the railway operations of the Company had settled into a smooth routine. In 1906, 12,140 tons of gilsonite were hauled south from the mines to the R.G.W. at Mack. This amounted to over 68 per cent of the total revenue tonnage moved by the railroad that year, but it was only a beginning. Six years later the gilsonite traffic peaked out at 34,511 tons for the year, nearly 85 per cent of the freight over the line.[18] Obviously the glossy black hydrocarbon was, for all practical purposes, the only reason for the existence of the Uintah Railway and would continue to be so. Efforts to develop other sources of traffic were only a sideline for the management. The major job was moving the gilsonite.

Little was allowed to interfere with the steady movement of the ore. The engine and train crews quickly became adept at hoisting it over the pass and on down to the standard gauge at Mack. And the shop forces at Atchee grew skilled at keeping the locomotives and rolling stock in tiptop condition for this demanding work. Only on rare occasions did nature throw a roadblock in their way.

Gravity, as on any mountain railroad, was an enemy, but the little Shays and side-tankers and the men who ran them regularly overcame this foe. Rock and mud slides were not uncommon during wet seasons, and they proved to be problems at times. Until the big slide above Shale Tank in 1929, however, these were usually not serious, and they could be quickly cleared from the tracks with a little help from the section crew. And then there was snow!

The first two winters were easy ones for the Uintah. That's the way it is in the Rockies. The really heavy snowfalls and crippling storms are more the exception than the rule. One or two Shays shoving a wedge plow could keep the line over Baxter Pass open with relatively little trouble most years. But even when the snowfall was rather light, it seemed the wind would never stop blowing up on the pass. Cuts would often fill with drifting snow almost as soon as they were plowed out. And when the really big blizzards came — the ones the men talked about for years afterward — there was a real battle to be fought. The opening weeks of 1907 brought the first of those big storms.

In just two years Vernal and the other communities in the Uintah Basin had come to rely upon the new railroad and its connecting stage line for practically all communication with the world outside. As long as the mail came in on schedule, everything was fine. But when snow blocked the track and the mail stopped coming, that made news. Some idea of the snow problems which the railroad encountered that January, and of the people's dependence upon rail transportation in those days before paved highways, may be gained from the following accounts published in the Vernal *Express*. They appeared in three successive issues, the first, under the headline "Delayed Mails" on Saturday, January 12, 1907:

> Last Saturday night and Sunday a heavy fall of snow on the Book Mountains caused a blockade on the Uintah Railway at the Baxter Pass, which, in spite of the strenuous efforts of the Uintah Railway company to get its trains through, lasted until Tuesday night. Vernal was without mail communication Monday and Tuesday. Prof. J. H. Paul and the students who left Vernal Saturday as well as Hon. John N. Davis, who left Vernal Monday morning, were delayed at Dragon until Tuesday night. The blockade is the first interference with the mail service between Vernal and the outside world that has occurred for years. The people took the matter philosophically as one of the unavoidable interferences to which railway traffic is subject in the winter season. The mail came in as usual, Wednesday night.[19]

By the following Saturday the situation had worsened considerably, and the story which appeared top center on the front page of that day's *Express* is quoted as follows:

One of the earliest know pictures of a train on Baxter Pass, above, shows Shay No. 1 heading down the hill with three cars. The man standing in the snow with his back to the camera is E. A. "Al" Grove, the Uintah's first superintendent. In the photo below, a little more snow, although still not enough to cover the bare branches of the scrub oak, is evident as two steamers blast up the hill nearing Shale Tank with a single passenger coach. *(Top: W. A. Banks Collection; bottom: F. A. Kennedy photo from J. L. Booth Collection)*

UINTAH RY IN WINTER

DELAYED MAILS

TRAIN HUNG UP IN 25 FEET OF SNOW

120 Miles Separates Vernal from the Great Rail-
roads and the Outside World, and the Roads
Blocked with 25 feet of Snow in Places — No
Mail for one Week.

No mail since last Saturday night and the
prospect of several more days without mail
communication from outside points is the way
Vernal is situated as we go to press.

The cause is a snow blockade on the Baxter
pass, the highest point over which the Uintah
Railway passes. The train made the journey
from Dragon to Mack last Saturday morning
but on the return trip the train with two engines stuck in the snow about half a mile this
side of the summit and was soon unable to
travel either way.

The passengers on board were Captain
Cooley, manager of the Uintah Railway Company, two other employees of the company and
three drummers. Two of the latter, viz: John
H. Crane, of Provo, F. E. West, of Ogden, have
since arrived at Vernal, after a most entranc-
ing experience which they appear to appreciate
very much. These passengers remained on the
train from Saturday until Monday, when they
were able to make their way to McAndrews
through the assistance of the Greek section
hands.

Since that time, owing to the continuous
storm and wind all efforts to extricate the train
have proven futile, though every available man
has been at work endeavoring to clear the track.

The people seem to appreciate the condition
which the company has been suddenly and un-
avoidably placed in. Though the old residents
seem to think that it would have been possible
to bring the first class mail over the pass on
snow shoes. This is the longest period that this
community has been deprived of mail facilities
since the winter of 1879.

As things turned out, the blockade was broken
the day after the above article was published,
when the storm ended. John McAndrews described the railway's snow-fighting efforts to the
editor of the *Express,* and this account appeared:

The snow blockade on the Uintah Railway,
at the Baxter Pass was finally broken last Sunday and the first mail, consisting of fifty-nine
bags of mail matter, was delivered at the Vernal Post Office, Monday night. It was the first
that had been delivered since the preceding
Saturday.

Mr. McAndrews, of the Railway Company,
stated upon his arrival here that the cause of
the trouble was the heavy wind accompanied,
at intervals, by heavy snowstorms that rendered
all their work useless until the storm abated last
Sunday morning. The company had 75 men at
work on this end of the blockade and all obtainable men on the other end, but until the storm
ceased the wind filled in the drifts as fast as
the snow was shoveled out, thereby undoing all
their work. It was also almost impossible for
the men to endure the cold as the wind was so
fierce and the temperature so low. They were
not long getting out when the storm ended. Mr.
McAndrews pronounces this the heaviest winter
he has ever seen in this section of the country.
The company is well equipped for handling
snow. Two snow plows and five locomotives
were employed in breaking the blockade. The
trains have been making regular trips since
Sunday.[20]

So it was that January of 1907 gave the Uintah railroaders their first real taste of winter railroading. They were to know more of the bitter
wind and stinging snow as the years went by.
The next winter was ushered in on the night of
September 29, 1907, when the first snow of the
season put a white sheet over the divide at Baxter Pass. But as the season developed it amounted
to little more than that. There were no big storms
on the Book Cliffs and no blockades that winter.
But then, after this respite, the winter of 1908-09
hit the little railway with greater fury than ever.

First, there were the small storms, leaving
their accumulation of snow on the pass and occasionally tying up the railroad for a day or two.
Then, on top of the snow that had already fallen,
came the blizzards to deposit more snow and
blow it across the mountain for days on end,
drifting in front of and around any train that
might attempt to defy the storm's wrath. The
sequence of events as the winter unfolded is interesting to relate.

Even before the snows came, "heavy moisture" softened the roadbed and caused a derailment of an engine and three cars about fifteen
miles north of Mack, on October 25th. The fireman, Roy Miller of Fruita, Colorado, was severely
scalded and bruised in the wreck, and the toes of

Uintah Railway Claim Agent Frank Kennedy went out with his "5x7" view camera on winter days as well as summer ones. Here he caught Shay No. 1 in the siding at Baxter Pass. Later (below) a gang of Uintah section men pose on the Shay for "Judge" Kennedy after they had helped clear the line. *(Both: J. L. Booth Collection)*

one foot had to be amputated. None of the passengers on the train were injured, though.[21] Two more months passed without incident, and then the storms started.

In its weekly issue dated December 18, 1908, the Vernal *Express* reported that a fierce storm had been raging for two or three days and that traffic had been delayed. The snow had drifted to such proportions, six feet in some places, that the stage failed to arrive in Vernal. Bob Johnson, the driver, had made it some distance beyond the Green River, but was then forced to turn back after he'd very nearly tipped over several times when he'd missed the road in the dark. Johnson resumed his trip the next morning and reached town about 11:00. The same day's stage from Vernal to Dragon was similarly delayed before reaching White River, and the following morning superintendent John McAndrews took the mail out himself on his buckboard to keep the schedule.[22] Elsewhere in the same issue the editor noted that the Uintah Railway Company was way behind on the delivery of freight, owing to the bad condition of the roads. Some merchants were complaining that all of their Christmas goods were not in yet. The company's Green River ferry at Alhandra had "been having all sorts of trouble the past two weeks." It seems the river had been frozen just enough to keep the ferry from running, and yet the ice was not strong enough to bear the weight of a team and wagon. Therefore a number of loads of incoming freight had piled up on the other side of the river. All mail and express were being transferred over by hand, and the passengers were walking across the thin ice.[23]

Only three weeks later the local merchants were notified that they would have to pay a slightly higher freight rate. The Dragon to Vernal rate was increased from 60 cents per hundred to 65 cents per hundred pounds, with corresponding increases in the rates from Dragon to other Basin points.[24] General Manager M. W. Cooley, in an advertisement, stated, "we have always lost money on our wagon hauls, and to cover such loss we are obliged to raise our wagon rates 5 cents per hundred pounds. We feel that this explanation is due and that reasonable objection cannot be made to an increase that means simply hauling at cost."[25]

Not long after came the first blockade of the winter. The *Express's* correspondent in Dragon wrote the following for the paper:

> The Uintah Railway was blocked last week and we were without mail for a couple of days. Sunday morning all hands from the mine left for the summit to clear the track, but before they got to their destination two engines pushing a snow plough came down the hill and nearly buried the crew in snow, as they scampered out of the way of the engine. Half of the crew returned to camp for the night while the other half went over the summit to shovel snow. Monday morning the men again were taken out to shovel on the north slope. Traffic is now again restored.[26]

The railroaders and the gilsonite miners were, of course, entirely dependent upon one another. At times like these the Railway was fortunate to be able to recruit the miners to help keep the track clear. For the Uintah Railway's section hands, many of whom had been born in Greece, shoveling snow was a full time job for a number of weeks many winters. It was not always a safe job, either, for the laborers or for the engine and train crews. Bucking snow with a wedge plow coupled in front of a Shay or two could be a dangerous business. On occasion the snow between the rails would pack up and form ice, and derailments became common under such conditions. Then, too, the slick rails and heavy gradient offered every chance for a runaway. On Wednesday, February 10, 1909, the first two deaths in the railway's short history occurred, and at least in part were a result of the storm. Here's the story:

TWO KILLED

———

Engineer Joseph Lane and Unknown Greek Met Death in Wreck on Baxter Pass.

———

Engineer Joseph Lane and a Greek whose name, other than "Nick" is unknown, were killed in a wreck on the Baxter pass on the Uintah railroad Wednesday, while working with a crew shoveling snow from the tracks. The crew foreman and two other Greeks were seriously injured.

The engine got from under the control of the engineer in some way and shot down the mountain side at a fearful rate of speed. It rolled over and over many times and when it

Just about ready to leave Mack is this happy crowd of employees and their families and friends (above). No doubt the girls' white dresses were not quite so white when the train returned the weary celebrants home many hours later. Another Fourth of July excursion train (below) stops at Lone Tree Curve on its return trip from the picnic grounds at Columbine. The year is 1905 or 1906, and the new Shay on the point is No. 3. The engine and train crews donated their services for these holiday trips, and the company supplied the train. *(Both: F. A. Kennedy photos from Denver Public Library Western Collection)*

stopped there was nothing left but scrap iron. The wreck occurred on this side of the pass.

Joseph Lane was a man about 50 years old. He leaves a wife and one child who were in Denver at the time. Nothing is known of the Greek, who was killed, or of those who were injured.

The tracks were cleared late Wednesday and a train from Mack reached Dragon at midnight.[27]

The engine involved was Shay No. 3 — its throttle pierced Lane's chest. A witness to this accident, William Cook, later related that the engine had been pushing a plow which hit the packed snow so hard that it lifted the engine right off the track and started it rolling down the mountainside. Cook also stated, in an interview nearly fifty years after the wreck, that "Nick" had not been killed, but that he lost three fingers as the engine rolled over.[28] The *Report of Accidents issued by The Colorado State Railroad Commission* for 1909, however, confirms that "One trainman and one other employee were killed" on the Uintah Railway that year.

By the following week things had gotten worse rather than better. The mail had not arrived in Vernal for nearly a week, and Editor Hillman was not quite so philosophical about the delay this time. Here is what he had to say on the front page of February 19th's paper:

AFTER SEVEN DAYS

First Mail For Week Due Today — Blockade on Baxter Pass Was Very Serious.

One of the most interesting events of the week will be the arrival of the mail from Dragon, the first since last Friday night, February 12. There has been another blockade on Baxter pass and it has been a bad one. From 75 to 100 men have been bucking snow every day and almost as fast as they got it out of the cut the wind blew it back again. The drift was something like two miles long and some times it was as much as 20 feet high.

An accumulation of mail and passengers piled up at Mack and Dragon to awful proportions. The passengers at each end grew very impatient, especially those who had been there since last Friday and more than one thought seriously of walking across. In fact more than one tried it. R. S. Collett, who left here last Sat-

urday tackled snow shoes part of the way and reached Mack Monday. Horace Coltharp who has been in Mack since last Friday has kept a regular trail for some distance on the other side, trying his luck toward the summit of the pass. In some places the snow was almost up to his head.

The first train to reach Dragon was a coal train on Wednesday afternoon. The people of the valley are very patient but there is a limit and they will begin to wonder one of these days why the Uintah Railway company does not transfer the mail from one end of the blockade to the other on snow shoes. Uncle Sam usually figures that nothing must delay the United States mail except fire or water.

It appears that very few passengers were as determined as the Messrs. Collett and Coltharp. The Uintah Railway hotels in Mack and Dragon were warm and comfortable places when the blizzard was raging up on the pass. And despite the good editor's suggestion, there is no evidence that the Uintah ever used snow shoes to supplement its Shays on Baxter Pass. The company's single-minded efforts to reopen the line were costing enough as it was.

Late in February, 1909, it was estimated that the blockades on Baxter would cost the Railway more than $10,000 for the winter.[29] The following week in a letter to the editor, George Billings of Dragon stated he had been reliably informed that the blockade had cost the Uintah Railway people over $30,000 so far. Writing in response to the criticism of the company, "as a citizen and observer of what is actually being done and in justice to what [he considered] as extraordinary efforts," he felt the public should know the exact situation. "Since February 1, or about that date," he wrote, "they, the Uintah Railway people, have had a continual battle with the snow on Baxter pass and to my certain knowledge have been expending from $400 to $1,000 per day bucking and shoveling snow, and each succeeding day on getting to the pass finding things in about the same condition as on the previous morning and have succeeded only in getting about three trains over in that time, but they are at it still."[30] They didn't seem to be discouraged, Billings continued, and "with Captain Cooley to the front urging them and encouraging them on, the common laborers getting from $4 to $6 every day, they would come

At McAndrews (above) and at Mack (below) these pictures give an impression of the Uintah's passenger business. The excursion party at the lake requiring two coaches for accommodation was highly unusual. Most days the single combination car was sufficient for all the riders that showed up. The scene (below) was typical — combine No. 1, a few sacks of mail and a handful of passengers — and most of the passengers were employees rather than paying ones! *(Above: J. Horace Erwin photo from D. H. Gerbaz Collection; below: F. A. Kennedy photo from Denver Public Library Western Collection)*

out and work . . ." Great credit was due both the company and the individuals, Billings felt.

Even after all that, the railroaders' troubles were not quite over that winter. As late as Sunday, March 7th, the train failed to arrive in Dragon. It had snowed all day making traffic over the pass impossible. This time the drifts were cleared by Monday morning, though.[31] Later that month ice breaking up on the Green River took the Ouray ferryboat out, but the stage-road bridge over the White remained safe. When asked where the ferryboat was, W. D. Halpin, assistant secretary & treasurer for the railway, replied that he thought most likely it was nearing the Gulf of California, as they had never heard from it.[32]

But the life and times of a railroad are, of course, not composed entirely of misfortune, storm skies and drifting snow. Every winter was not a hard one, nor was every day a winter day. By June 30, 1909, the thermometer read 100 degrees in the shade at Dragon, and nearly everyone in

camp was contemplating spending July 5th on Baxter Pass. There were still a few snow drifts to be seen up there. Despite a severe rain storm in Dragon on Sunday, the 4th, the holiday excursion train the next morning took about forty people with well filled picnic baskets up among the pines on the pass. "Every one reported a good time."[33] Such was life for the Uintah's people. Tens of thousands of tasks performed by a hundred and more men merged, day after day, to become the history of a railroad. It might have been Roy McCoy laying a fire on the grates of a Shay as the dark sky gradually lightened in the east, or maybe George Komatas and his gang replacing ties in the canyon below Carbonera. It was Jim Booth transmitting the orders instructing an extra freight to wait at Wendella until No. 2 cleared, or Vic Earp applying a little more air as his Shay eased a string of flats into "Hairpin Curve" above Lake McAndrews. These and many more men were the Uintah Railway!

Holiday train and Uintah vista between the east switch at Baxter Pass and milepost 34.
(*F. A. Kennedy photo from C. J. Neal Collection*)

71

Lake McAndrews proved an attractive subject for more than one photographer. The Denver & Rio Grande's company photographer, George L. Beam, recorded this scene on an "8x10" glass negative about 1910. Beyond the Mack rail car and the icehouse, three different levels of the railway climbing towards Baxter Pass can be seen.

(D.&R.G.W. files, courtesy of Jackson C. Thode)

Chapter Four

High Freight Rates and First Complaints

Snow drifts and the severe gradients on Baxter Pass were not the only problems which confronted the Uintah's management. In April of 1907 the American Asphalt Association, a smaller competitor of the Gilson Asphaltum Company in the mining and selling of gilsonite, registered a complaint against the Uintah Railway Company with the Interstate Commerce Commission. They alleged that the railway, wholly owned, as was the Gilson Company, by the General Asphalt Company, had set a rate of 50 cents per hundred pounds, or about $15 a car, to transport gilsonite from Dragon, Utah, to Mack, Colorado, and that this rate was unjust and unreasonable. Among other things, it was pointed out in the complaint that sheep were carried the same distance by the Uintah for $14 per carload.[1] Commissioner Prouty of the I.C.C. held hearings on the complaint early in November at Denver and thereupon granted the plaintiff thirty days to prepare a brief and the defendant fifteen days in which to answer it.[2] The resulting Report of the Commission in the case, "American Asphalt Association v. Uintah Railway Company; Submitted December 20, 1907, Decided March 11, 1908," though not included here, makes interesting reading. Sixteen pages in length, it set precedents which would affect the Uintah for years afterward.

The I.C.C. examiners were quick to observe that the General Asphalt interests built the Uintah Railway for no other purpose than to haul gilsonite from their mines, and that it was a rather expensive railroad to build and operate. The abstract preceding their Report sums up the decision of the Commission:

> Where a railroad has been constructed for a special purpose, and does not form part of any general industrial development, it does not stand in the same relation to the public as a railroad chartered and built for general purposes, and the reasonableness of its rates must be determined by the financial returns which they produce rather than by comparison with rates in effect elsewhere.

> *Held,* That under the peculiar circumstances of this case a rate of $8 per ton is a reasonable charge to be imposed by the defendant for the transportation of gilsonite, a low-grade commodity, a distance of 54 miles.

A number of points are then brought out in the Report to substantiate the decision.

The complainant, American Asphalt Association, insisted that the rate of 50 cents per hundred pounds or $10 per ton, charged since the Uintah had opened for operation some two years earlier, was inherently extortionate for hauling a commodity like gilsonite a distance of only 54 miles. It was noted that the rate of the Denver & Rio Grande for gilsonite shipped from Mack to St. Louis, a distance of 1,313 miles, was only $7.75 per ton. The I.C.C. thought, however, that the Uintah's rate should not be fixed by comparison with other rates then in effect, since the road was constructed for the express purpose of bringing out gilsonite and practically for no other purpose. On the other hand it was especially important, because of the competitive relationship of the par-

The "Union Depot" at Mack was in a convenient location between the standard-gauge main line of the Rio Grande Western and the narrow-gauge Uintah track. At the depot (below) waiting for the train, two members of the party have traded derby and sunbonnet for "Judge" Kennedy's benefit. *(Both: F. A. Kennedy photos; above: V. L. McCoy Collection; below: J. L. Booth Collection)*

ties in the case, that a rate be set that was reasonable and just for both the complainant and the defendant.

It was evident that the General Asphalt combine had the power to set an arbitrarily high freight rate and then sell the gilsonite it mined at a cost less than that of production including transportation. The profits made on the rail haul would more than offset any loss from selling the mineral at "less than cost." It made no difference to the parent concern which of its subsidiaries made the final profit. Thus the "Asphalt Trust" could put its gilsonite on the market at a price which must inevitably drive its competitor out of business altogether. On the other hand, if the charge for transportation was less than the cost of furnishing same, the end result would be exactly the opposite. The Uintah Railway Company would lose upon what it transported for both the Gilson Asphaltum Company and the complainant American Asphalt Association, while the Gilson Company earned money only upon its own tonnage, the total result being a loss to the controlling General Asphalt Company.

Having shown the necessity of setting an equitable rate, I.C.C. Commissioner Prouty then settled down to the task of establishing the cost of building and equipping the railway, and of determining the net operating revenues which would seem to yield a fair rate of return on that initial investment. A statement introduced by the president of the Barber Asphalt Paving Company gave in detail the original costs of construction, not including buildings and equipment. In round figures, this construction cost was $510,000 and it was stated to be in all cases actual payments of cash made under contract to construction companies in which no person connected with either the Barber Company or the railway company had an interest. In short, the railroad was constructed upon the best terms possible by a party possessing ample financial resources.

Among the items making up the total construction cost was one for legal expenses of $11,000 and one for general expenses and incidentals of $31,000. Both these items were thought to be abnormally large, but then there was no item shown for interest, which Commissioner Prouty thought might properly appear in the total.

When the railroad was put into actual service it was found that certain improvements and additions were necessary, the cost of which came to $47,000. Some of the rail originally laid on the steepest portions of the line over Baxter Pass was too light and had to be replaced with heavier steel. Certain curves, such as the one at Moro Castle, were found to be too sharp. At considerable expense the curvature at these locations was reduced, so that the maximum curves on the line would be about 65 degrees. The cost of equipping the new railway with locomotives and rolling stock amounted to $88,000.

Two additional rather large items of cost listed by the defendant became matters for argument in the case. These were the expenses of $63,000 for various buildings constructed along the railway, and roughly $100,000 for building the toll road from Dragon to Vernal and Fort Duchesne and providing the freighting and staging outfits and buildings connected with it. The $63,000 figure was for the office at Mack, a boarding house at Dragon and certain cottages for housing employees, the propriety of which was not questioned, and also included $17,000 for the hotel at Mack, $18,000 for the hotel at Dragon, and $9,000 for furnishings. The complainant claimed that the cost of these two hotels and their furnishings ought not to be included as a part of the cost of the railway. But Commissioner Prouty ruled in favor of the railway company on the basis that a considerable amount of revenue was derived from its passenger business. ". . . It must be evident that no passenger business could be done in this desert country without the provision of some means of caring for passengers at the hands of this railroad."[3] The wagon road and staging operation, however, was judged not to be a legitimate part of the cost of a railroad built and operated for the main purpose of bringing out the gilsonite. In this matter the I.C.C. noted that a significant portion of the railway's revenue came from the transportation of commodities and persons between Mack and Dragon which came from or went on to Vernal or Fort Duchesne and would not have been handled by the railroad unless some provision was made for transporting them beyond Dragon. It was further noted that the freight and stage line operation was being conducted at

Although a traveler arriving in Mack didn't have much choice of lodging, few could have been disappointed with the Uintah Hotel. The dining room and the lounge were warm and inviting, the food was good, and the rooms were clean and comfortable. The stuffed birds and mammals added a note of interest, too, particularly for dudes from the East. (*Both: V. L. "Roy" McCoy Collection*)

a very material loss. The Commission reasoned that the complainant association should not receive the benefit of revenue from rail traffic resulting from the stage road connection, nor, on the contrary, should it sustain the burden of the poor business management on the part of the defendant in undertaking a losing operation. Thus the wagon road and everything connected with it were eliminated from the calculations. It was found this could be done with reasonable accuracy.

The total cost of the Uintah Railway, then, was found to be somewhat in excess of $700,000. This, the I.C.C. thought, could "hardly be regarded as an extravagant valuation for the building and equipment of this property, including its hotels."[4] They refused to allow an additional $150,000 which the defendant claimed would have been the increased cost of reproducing the railway at the date of the hearing, only some three years after the actual construction. The I.C.C. then continued on to determine the railway's earnings and compare them with the capital investment in the line.

The first statement furnished, for the year 1905, showed total earnings of $156,000 and total expenses of $154,000, but did not show the stage line earnings and expenses separate from those of the railroad itself. Instead, among the earnings was an item termed "Miscellaneous" amounting to $28,000, and there was a corresponding $61,000 entry among the operating expenses, which, Commissioner Prouty thought, seemed to fairly well represent the earnings and operating expenses of the stage line. Deducting these two figures, the Railway's gross earnings for 1905 were $128,000 and the operating expenses $92,000, leaving a net income of $35,000. There was no way, however, to determine the portion of the $128,000 earnings which resulted from freight and passengers which would not have been carried by the Uintah Railway but for the operation of the stage line. The financial statement submitted for the following fiscal year was more complete and detailed, so the commissioner went on to examine it. After briefly wondering why the fiscal year of the company was set up to end on the 31st of January, he published the following statement as a part of the "Report of the Commission":

For twelve months ending January 31, 1907.

Gross earnings, railway division:

Freight	$157,440.26
Passenger	11,089.99
Express	813.24
Mails	2,959.97
Telegraph	1,847.41
Telephone	295.70
Hotels	680.50
Real estate	2,059.67
Miscellaneous	555.72
Total earnings	$177,742.46

Operating expenses, railway division:

Maintenance of way and structure	$ 36,793.92
Maintenance of equipment	16,106.98
Conducting transportation	38,102.33
General expenses	29,122.11
Total expenses	$120,125.34
Net earnings	$ 57,617.12

During this same period earnings from the wagon operations were $47,000 and expenses were $90,000, leaving a deficit of $43,000. These figures, for the reasons already noted, were not to be considered in determining the income from rail operations. Furthermore, based upon a detailed statement showing the different commodities carried both north and south over the Uintah Railway during the twelve months in question and the amount of revenue derived from each commodity, the I.C.C. determined that probably $20,000 of the road's earnings arose from traffic which would not have been obtained but for the teaming operations of the company. Accordingly, that $20,000 was deducted from the reported earnings, leaving the gross earnings for the period at $157,742.46. It had already been decided that, since most of this traffic was of a back haul nature and thus being carried aboard cars which would otherwise be returning empty to the mines, it could be transported without practically any additional expense to the defendant.

An objection was then raised by the complainant regarding the item of general expenses contained in the above statement, which was said to be too large. After hearing testimony on the matter and examining the general expenses for other years, the I.C.C. found the complainant's position well taken and decided the amount of general ex-

A pair of horsemen pause in front of the Uintah Railway office in Mack on their way home from a shopping trip. Below is the only known picture of the inside of that same office building. There's a fire in the stove and the calendars on the wall place the date as December, 1908. The Uintah employees seated from left to right are Haywood Brown, Joe Perry and W. H. Haun. (*Both: F. A. Kennedy photos from J. V. Kelly Collection*)

penses ought to be reduced by at least $10,000. This left the operating expenses at $110,125.34 and the net earnings at $47,617.12.

This net was seen to be a yield of about seven per cent on what the Commission regarded as the fair money value of the property. It could hardly be claimed that such a return was excessive, they stated. The feeling was that, "While the Barber Company with its strong financial position could undoubtedly furnish that money for considerably less than seven per cent, there are elements of uncertainty in the investment which would fairly entitle that company to at least this return."[5] It was also apparent that any material increase in the rate of the gilsonite shipments would bring about an increase of gross revenues without a corresponding increase of operating expenses, and thus would compel the I.C.C. to impose a reduced rate on the commodity.

This was exactly what happened within the following eight months. The statement below shows earnings and expenses for the eight-month period from February 1 to September 30, 1907:[6]

For eight months ending September 30, 1907

Gross earnings, railway division:

Freight	$175,951.45
Passenger	8,766.96
Express	620.00
Mails	2,312.24
Telegraph	823.55
Telephone	285.08
Real estate	1,618.60
Miscellaneous	94.15
Total earnings	$190,472.03

Operating expenses, railway division:

Maintenance of way and structures	$ 25,013.47
Maintenance of equipment	15,729.10
Traffic	440.15
Conducting transportation	27,726.29
General expenses	9,733.77
Total expenses	$ 78,642.78
Net earnings	$111,829.25

During the same eight months the earnings from wagon operations of the company were $35,000 and expenses $50,000, for a deficit of $15,000. Based upon a statement showing com-

modities shipped over the railway and the revenues therefrom, it seemed probable that the total earnings would have been $20,000 less were it not for traffic which came to the Uintah via these wagon and stage lines. The I.C.C. continued to assume that since this traffic, especially the freight traffic, was handled without appreciable additional expense to the railway, the operating expenses ought not to be diminished on this account. The net earnings were therefore decreased by the $20,000, making them $91,829.25 for the eight months. It is readily seen that this net was nearly double that for the entire preceding year!

The Commission's "Report" went on to note that during the eight months in question the defendant transported 14,738 tons of gilsonite, from which it derived revenues of $147,380, at $10 per ton. Had this been carried at $8 per ton the net revenue of the company would have been further reduced by $29,476, leaving a net income for the eight months of $62,353.25. This, it was thought, was as great as the earnings of the defendant should have been for the entire twelve months.

The Uintah Railway lawyers countered by contending that the period covered was one of unusual commercial prosperity and activity and that similar results could not be expected over a series of years. The I.C.C. found it probable, however, that the operation of the property was extravagant during the first two years and also that the already numerous uses for gilsonite would continue to increase. It judged, then, that the road ought to be able to earn upon a basis of $8 per ton a fair return on the investment in the property. Everything was seen to depend upon the quantity of gilsonite transported. Ample opportunity was left for an appeal by the railway and a rehearing any time there should be a significant decrease in the quantity shipped.

With that the case was settled. An order was issued directing the Uintah Railway Company to establish and maintain for two years a rate of $8 per ton for the transportation of gilsonite from Dragon to Mack. Actually, the rate would stand at essentially that level for quite a few years to come. A claim for damages asked by American Asphalt Association because of the previous $10 per ton rate and also for other alleged violations

79

The big fire of February, 1908, at the Dragon Mine left its telltale plume of smoke visible for miles. *(Fries photo from W. A. Banks Collection)*

of the act to regulate commerce was not upheld by the I.C.C. No evidence submitted at the trial tended to show any damage to the complainant by reason of the other infractions of the act which he alleged, and the Commission was of the opinion that no reparation should be allowed on account of excessive freight charges.

Shortly after the preparation of the I.C.C. report but before March 11, 1908, when the case was decided, a communication from the Uintah Railway attorneys stated that during the last few months shipments of gilsonite had declined 25 to 30 per cent, and further that a recent explosion and fire in the mine of the Gilson Company at Dragon would result in a virtual suspension of that company's shipments for some time to come. Upon receiving this news, the Commission did not see fit to change the conclusion reached, but did note that these facts confirmed the impression that, in view of the many uncertainties surrounding the operation of the property, the $8 rate established was not excessive.[7]

As had been mentioned by the attorneys in their report to the I.C.C., there was great concern by the Uintah management and employees over the explosion and fire in the Black Dragon mine on February 12, 1908.[8] Starting at 1:10 that morning a series of explosions rocked the area, hurling mine timbers for as much as two thousand feet and killing instantly the two Greeks who were the only men at work in the mine during that shift. The intense heat from the burning gilsonite made it impossible to even approach the entrance to the open vein for days, and the red glow from the fire was visible in the night sky at Vernal, 68 miles away.[9] The bodies of the two miners were not found and recovered for another 14 months, having been entombed by the molten gilsonite which flowed into and filled the drift where they were working.[10] The fire continued to burn for months afterward, growing fierce at times and then seeming to die out again. Over two and a half years later the Vernal *Express* reported that the same fire had broken out anew after smoldering for some time in the Cumberland tunnel of the Dragon mine.[11]

Since the Black Dragon Vein had been the source of most of the gilsonite hauled out over the Uintah Railway since its completion, a serious impact on traffic and revenues might have been expected as a result of the disastrous explosion and fire. Such turned out not to be the case. Within a month of the explosion a new mining camp was started on the same vein where the fire still burned, but about two miles to the west. It was expected that 25 or 30 men would be working there within a short time. Also, a force of men was sent over to work the veins at Bonanza, north of the White River, although Superintendent John McAndrews told the Vernal *Express* they would have been sent there whether there had been an explosion at the Dragon mine or not. The Gilson Asphaltum Company had big orders coming in, and the eastern demand for the mineral was reported to be growing every year.[12]

Evidence of this growth appeared in the *Annual Report to the Stockholders of the General Asphalt Company for the fiscal year ending April 30, 1909*, in which the following figures showing the amount of freight moved over the Uintah Railway were published:

	1906	1907	1908
Tons of gilsonite hauled south	12,140	19,198	19,785
Tons of merchandise hauled south	973	716	951
Tons of merchandise hauled north	4,648	6,658	9,069
Total tons moved	17,761	26,572	29,805

It seems likely, though, that the growth in the gilsonite traffic would have been significantly greater during 1908 were it not for the explosion and fire at the Dragon mine. No doubt the officers and employees of the firm were working to increase the business. In 1909 the quantity of the glossy black mineral hauled south over the Uintah would be 27,217 tons. In 1910 it would increase further to 34,321 tons and in 1911, to 34,511 tons, the high point for some years.

For some reason not readily apparent, in its *Annual Report to the Stockholders* for 1911 the parent General Asphalt Company changed the second and third lines of its report of Uintah Railway traffic to reflect "Tons of miscell'us freight hauled" rather than "Tons of merchandise." The difference is not made clear, but the results were as follows:

The frigid winds have left ridges in the crusted surface of the snow and frosted the trees on the hillside with white. Three Shays (above) half hidden behind the snow they have cleared are ready to head their plow down the west side of Baxter Pass toward Wendella and Dragon. The picture below was also taken on top of the pass, but the wind is not blowing so hard. *(Both photos: Robert O. Perkins Collection)*

	1907	1908	1909	1910
Tons of gilsonite hauled south..	19,198	19,785	27,217	34,321
Tons of miscell'us freight hauled south	715	903	659	1,226
Tons of miscell'us freight hauled north	3,417	3,408	3,691	6,000
Total tons moved.	23,330	24,096	31,567	41,547

Perhaps the earlier figures included freight, such as coal and water, which was moved for company use.

So, as the first decade of the century drew to a close, the wind-blown smoke plumes of the Shays were seen more frequently on Baxter Pass. The railroaders were becoming gradually more proficient with each passing day in the job of moving the trains over the big hill. Nevertheless, accidents of various kinds, some rather serious, were not infrequent during these years. On January 22, 1908, one of the stage coaches had been destroyed by fire near Dragon, burning some of the mail aboard. Months later the government decided that the contractor would have to pay for the registered letters which had been burned. All told, these registered letters had contained only $6.90, so stage road Superintendent John McAndrews paid for them.[13]

The following August, McAndrews himself was hurt in an accident. A very severe rain storm the middle of that month had done considerable damage to both the railroad and stage road bridges along Evacuation Creek on both sides of Dragon. The railroad bridge near Davis Spring was rendered impassable, and the train was held until the bridge could be repaired. Passengers and mail were transferred across and brought into Dragon on the Mack rail car. Several of the bridges on the stage road were entirely demolished.[14] A week later, while supervising repair work on one of the bridges just out of Dragon, "Mr. McAndrews was standing near the edge of the bridge and in some way fell off backward into the wash a distance of about thirty feet. One of his ankles was badly sprained and he was considerably bruised about the body."[15] Internal injuries, thought serious at first, were only slight. Three weeks later McAn-

drews was getting around on crutches and no doubt watching his step a little more carefully.

As mentioned, the first fatal accident on the railway happened when Engineer Joseph Lane and a Greek section hand named Nick were killed while bucking snow on the pass on February 10, 1909. The second one, less than eleven months later, also occurred while bucking snow on Baxter Pass, although the immediate cause this time was low water in the boiler. Here is the story as it was published in the Vernal *Express* the same day it happened:

TRAINMEN SCALDED ON THE UINTAH RY.

The crown head blew out of an engine on Baxter Pass this morning at 3 a.m. and scalded to death Fireman Samuel Hancock and Roadmaster W. D. Sutton.

Last Saturday night the heavy wind storm filled all of the cuts on the Uintah Railway on Baxter Pass with snow and Vernal was without mail until Thursday night, when three sacks of letter mail came in. All week the Uintah Railway people have been bucking the snow, and as fast as the force of 100 men shoveled the snow out, it drifted back in. Wednesday night they got through to Dragon with one engine, which carried all the accumulated mail and ten passengers, all men, as the road officials would not allow the lady passengers on the engine. The engine went back to Mack yesterday, and started on the return trip to Dragon last night and at Shale, the other side of Baxter Pass, it got stuck in the snow drifts. Here is where the crown head blew out, scalding the men. Roadmaster Sutton died instantly and Fireman Hancock died while he was being taken back to Atchee. Hancock was a new man on the road, but W. D. Sutton had been with the Uintah railway several years and was a very popular official. He came here from Ohio, and had been a train dispatcher in that state before coming west.

Dr. Christy and Louis Kabell came over the pass on this same engine the trip before it blew up, and you can bet that they are shaking hands with themselves as well as their numerous friends. There were about thirty passengers at Dragon waiting to get over and there are about that many here in Vernal waiting to get out as soon as the road is clear, but the agent here is not selling tickets yet.

It was reported that there were thirty passengers down at Mack, and many of them went to Grand Junction until the road was opened.[16]

A section gang's pump car makes a good, if somewhat unusual, place for a family portrait. Here Mrs. Perkins and Mr. and Mrs. Kelley of Atchee pose with their children. The time is the summer of 1910. Below, with Lake McAndrews, the section house and the icehouse for a background, one of the Baldwin 0-6-2Ts with its characteristic single car chuffs towards the "Hairpin Curves," Columbine and Baxter Pass. (Top: Robert O. Perkins Collection; bottom: F. A. Kennedy photo from V. L. McCoy Collection)

In their account of this tragic accident the following day, the Grand Junction *Daily Sentinel* gave a few other details. The engine, most likely one of the two Baldwin 0-6-2 side-tankers, had been pulling a single coach filled with passengers up the pass. "The snow was so deep," the paper reported, "that the train moved with difficulty. The water in the boiler was entirely evaporated before the engineman discovered it; the crown sheet melted, and a terrible explosion followed."[17] On the engine, besides the two men who were killed, was engineer Shoeman. He was thrown high in the air by the explosion, but escaped fatal injuries.

That storm during the opening days of January, 1910, was the last big one to hit the Uintah for six years. It was not until the following Wednesday evening, the 12th, when 42 sacks of incoming mail were delivered to the Vernal post office, that the blockade had been cleared and trains were going through. There had been several snow slides this time, something which had never been encountered on Baxter Pass before. A few warm days late in December had melted and settled the snow, which then froze as the blizzard came. The new snow that fell had nothing to cling to and would break away and slide down the mountain side. If the railroad happened to be in the way, it was buried deep in snow. Passengers arriving in Vernal were able to relate "some chilly experiences of being hemmed in 24 hours at a time between two snow slides. The wind was so fierce that the workmen could only shovel a few minutes at a time and would have to get in the car to warm their benumbed fingers and faces. When there is any wind moving at all, Baxter Pass gets more than its share and when there is any loose snow it soon drifts into the low places."[18]

That one blizzard was not quite the end of the railroaders' troubles for the winter, though. Little more than two weeks later the paper's correspondent in Dragon wrote the Vernal *Express*, "The engine of the passenger train ran off the track between Mack and Baxter Pass Friday the twenty-eighth and did not arrive here until early Sunday morning."[19] Then, the following Wednesday there was a 15-foot snow slide between Baxter Pass and Lone Tree curve, sometime after the southbound passenger train had passed that morning. The train, due to return to Dragon that evening, didn't make it back until Friday evening, 48 hours late.[20] Just a few short delays!

In contrast to derailments and snow blockades, many activities of a more normal and routine nature were making up the day-to-day life along the Uintah. Among other things, the company was busy putting up its summer supply of ice during the same weeks the trains were having such problems making it over the Pass. This was, of course, a job that took place every winter when the ice got thick enough on Lake McAndrews. Big blocks were cut from the frozen surface of the lake and stacked in the icehouse next to the track along the shore. During the next few weeks a new proprietor was hired for the Uintah Hotel at Dragon, and, not long afterwards, a new hotel cook. Meanwhile, 1.3 miles up Camp Gulch at Dragon mine the hotel was being fixed up and enlarged to accommodate more employees.[21] Every few weeks, especially during the winter and spring months, a Saturday night dance at the hotel in Dragon or in Mr. Jensen's store up at the mine would provide welcome entertainment for the miners and railroaders and their womenfolk. As the days grew longer and warmer, a Sunday afternoon softball game or a family picnic in the shade of the aspen up at Columbine were the pastimes which the men and women looked forward to.

Another diversion for some of the men, and one definitely not subject to the approval of the railway and mining companies, was provided by a saloon or two in Dragon and another west of the tracks near Salt Wash in Atchee. No doubt there were mixed feelings among the townspeople when, early in February of 1910, Mr. Odem's saloon on the north side of Dragon burned to the ground after a gasoline stove exploded. At least the money and a stock of liquor in the cellar were saved from the flames.[22]

Probably motivated in part by a desire to keep the men out of the saloons, the wife of General Manager M. W. "Captain" Cooley was instrumental in establishing a public library in Dragon. Mr. T. M. McNeil was the librarian and Mrs. Cooley the principal patron, and the library comprised nearly 300 volumes by April, 1910, with more on the way. In addition, the usefulness of the library was not confined to Dragon. Anyone along the Uintah Railway route or in the neighboring

country could apply to borrow a book and the book would be sent over the Uintah without charge. Many stockmen and miners in the region were reported to be availing themselves of this opportunity.[23]

Three months to the day after fire destroyed Mr. Odem's saloon another conflagration struck Dragon, and this one was considerably more serious. The Uintah Railway's warehouse burned to the ground Monday, May 9, 1910, and hundreds of tons of freight in the building were consumed. The loss, estimated to be in excess of $15,000, was the greatest loss by fire ever experienced in northeastern Utah up to that time. With some amount of gilsonite stored inside, the dry frame structure burned fiercely, and the heat was intense from the start. Three minutes after the fire began, spectators reported, the building was doomed. Gasoline tanks which were nearby soon became heated and exploded loudly, adding more fuel and danger to the blaze.

A spark from a locomotive started the fire, although there was disagreement whether it was from a freight engine or the engine of the passenger train which had pulled into the station shortly before 5:00 that afternoon. The spark fell onto a pile of gilsonite sacks, or sacked gilsonite according to the other reporter, and the resulting fire spread quickly to the adjacent warehouse. Bucket brigades were able to save the baggage, express and telegraph buildings nearby, but the warehouse and freight storerooms and loading platforms were entirely consumed by the fierce blaze. There had seldom been more goods stored in the warehouse awaiting transshipment than there was at the time, adding to the losses. Among the merchandise destroyed was a carload of sugar, a car of soap, a car of wire and two cars of water pipe destined for installation in Vernal. The pipe was of the wooden variety and thus added to the flames along with the considerable amounts of dry-goods and groceries.

Happily, no one was injured. An engine was able to remove all the cars that were between the freight house and the gilsonite storage houses, thereby saving the major portion of the gilsonite stored awaiting shipment. The buildings were all insured and there was some insurance on the contents, so the loss to the railway was not as great as it might have been. Within two or three days the company was informing merchants and other shippers that it would stand behind all losses, and that claims for the losses would be paid just as quickly as adjustments could be made.[24]

A month and a half later the Denver & Rio Grande depot and warehouse at Price, Utah, burned to the ground, also with heavy losses. Price was the transshipment point for much of the freight moving to and from the Uintah Basin, especially the reservation towns of Roosevelt and Myton to the west of Vernal. It seemed very strange that both Price and Dragon should have such similar fires affecting the Basin interests within such a short time.[25]

Just a week or two after the big fire at Dragon the Uintah Railway management disclosed that automobiles would be brought in, on a trial basis, to haul the passengers, mail, freight and express between Dragon and Vernal. Ever interested in progress and efficiency, the company said it was willing to replace the horse-drawn stages and freight wagons with automobiles provided the people of the valley would put up half the expense of building a good automobile road in the valley. On Thursday, May 26, 1910, the first of the autos rolled into Vernal at 11:45 a.m. with a load of mail and some passengers. Its arrival was witnessed by a good crowd of local businessmen, and the mail was distributed and ready for the people during the noon hour. The auto left shortly after noon for the return trip to Dragon taking the mail and three passengers. Later that same eventful afternoon the express truck arrived from Dragon loaded with trunks. The speedy service, getting passengers into Vernal in time for lunch, was a welcome improvement over the previous all-day stage journey.[26]

Less than two weeks later the Uintah County commissioners received a delegation consisting of General Manager M. W. Cooley and John McAndrews of the railway company, together with fourteen Vernal businessmen. Cooley explained the desire of his company to continue the automobile service and to increase it as business demanded, but went on to point out that the only hindrance was the condition of the road between Vernal and the Green River. The company's toll road covered the remainder of the distance to Dragon and was

There's nothing like a slice of watermelon after work on a summer day. The year is 1911 and the railroaders about to enjoy the sweet, juicy melon are, from left to right, Shorty Dixon, Conductor Jessie Yount, Master Mechanic W. H. "Bill" Chambers, Lyle Ridenour and Engineer Richard Griffith. (Mrs. E. H. Whyler Collection)

Scott Shafer is leaning against the lathe in the shop at Atchee. As the Uintah's master mechanic some years later, Mr. Shafer would help design the articulateds and supervise construction of Shay No. 7.
(J. V. Kelly Collection)

Shay No. 4, one of the pair purchased in 1910 from the Argentine Central Ry., is at the top of the pass with the section men and the snow spreader in this 1913 photo. (Robert O. Perkins Collection)

in fine condition. Captain Cooley offered to send the railway's civil engineer over to Vernal, at company expense, to estimate the cost of a good road, and he said they were willing to help build the road. The county commissioners replied by stating the county was unable to spend very much money on roads at that time. However, a committee of three men was appointed to join with the railway's engineer and the county surveyor in selecting the best road out of town and estimating the cost.[27]

By early August the Uintah Railway people had graded their part of the new road but little had yet been done on the rest. On August 24th a big freight auto made an initial trial run to Vernal, bringing in over three tons of freight and then treating Vernalites to demonstration "joy rides." Before another week passed, though, the company had called attention to the fact that they did not yet own this freight automobile and did not expect to buy one until the people got busy and built some roads so there would be some justification for the expense.[28] But satisfactory roads weren't built, so the relatively small amounts of freight which the railway company carried beyond its end-of-track into the Basin would continue to move in covered wagons behind teams of horses for some years to come.

An unfortunate incident happened just a month after the freight auto demonstrations when a four-year-old boy fell to his death under a wheel of one of the railway wagons. Little Harvey J. Wimmer and his sister Leona, aged six, were out playing near their home on Vernal Avenue when they decided to hitch a ride on a passing freight wagon. They climbed on to the tongue of the second trailer, a Studebaker wagon, and rode for a ways. At a point near S. P. Trim's residence the girl got off and called to her brother to do the same. He rode a little further, then while alighting from the tongue of the trailer he lost his balance and fell under the wheel, which passed over his head. A neighbor carried the limp body to the Trims' lawn, but within half an hour all breathing had ceased.[29]

To the southeast of Vernal and the toll roads, the railway's primary job of hauling the gilsonite out over Baxter Pass and down to the standard gauge at Mack was going on as usual, and the tonnage was increasing each year. When the figures for 1910 were in, they showed that 34,321 tons of the glossy black hydrocarbon had been moved south during the year. This was a considerable increase over the previous year's 27,217 tons and almost double 1908's figure of 19,785 tons.[30] With the fatal boiler explosion on the pass

The second ex-Argentine Central Shay, No. 5, stands by the Atchee water tank with tanker No. 21 ready to double-head a two-car passenger train up Baxter Pass. (Baldwin Locomotives *magazine, from Colorado Railroad Museum Collection*)

No. 5 and No. 21 (top) working two cars up the 7.5 per cent between Moro Castle and Shale. One of the most dramatic shots ever taken of operations on the 7.5 (center). Two Shays, seven cars and a four-wheel caboose pound upgrade less than two miles away on the other side of the pass at milepost 35. (*Top: Baldwin Locomotives* magazine, *Margaret Romager Collection; center: Otto C. Perry; bottom: F. A. Kennedy photo from V. L. McCoy Collection*)

early in January and the warehouse fire at Dragon in May, the year 1910 might have seemed an inauspicious one for the Uintah, but it did turn out well from a production standpoint.

Also, among the more promising events of the year, especially for the operating men, was the arrival of two more Shays, the first additions to the locomotive roster since the railroad was brand new, five years earlier. Slightly less than five years old themselves, these two engines were purchased from the Argentine Central Railway, another Colorado narrow-gauge line. The A.C. had been built in late 1905 and early 1906, being started shortly before the Uintah was completed. It ran its Shays up and down 15.9 miles of almost constant six per cent grade from Silver Plume to a point near the summit of Mount McClellan at an elevation above 13,000 feet. Being built partly to serve the silver mines of the East Argentine Mining District and partly in anticipation of a heavy tourist traffic, the Argentine Central was never as financially successful as the Uintah and would cease operations by 1917.[31] The two secondhand Shays were renumbered 4 and 5 by the Uintah Railway and were

promptly put to work lifting freights over the pass. One of them, the No. 5, would still be on the property when the Uintah ceased to run.

As 1910 entered its final weeks only minor difficulties arose to interrupt the bright days for the Gilsonite Route. The long-smoldering fire which broke out anew in the Cumberland tunnel at the Dragon mine didn't affect the gilsonite traffic since that tunnel had been abandoned since the big explosion and fire early in 1908. The other tunnels at Dragon were safe, and mining operations were being switched away from Dragon to veins a few miles farther north anyway. On November 23rd the passenger coach was overturned as the northbound train was climbing Baxter Pass, and traffic was blocked for some time. Happily, no one was hurt, though, and the delayed mail arrived the next day.[32] As of the same date one of the company's automobiles had been laid up for several days with a broken axle. Then, about the end of the year a new 12 passenger Mack auto arrived and was placed in service north of Dragon.[33] And so went the little things. The coming year would bring more significant events.

Climbing the hill above Columbine, seen far below in the valley, Baldwin 0-6-2T No. 20 with the passenger train presents the classic picture of Uintah railroading. (*F. A. Kennedy photo from J. L. Booth Collection*)

With ties of standard-gauge dimensions already in place, the Uintah track looks perfectly suitable for widening to standard gauge as it follows Evacuation Creek between shale cliffs into Watson. *(George L. Beam photo from Library, State Historical Society of Colorado)*

Chapter Five

Extension to Watson and Rainbow

In February of 1911, during the line's seventh year of operation, the news broke that the Uintah Railway was planning to start work on an extension of its line. The papers said that reports from the East indicated the Barber Asphalt Paving Company, which owned the Uintah, had sold $3,000,000 worth of bonds "for extending the road north to Bonanza, and constructing a tunnel through Baxter pass, thus greatly reducing the grade of the present line and making it practicable for the handling of general freight." It was also stated, the Denver newspaper continued, "that the company contemplates the extension of the line north to Vernal, Utah, tapping one of the most fertile fruit sections in the West and making it directly tributary to Denver markets."[1] Describing the Uintah as "a narrow gauge line of almost impracticable grades and curves," the paper then disclosed that crossties of standard gauge size were even then being used as replacement ties by section gangs repairing the company's track. By drilling the proposed tunnel under Baxter Pass and widening the rest to standard gauge, it was claimed, the line would offer a feasible route for an extension west to Salt Lake City. It was said such an extension was actually being contemplated by the owners of the line.

Actually, talk of extending the Uintah Railway was not a new thing. Indeed, the newspapers of the period generally filled more space with stories of proposed railroads and railroads that were "beginning construction" than they did with the news that such railroads were actually completed!

The first evidence, though, that the Uintah was seriously contemplating the extension of its steel beyond Dragon had appeared some 28 months earlier, in September of 1908, with the news that a surveying party was then in the field north of the White River. The company was actually investigating the costs that would be involved in building its line on to tap the large gilsonite veins at Bonanza, 47 miles from Vernal. But the writer for the Vernal *Express* began his article, "There seems to be no doubt but that the Uintah Railway Company will eventually build the road into Vernal."[2] There were big plans, to read it in the paper. The survey party, headed by Mr. Longaker, had already surveyed for the bridge spanning the White River — and a wonderful structure it was to be. It would be 900 feet long, extending from one cliff to the other, about 480 feet above the water. Why would the company build such a bridge if it did not plan to lay track on in to Vernal? was the question posed by the paper. The same article went on to state, as an indisputable fact, "The present road from Mack to Dragon is to be made a standard gauge." As things turned out, the big White River bridge would never be built, nor would Baxter be tunneled nor the Uintah Railway widened. But the rumors would continue for years.

Another rumor, coming "Unofficially, but with the very strongest reasons for our belief," via the Grand Junction *Sentinel*, stated that there was a well formed plan for the Colorado Midland Railway to connect with the Uintah. The western end

Before 1911 and as late as 1922, surveyors were at work plotting the location of a tunnel below Baxter Pass. The findings of each survey party were essentially the same — the job would be very expensive! Here Civil Engineer Walton, on one of the later surveys, picks his way across typical Baxter Pass terrain with his transit on his shoulder. (*A. T. S. Stoney photo from Bruce Angus Collection*)

A popular leisure-time activity for many of the railroaders was hunting. The photo below shows a Christmas Day hunting party on the cliffs overlooking the Grand River (now the Colorado) near Mack. (*F. A. Kennedy photo from J. L. Booth Collection*)

of the Midland at Grand Junction and the eastern end of the Uintah at Mack were less than twenty miles apart, and were the gauge widened and the Baxter Pass tunnel built, the Uintah Railway would have been a most logical stepping stone for the Colorado Midland on its way west. Talk of building such a connection, perhaps utilizing the Grand Junction and Grand River Valley Railway, an electric interurban line between Grand Junction and Fruita, was heard in the area for quite a few years. The first mention of such plans by the papers was in March of 1909, some 16 months before the G.J.&G.R.V. was completed.[3] From then until 1917, when serious-sounding statements from the Colorado Midland headquarters announced a revival of the old plans, such talk was heard every few months. It ceased abruptly in 1918 when the Midland was closed down and abandoned after the United States Railroad Administration diverted all its through traffic.

In February, 1911, though, the news was about the Uintah Railway. Actual construction was to begin in a few days, the *Express* reported, on the extension from Dragon to the Temple mine, about 12 miles northwest of Dragon. "The increased business of the Gilson Asphaltum Company," the paper continued, "has made this move necessary as they were unable to produce enough ore from the Dragon mine to fill their orders."[4] The reporter then went on at some length telling of the seemingly bright possibilities that the line would be continued right on down Evacuation Creek and into their own valley, and he recounted the plans for tunneling Baxter Pass in preparation for a greatly increased traffic. By mid-April the surveying had been completed and dirt was moving on the 12-mile extension. Although the rails were to be spiked down only three feet apart, standard gauge ties were being used. This fact in itself was thought significant. The construction work was being done by the Wasatch Construction Company of Salt Lake City. Senator Reed Smoot, Mr. Jesse Knight and Mr. Frank E. Baxter were the heads of this company, and Frank Baxter was also the company's engineer in charge of the work.[5] This was the same Frank Baxter who had in 1903 and 1904 surveyed and laid out the Uintah's line over the pass that bears his name.

As the spring and summer progressed, sixty-pound rail was spiked to the ties, and the line pushed farther down the valley of Evacuation Creek. A steadily descending grade of 1.1 per cent was held for the entire 9.6 miles from Dragon to the end of track which was located on a shelf of land formed where a normally-dry wash exited from its gully to join the canyon cut by the creek. As Evacuation Creek made its way northwest towards its confluence with the White River it had gradually cut its way into a deeper, more confining canyon. Irregular, eroded cliffs of oil shale on both sides left the contractors very little room in places to grade a shelf for the track above the stream. Needless to say, washouts were not uncommon along this portion of the railroad. Fortunately the summer thunderstorms which sent walls of water roaring and cascading down the dry washes and canyons were infrequent in this rather arid country.

A handful of buildings was erected near the end of track in the canyon and a new town came into being. Named Watson in honor of the civil engineer, Wallace G. Watson, who laid out the extension from Dragon, it would never be a very big place. More important was the mining camp of Rainbow up on the mesa about four miles to the southwest. A branch to these newly opened mines was built from Rainbow Junction, about two-thirds of a mile from Watson. It twisted and snaked up a narrow gully climbing grades as steep as 5.1 per cent in places, gaining 837 feet of elevation in the 4.1 track miles between the Junction and Rainbow. Near the end of the branch the track made a sweeping curve crossing over the gilsonite vein twice. Large burlap sacks of the mineral were hoisted from the depths of the vein where they had been filled, and loaded onto push-cars, which then were run out along a platform adjacent to the railroad. The sacks weighing from 150 to 200 pounds each were then slid down a plank onto the waiting flat cars. Nearby was a wye where the engine turned for the return trip. Also the town of Rainbow was built for the miners; two rows of small but adequate houses, many of log construction, faced each other along the ridge near the mine.

Rainbow was to be the source of the better part of the Uintah's traffic from then on. Although

Nearly all of the new town of Watson, Utah, is seen in the two photographs on this page. The big building with the sign on the end is the Uintah Railway station and freight house. Just to the left and across the tracks, in the photo below, is the Watson Hotel. The road at the bottom of the narrow canyon in the foreground (below) led up the hill to Rainbow and it was definitely a road that required caution on the part of the driver. On one occasion a traveling salesman's auto was caught and demolished by a flash flood, and another time a Ford roadster driven by the Uintah's agent at Watson, W. H. Bair, met a Chrysler head-on in the canyon, completely wrecking both cars and injuring the agent and his son. *(Both: F. A. Kennedy photos from C. J. Neal Collection)*

The town of Rainbow was just eleven years old in 1922, when the picture above was taken. Baldwin Mikado No. 30 (below) was built the same year as were the town and the branch railroad, and she spent her entire twenty-eight year lifetime on the Rainbow branch and the connecting Uintah main line between Watson and Wendella. Below we see her on the branch to the Thimble Rock Mine, with some of the other mines at Rainbow in the background. *(Top: Charles J. Neal Collection; bottom: F. A. Kennedy photo from D. H. Gerbaz Collection)*

Six loads of recently-mined gilsonite (above) are ready to go down the hill to Rainbow Junction and on to Wendella behind Mikado No. 30. The picture below, taken from a point farther southeast along the Rainbow Vein, includes the above location in the middle distance. It is a particularly good illustration of how a single gilsonite vein runs for miles across the Uintah Basin. *(Both photos: F. A. Kennedy, from E. Victor Earp Collection)*

the line to the camp was not completed until late in the year, mining had been going on there since the beginning of 1911. This necessitated a wagon-haul and double handling of the sacks of ore for a few months, cutting into the company's earnings. But, never one to miss an opportunity, the company quickly applied to the Utah authorities for a reduced tax valuation on their properties because of these reduced earnings, and it was granted.[6]

Meanwhile, the former terminal of Dragon was waning. By mid-August Myron Mott, who had been operating a barber shop there, was in Vernal looking for a new location to establish his business. He reported that business was very slack in Dragon, owing to the reduced output of the mines there and the moving of the railroad's terminal to Watson.[7]

Early in the year the Uintah had received a brand new Consolidation from the Baldwin Locomotive Works for use between Mack and Atchee. Numbered 11, it was the second engine to bear that number on the roster. The first No. 11, the 1880 Baldwin Consolidation which had been purchased from the D.&R.G. in 1904 to become the Uintah's first engine, was retired from service when the second No. 11 arrived on the scene. This left not an engine on the road which was more than seven years old, and only the two ex-Argentine Central Shays which were secondhand. The second No. 11, incidentally, was built to exactly the same plans as the seven-year-old No. 10, which it joined in service on the Mack-Atchee portion of the line.

About the time this new Consolidation arrived from Baldwin, and as construction was getting started on the extension to Watson and Rainbow, another order was placed with the Baldwin people. It seemed that General Manager Cooley and Master Mechanic W. H. Chambers were reluctant to have the slow-moving Shays run any farther than necessary beyond Wendella, at the base of the five per cent grade on the north side of the big hill. So, to handle the expected traffic on the north end they ordered an outside-frame Mikado, considerably bigger and heavier than any engine yet on the line. The Mike, in fact, would be more than twice the weight of the 2-8-0 which had just been delivered. When she was completed

in September, 2-8-2 No. 30 with her tender was shipped west to Mack aboard a couple of standard gauge flat cars. Unloaded there, the No. 30 was run up to Atchee on her own wheels. Once there, to get her past the impossible 66-degree curves on the pass, she was jacked up and her rods and driving wheels were removed. A set of tender trucks was rolled in and fastened below the leading and trailing trucks, and in that ungainly position the new Mike was hauled over Baxter Pass by a Shay. As would be expected, this unusual movement was remembered by the men many years afterward. The No. 30 was reassembled at Dragon, after her trip over the hill, and placed in service. Never again for all her 28-year life did the Mike see the other side of Baxter Pass. When repairs were needed the shopmen would go over to Dragon or Watson to work on her. Once when she needed a new firebox the pieces were brought down to Atchee, the plates welded on and the job returned to Watson for assembly.[8] Finally, after the railway was abandoned in 1939 she was cut up by the scrappers and the pieces hauled back over the hill and shipped out to the furnaces at Pueblo.

Additional freight cars would also be needed, the management decided, to haul the increasing amounts of gilsonite which they hoped would come up from the mines at Rainbow. Flat cars were the thing, so rather than ordering them from an outside builder the Uintah Railway men went right ahead and started building their own in the Atchee car shops. Since the line was built in 1904, the Uintah Railway had moved all its freight in its original complement of 37 cars, built for them by American Car & Foundry Co. of St. Louis. By types, these consisted of 8 box cars, 5 stock cars, 12 flats and 12 gondolas.[9] Between mid-1910 when the flat car building program started at Atchee and April 30, 1913, when it was completed, the roster more than doubled. By mid-1913 a total of 79 freight cars were in service on the road.[10] Other than a handful of rectangular steel water tank cars built at Atchee around 1916 and a few cars rebuilt, there would be no more changes until 1920 when construction started on another 43 flat cars.

Just a few weeks before the opening of the extension and the new station at Watson, one of

The Rainbow branch had grades averaging around 4 per cent and running up to as steep as 5.1 per cent for nearly a mile. It was a challenge for any engine, but the No. 30 was up to the challenge, most of the time. Except once (below) when "Judge" Kennedy found her in an embarrassing moment on the ground just a few feet up above the switch at Rainbow Junction. *(Both: F. A. Kennedy photos from V. L. McCoy Collection)*

Pictures of the Uintah's Buick rail car are very rare. This one shows only portions of the 1916 Buick which was equipped with flanged wheels for railway use in 1922. That's Bruce Angus standing alongside, and Mrs. Angus with the pretty smile. (*Bruce Angus Collection*)

Without a doubt the least photographed engine the Uintah Railway owned was the second No. 11. This photo of the 1911 Baldwin 2-8-0 is the only known picture of the Consolidation. She was three years old at the time it was taken in Atchee. (*J. Horace Erwin photo from D. H. Gerbaz Collection*)

Two brand new flat cars and the men who built them stand outside the car shops at Atchee. The year is 1911, and lumber for more flats is on the ground. Other than the unique above-the-coupler position of the air hoses and the steel buffer plates at each end, they were just ordinary three-foot-gauge flats. *(Robert O. Perkins Collection)*

By 1911, the town of Atchee (opposite page) had grown. Besides the car shops and the schoolhouse, a section house and the saloon in the lower right corner had been added. A few outbuildings, outhouses and tents helped round out the community. *(Robert O. Perkins Collection)*

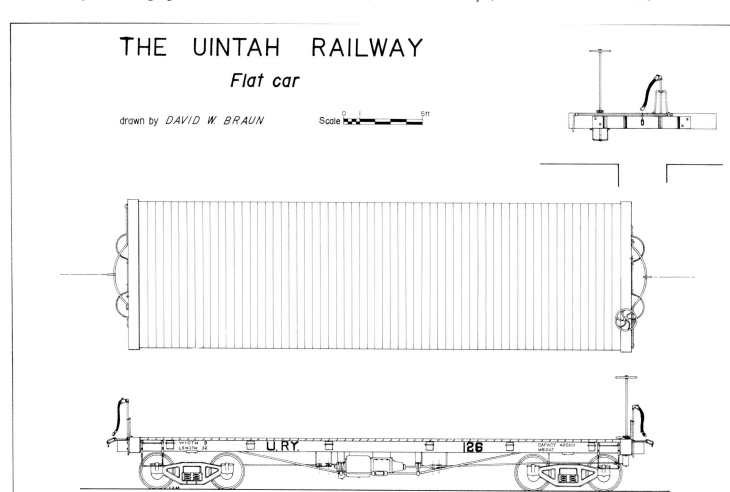

THE UINTAH RAILWAY
Flat car

drawn by *DAVID W. BRAUN*   Scale |—————| 5ft.

WIDTH 9
LENGTH 32   U. RY.   126   CAPACY 40000
WEIGHT

the best of the customers served by the company's stage and wagon roads disclosed plans for going out of business. It was the U. S. Army detachment at Fort Duchesne, Utah. The Fort, which had been established in 1886 to protect the Uintah Basin settlers from possible hostilities by the Utes, had served its purpose. Possibly the draining of the Uinta River by irrigation companies which thus cut off the supply for the military water system may have been a factor in prompting the Army's order to deactivate Fort Duchesne. Whatever the reasons, though, Captain Brees received a telegram from headquarters ordering him and his garrison to new barracks at Boise, Idaho. Sixteen men were to stay behind and remain in charge of the Fort. The remainder of the soldiers marched to Dragon and there, on Friday, September 15, 1911, boarded the only troop train ever run by the Uintah Railway. Thanks to the "5x7" camera of the railroad's claim agent Frank A. Kennedy, a number of excellent photographs of this train were preserved for posterity. Perhaps "Judge" Kennedy just wanted to be prepared in case any claims arose due to soldiers falling from atop box cars where they were riding!

There was some speculation that Fort Duchesne might be the logical place for the terminus of the Uintah Railway extension even then under

way in that direction from Dragon. Rumor had it that negotiations were already under way for the purchase of the Fort and all its excellent buildings and accessories by the railway people. When Captain Brees was questioned about this matter, prior to his departure with his garrison, he neither affirmed nor discredited the rumor.[11] A few weeks' time would prove the rumors to be just that, though. By the end of the following February the few remaining soldiers at Fort Duchesne, with Captain R. M. Nolan in charge, had disposed of the few Army goods and chattels still there and had left to join their command at Boise Barracks.[12]

Then suddenly, without warning, disaster and death struck the Uintah again. The passenger train, running many hours late due to trouble caused by abnormally heavy rains along the line, had almost made it back to its home terminal. The night was dark and stormy. Midnight had come and gone nearly two hours earlier. Running dead slow, Engineer George Lyman eased engine No. 10 out onto the trestle spanning Salt Wash two miles west of Mack. About halfway across, the flood-weakened bridge shuddered and gave way, catching the enginemen entirely unawares as the Consolidation dropped into the raging waters. As it fell the engine rolled onto its left side trapping and drowning Fireman Charles Pisano in the

Photographer Kennedy seems to have had a good time recording the passage of the Uintah's first and last troop train, on September 15, 1911. The soldiers, too, seem to be enjoying themselves — the view from atop the cars must have been good. The train itself is rather unique, containing all three of the ex-D.&R.G. narrow-gauge Pullmans separated by boxcar No. 204 and side-door caboose No. 01 to permit passage around the many sharp curves. One of those curves is "Hairpin Curve" at milepost 39 (below, opposite page). The picture above is near the same location. (Above, opposite page) is the only known picture taken at Wendella, while below on this page the men are unloading footlockers at Mack, preparing to transfer to the standard gauge. *(Left above: D. H. Gerbaz Collection; left below: V. L. McCoy Collection; above: E. V. Earp Collection; below: Denver Public Library Western Collection)*

As quickly as they come, the flood waters ebb, leaving only mud, destruction and death. This was the scene at bridge 2-A the morning after. Consolidation No. 10 lies on her side presenting a seldom-seen view of her brake rigging and blind center drivers, while the section men work to free her from the mud. The combine had been eased off the weakened trestle hours before, leaving boxcar No. 202 hanging precariously over the gap. (Both: *F. A. Kennedy photos from Denver Public Library Western Collection*)

crushed cab. A Greek section hand, C. M. Kipros, who had been riding the engine was also trapped and drowned in the wreck. Engineer Lyman, with his shoulder, ribs and a leg broken, was pinned in the wreckage of the cab with his head barely above the surging water. There he was held prisoner for two hours while rescuers tried vainly to reach him. Finally a Greek section man was anchored to a large rope and thrown out into the stream where he could get hold of the engine and help the badly injured engineer to safety.

The train consisted of the engine and one box car of ice, followed by the combination baggage-passenger coach. Fortunately, when the engine went through the trestle followed by its tender, the ice car hung perched on the brink. The 14 passengers aboard the combination were, needless to say, thankful. Things could have been much worse.

It was during the wee hours of Sunday morning, October 1, 1911, when No. 10 went through bridge 2-A. Not until Tuesday was the wrecked engine raised from the soft mud of the wash and the bodies of the fireman and the section man recovered.[13] The rains, reported to be the heaviest in many years, were not over yet, though. Bridge 2-A across Salt Wash had just been repaired when, on Friday, flood waters carried out fifty feet of it again.[14] Nor were the railway's troubles over when they had repaired the damage caused by the storms. Nearly two years later, on September 8, 1913, a damage suit asking $25,000 for the death of C. M. Kipros came to trial before the district court in session at Vernal, Utah. Brought by George N. Kipros of Salt Lake City, a relative of the deceased and administrator for his estate, the suit charged negligence on the part of the defendant company in that the bridge across Salt Wash was not properly constructed and maintained. The defense introduced rebuttal testimony to show contributory negligence on the part of the plaintiff. It was alleged that he had been warned to get off the engine and had not done so. Noted legal talent was brought in from Salt Lake City to represent both parties in the case.

The trial turned out to be the longest, up to that date, in the history of Uintah County. Starting Monday morning, the case did not go to the jury until about suppertime on Saturday. The jury was out until 2:00 a.m. Sunday when a verdict was agreed upon awarding the laborer's widow damages in the sum of $3,467. The widow lived in Greece and was preparing to come to the United States when the news of her husband's death had reached her. Kipros had been 35 years old.[15]

It was but days after the disastrous washout at bridge 2-A that the extension from Dragon to Watson was completed and opened for service. According to the *Rio Grande Service Gazette*, issued by the passenger department of the D.&R.G., it was to be completed October 15, 1911. No changes were to be made in the through fares to Vernal or Fort Duchesne.[16] The official opening for the new station of Watson was not until Sunday, November 19th, though. This brought rail service ten miles closer to Vernal and the other towns of the Uintah Basin and cut off twenty miles from the round trip for the company's teams carrying freight. In the two weeks prior to the official opening, the railroad had brought in a big sixty-horsepower truck to try it out in the freight service between Watson and Vernal. The truck made the round trip of 120 miles in three days and had a loading capacity of 6000 pounds. Painted on its side was the inscription "Big Chief — The Uintah Railway Fast Freight Between Dragon and Vernal." It was hoped that this truck would prove to be the right machine for the business. If it had, the company would have motorized the entire operation and laid off the teams.[17] As things turned out, however, horses would pull the Uintah Railway wagons for a few more years to come.

Even the passengers buying a Uintah Railway ticket to or from Vernal could not always count on traveling in motorized comfort during those early years of the automobile. The following account relates what happened on the first day of April of 1912:

"INNOCENCE ABROAD," OR
"WATSON AM A HARD ROAD"
———

The king of the Mischievous imps who preside over All Fool's Day must have directed the destiny of the passengers over the Dragon road Monday. There were ten passengers registered out from Vernal, two autos were to go. The first started on time, went around to the post-office

107

"Judge" Kennedy has moved in with his camera for a close-up of the Rainbow Mine.
(Top: C. J. Neal Collection; bottom: V. L. McCoy Collection)

and broke down. Then there was a discussion as to who should stay until the next day. After much telephoning on the part of the agent, it was decided to load four people on the one remaining auto and the others on a stage. The auto was to carry the four to Kennedy's then return to meet the other passengers at Alhandra. Another auto was to come from White river to pick up the passengers at Kennedy's. But here the imps began to show their real class. The auto from Vernal had just delivered its passengers to a stage driver who came out from Kennedy's to meet him and turned to go back to Alhandra when, snap! went an axle on the car. Then the imps at White river got busy, and the car which was to go to Kennedy's broke down before it got out of the river bottom. This left both parties to continue the journey in the old style — by stage. When the first party reached White river they were cheered by the sight of the "big auto" on the farther shore. After crossing the river, some walking planks across the unfinished bridge, others tumbled in the bottom of a lumber wagon among a lot of suit cases and mail sacks, they were given their choice, to wait for the other party and all continue together in the "big auto," or continue toward Watson in the stage. Thinking it an off day for automobiles, they decided to continue by stage with the hope that the auto would overtake them. But all the craning of necks and straining of ears failed to disclose the car. At Watson the first happy surprise of the first party awaited them. Mr. Dalvie was there with his autocar and kindly offered to take the party on to Dragon. The ride was delightful; and the dinner at the Dragon Hotel tasted like ambrosia. Riding from 7 a.m. to 5 p.m. without dinner is good for the appetite. The second party in the "big auto" reached Watson about five, and taking the train reached Dragon about an hour after the first party. The trip over the mountain, and Baxter pass in the moonlight was pronounced by everyone, ideal but all were glad of the comforts of the Mack Hotel at the end of the journey. When it came to getting up at three a.m. to take the Salt Lake train the spirits of the women of the party flagged, but the men with characteristic energy tore themselves from the realm of Morpheus — and took No. 5 while the ladies waited for No. 3 at noon.[18]

Happily for everyone, not every day was like that one. It might have been years before some of those travelers even considered starting out on April 1st again! Not many months later, though, there was another such day. On October 29th the northbound party of passengers, including principal Oliver B. Loud of the Wilcox Academy in Vernal, first saw the engine of their train tip over, and then the replacement engine break an axle. Next, the small auto sent out to rescue them suffered a broken spring. Then Captain Cooley, the Uintah's general manager, took the group aboard his private railcar and brought them safely to Watson, from which point after a series of experiences they finally reached Vernal at 3:00 the next morning behind a four-mule team. One of the railway's employees is reported to have remarked that day, "There is no such word as monotony in the Uintah Railway's dictionary; we give our passengers variety instead." Principal Loud was not hesitant in vouching for the truth of the man's statement![19]

Although the line's small passenger business occasionally provided newsworthy, or at least humorous, copy for the local papers, the Uintah's primary job, as always, continued to be moving the gilsonite. During November, 1912, 312 carloads of the mineral, at 15 tons to the car, were hauled over Baxter Pass to Mack. This included the output of the American Asphalt Association as well as Gilson Asphaltum Company. The latter firm employed 65 men in their mine at Rainbow digging from five to seven cars of ore per day. Over 200 men were employed directly by both the Gilson Company and the railway, and it was conservatively estimated that the combined payroll came to $500 per day, $15,000 a month or $180,000 a year. Additional scores of people depended either directly or indirectly upon these employees for their support. All told, the gilsonite industry was the major contributor to the economy of this very sparsely settled corner of the West.[20]

Of course not all the Uintah's freight tonnage was gilsonite. By early August of 1912 the last of that year's clip of wool from the Uintah Reservation and the Vernal area, 1,036,323 pounds of it, had been shipped from Watson. Enough to fill thirty-four standard gauge cars, the shipment included about 170,000 fleeces for which the sheepmen received an average of a little more than one dollar per fleece. About nine-tenths of the quantity was shipped to Boston while the remainder went to Philadelphia.[21] On occasion the sheepmen also found the railway useful when transporting their

Rainbow mine. This particular portion of the vein was known as the Pigeon Toe Claim. (Above) we see two men hoisting a sack of gilsonite up from the vein; (below) the men who worked the mine, with their picks for loosening the ore and empty burlap bags and coils of twine for sewing up the bags when they were full. *(Both: F. A. Kennedy photos from C. J. Neal Collection)*

flocks from winter to summer pastures, or back again, but more frequently trail drives did the trick and saved the freight bill. Although sheep and the wool from their backs were second only to the gilsonite as a traffic source during most of the years the Uintah Railway operated, it was a seasonal traffic and never brought in consistent revenue.

After an eventful year in 1911, things pretty much settled down to a smooth routine on the line for a few years. At least not very much of a catastrophic nature occurred to make news. Spring floods did take out the White River bridge at Ignacio on the Watson-Vernal toll road in March of 1912, delaying the mail for a couple days and the freight wagons for a longer time. Even this, though, was something which had almost become routine (although never welcome) for the Uintah.[22] Just a couple of weeks later the railway was blocked by two mud slides, one on either side of the summit. Although these might have been a forewarning of the far more serious slides which would plague the line in the 1920s, not much thought was given them at the time. No damage had been done to the track, and the trains were soon moving again.[23]

Practically the only other event of much significance for the Railway during the next few months was the increase in the company's capital stock, approved May 7, 1912. An amendment to its articles of incorporation, filed in the secretary of state offices in both Colorado and Utah, increased the stock from $1,750,000 par value to $2,250,000. Most companies, of course, issue stock prior to an expansion of their business in order to finance that expansion. The Uintah Railway, at least on this occasion, did things backward! The stock increase was authorized some six months after the extension to Watson and Rainbow had been finished. Since all the railway's stock, except

for five qualifying shares held by the five directors, was owned by the parent Barber Asphalt Paving Company or its parent General Asphalt Company, it didn't matter much anyway. Apparently the management was more concerned with possible future I.C.C. valuations of the property for rate-making purposes than with any other reasons for issuing stock.

And so the next three or four years passed smoothly and quietly for the Uintah. The talk in Colorado and Utah was mostly of other railroads. In 1912 the Provo & Eastern Utah Railway Company announced plans to build east from Provo through the Uintah Basin. It was to run to Vernal and Jensen and thence on to Craig to connect with the Laramie, Hahns Peak & Pacific Railway which was even then extending its rails towards northwestern Colorado.[24] But the former never laid a rail and the latter ceased construction at Coalmont, Colorado, some 111 miles from Laramie, and was soon in receivership. As the Denver & Salt Lake pushed its rails west from Steamboat Springs to Craig in 1913, hopes were expressed in the Basin that it would continue on west to the Salt Lake of its new corporate title. But this was not to be, either. The Moffat Road laid its last rails at Craig. The mighty Denver & Rio Grande, too, considered building into the Basin on more than one occasion. In 1913 a party of D.&R.G. surveyors made a preliminary survey from Meeker, Colorado, west through the White River valley to Dragon.[25] Again, late in 1915 a Rio Grande survey crew was in the field running a line from Thistle Junction, Utah, into the Basin. This party, with D.&R.G. locating engineer C. L. Milton in charge, had reached Randlett and was running a branch survey to Vernal.[26] But nothing ever came of any of these plans or schemes. The Uintah remained the only railway ever to penetrate its namesake Basin.

The Uintah Railway climbs towards Columbine and Baxter Pass. (*George L. Beam photo, from D.&R.G.W. files courtesy of Jackson C. Thode*)

Chapter Six

Bricks by Parcel Post

An interesting new era for the Uintah Railway dawned on New Year's Day of 1914, when a government ruling increasing the weight limit of a parcel post package to fifty pounds went into effect. The previous month the railway company had handled a record amount of 36,000 pounds of mail coming to and from the Vernal post office. But that record didn't last long! By the end of January nearly 75,000 pounds of mail had been moved to and from the county seat that month. And this was just the start. It was estimated that the Vernal post office would handle nearly 2,000,000 pounds of mail before 1914 was over. One local firm alone indicated that it might order 500,000 pounds shipped by parcel post during the year.[1]

The post office charged the patron just five cents for the first pound and one cent for each additional pound for carrying parcels within the first and second zones. But, while the parcel post zones were measured "as the crow flies," mail to the Uintah Basin frequently traveled a circuitous route. Parcels sent from Salt Lake City to Vernal, for example, usually moved via Mack, Colorado, traveling the final sixty miles from Watson on the Uintah Railway trucks or freight wagons. By June, 1916, "at a very conservative estimate," the government was reported to be "losing between $25,000 and $30,000 annually by being compelled to haul in parcel post at a loss to the Uintah Basin from Watson and Helper, Utah."[2] In reality Uncle Sam was footing part of the grocery bill of every family living in the Basin.

It hadn't taken the local merchants long to realize they could save considerable money by using the parcel post. The doubling of the amount shipped by mail that first month wasn't accidental! Within days of the January 1st change in service a Duchesne firm had ordered 30,000 pounds of cement — a carload lot — by mail. The town of Duchesne in the western part of the Basin was in the second zone from Salt Lake City, and packages weighing fifty pounds could be sent from the city to Duchesne for 54 cents. The freight rate at the time was 40 cents per hundredweight on the railroad from Salt Lake City to Helper, plus $1 per hundredweight for trucking from the railroad to Duchesne. Thus the consignee could save 32 cents per hundred pounds by having merchandise come in by parcel post in fifty pound lots.[3]

Soon all sorts of commodities were flowing into the Uintah Basin courtesy of the U. S. Post Office. Although most were incoming, there were some shipments headed for the outside world, too. One spring day in 1915 the Acorn Mercantile Co. of Vernal shipped out 1,000 dozen eggs by parcel post to Grand Junction and Salt Lake City, thus opening up a new market for the farmers of the area.[4] Another profitable cash crop for the Mormon settlers was honey. Within a 24-hour period in March, 1916, the Vernal post office received 28,500 pounds and shipped out 6,800 pounds. The outgoing shipment was honey from the Hampton farm. On another occasion the outbound mail included 85 sacks of copper ore.

The Bank of Vernal (top) as it appears today. The center photo shows the Bank of Vernal or Coltharp building under construction in 1916. At the left are some of the bricks, telephone parts and supplies that were scattered during the wreck of the Uintah Railway mail truck on July 13, 1916. *(Charles J. Neal Collection)*

The packages coming into the Basin included as diverse an assortment of items as can be imagined. Groceries, blacksmith tools, automobile parts, hardware, nails, pitchforks, brooms, water hydrants, fresh strawberries and cherries, fruit jars, auto tires and feather beds were just some of the things received at the Vernal post office. One day 10,000 pounds of salt, 12,500 pounds of flour and 8,800 pounds of sugar all arrived at once!

Practically all the parcel post moving into the eastern part of the Uintah Basin was hauled by the Uintah Railway Company. By April of 1916 this amounted to 728,000 pounds during the previous six months. In addition, the company moved about 40,000 pounds of regular mail in that period. The Duchesne Stage & Transportation Co. had the contract for the mail and parcel post from Helper to towns in the western part of the Basin and hauled approximately 787,000 pounds of parcel post plus about 60,000 pounds of mail during the same six-month period. The government was paying the railway 1.5 cents a pound for hauling the parcel post from Watson to Vernal, but never received more than 1.08 cents per pound postage on each fifty-pound package. Thus, Uncle Sam was losing 0.42 cents on every pound hauled, in addition to what was paid for transportation charges from point of shipment to Watson.[5] When the parcel post flood began in January, 1914, things were even worse for the government. The Uintah was then carrying the mail under a fixed price contract and received approximately 4.5 cents per pound for it that month, down from about 9 cents per pound the month before.[6]

This deluge at the taxpayers' expense might have continued for years had it not been for the bricks. Late in the spring of 1916 the first of 13,700 pressed brick, reputedly the finest obtainable, started arriving in Vernal for use in the new Coltharp Building. The bricks were purchased in Salt Lake City, and enough were obtained to construct the entire front of the new business structure, the rest of the building being built of local brick. Needless to say, the pressed bricks came from Salt Lake by mail — nearly 35 tons of them! Including the postage, the bricks cost $90 per thousand delivered in Vernal. This was a significant percentage of the more than $30,000 the two-story building cost, but undoubtedly a necessary

cost in making it the finest commercial structure in the city. The ground floor was, and still is, occupied by the Bank of Vernal, and the second floor contained 24 office rooms.[7] Old-timers around Vernal still talk of "the bank that arrived by mail," and former Uintah railroaders remember how the bricks tied up the mail for weeks that summer. It seems the mailing address was applied to each brick individually, with a rubber stamp!

The morning of July 13th was not a lucky one. One load of bricks didn't quite make it to Vernal. A big Uintah Railway truck started up Lion Hill just past Alhandra loaded down with several thousand white pressed bricks and two small express shipments. Driver Sibley was making the difficult hill out of the Green River valley when, partway up, one of the drive chains broke. The truck immediately started backwards and the brakes failed to hold. It turned over and caught fire and was a total wreck. Some of the bricks could be used but most of them were a loss. The damages were estimated to be between $1,000 and $1,500, a considerable sum in those days. Happily, the driver was uninjured.[8]

The Post Office Department finally took action and called a halt in mid-November, 1916. Instructions were sent out to postmasters defining "large and unusual shipments" of parcel post matter, providing that not more than 200 pounds of parcel post mail thereafter was to be accepted for any one addressee on the same day. That effectively put a stop to the shipments of cement, flour and pressed brick enough for a building through the mails![9] A year later, though, the new desks and seats for the school house at Dragon arrived from Salt Lake City by parcel post.[10] Perhaps they were within the 200 pound limit?

Just before the deluge of parcel post reached its peak the Uintah suffered one of the worst, if not the worst, snowstorms in the railroad's history. At least E. Victor Earp, who was superintendent of the Uintah Railway in the final years of the line's existence, remembered it as the worst blockade he ever saw.[11] Since the washout at Bridge 2-A in 1911, there had been only one day that the line had been blocked. That was on January 26, 1914, when blowing snow and drifts closed the pass.[12] It was two years later, to the very day, when the big storm hit the Uintah. "We were

Shays 4, 3 and 5 (above) team up to buck through a drift at Lone Tree Curve in one of the most spectacular photos of Uintah Ry. snow-fighting operations. This storm in 1916 kept the line closed for eight days and was remembered years later by Uintah men as "The Big Snow." The same three Shays (below) as seen from above, appear to be almost buried in the white stuff. *(Both: F. A. Kennedy photos; above: Robert O. Perkins Collection; below: V. L. McCoy Collection)*

After the storm has passed and the tracks are cleared, the railway in winter takes on a peaceful appearance. The quiet is broken only by the trickle of melting snow and occasionally the rapid-staccato exhaust of a Shay in the distance, like the one below starting her train up the hill after taking a drink of water at Shale Tank. *(Both: F. A. Kennedy photos; above: R. O. Perkins Collection; below: V. L. McCoy Collection)*

Above, in front of the hotel in Atchee, and below, in front of the Uintah Railway office and the hotel in Mack, wet snow has coated the trees and left a fairyland scene. Most likely, though, the idea that they are in fairyland has not entered the minds of the crew aboard that Shay. There still is work to be done. *(Top: Ruby Luton photo from Bruce Angus Collection; bottom: F. A. Kennedy photo from J. V. Kelly Collection)*

sewed up for eight days," Vic Earp recalled. "It took us eight days to buck it out."

There had been heavy snowfalls late in December, breaking all previous records for the month in Grand Junction and leaving a good layer of the white stuff covering the Book Cliffs.[13] The heavy snows continued on into January, and by the 28th the snow was 26 inches deep on the court house lawn in Vernal. Up on Baxter Pass the wind was blowing fiercely and the snow was drifting.[14] By February 4th when a train, the first in nine days, finally made it through from Mack to Watson the snow on the pass was reported to measure nine feet on the level with many deep drifts.[15]

E. V. Earp remembered the storm clearly nearly a half century later. He had been promoted to the right-hand side of the cab not long before. One particular incident stood out. Here is the story in his own words:

> There were three engines of us coupled together leaving the top. We had, I don't just remember, we had three or four, maybe five, cars of ore. I was coupled to the train, and as we went around out of Lone Tree Curve I just saw through this blizzard that there was a big slide down ahead of us. So I whistled 'em down. So they cut off the two engines, the front engines, and went down and tried to go through it and they got stuck, and it took a long time to dig 'em out. By the time they got 'em dug out it was dark, so they told me they were going to put all three of us on, and then we'd come back and get the train. So we hit that slide just as hard as we could, and we just poked a hole through it, and it fell in behind us so we couldn't go back and get the train! So we went on into Atchee.
>
> The next morning the superintendent called the section crew at Baxter Pass, and told them to go down and shovel the snow out from around that train. We were going to come up and get it. The train was about half way between Baxter Pass and Shale. The section foreman walked down to Shale and called up and said he couldn't find the train! So we got to looking up from Atchee with field glasses, and it was piled all the way down the hill there, about half way down to where the track was down below. A slide had come down in the night, and wiped it off. And, if we hadn't got bored through that slide, we'd all have tied up right there for the night! We'd all have been in that snowslide!

Even the run-off from the snows that winter gave the railway some trouble, washing out stretches of track between Dragon and Watson early in March.[16] But washouts were more common during August and September. The summer afternoon thunderstorms which are characteristic of the arid Great Basin between the Rockies and the Sierra sometimes sent wild torrents of water rushing down usually placid Evacuation Creek, or down West Salt Wash on the other side of Baxter Pass, and 1916 turned out to be one of those years. A sudden storm August 13th was almost disastrous for some picnickers from Watson.

W. A. Banks, the Uintah Railway agent at Watson for many years, his son, B. Thompson and his wife and Ernest Heaton and his wife decided they would have a Sunday outing at Lake McAndrews. Accordingly they got together their lunch baskets, ice cream freezer and other necessities and went up on the afternoon train out of Watson and spent the afternoon and evening enjoying themselves.

A hard rain came up just as they started home but they thought nothing of it. The sky grew darker. They had a "go-devil" and expected to coast all the way home. The rain, however, had assumed the proportions of a cloudburst about three miles south of Watson and washed out about 200 yards of the track paralleling Evacuation Creek. Into this they plunged. The "go-devil" hung on the edge of the brink and did not go in. One of the ladies with a six-month-old baby in her arms was thrown out so that she was hanging upside down held only by her foot. Mr. Banks, although badly bruised, managed to pull her to safety. Mr. Heaton and the others were badly bruised too. Ice cream freezer, lunch baskets and all were thrown into the raging torrent. One of Mr. Banks' boys was also thrown in, and Mr. Heaton raced for 200 yards down the stream before he was able to drag him to safety.[17] Rather a close call!

After that, things went pretty well for the next couple years. There were more rumors about replacing the horses which pulled the freight wagons north of Watson with gasoline-driven motive power, but again, it didn't happen. Late in June, 1916, a new Holt caterpillar tractor arrived on the scene. It hauled over 17,000 pounds of freight

A handcar hooked on behind a train and taken to the top of Baxter Pass could coast to almost any point on the railroad. (Above) W. A. Banks, at the right behind the handcar, his wife and another couple and their children are ready with their picnic basket filled for an all-day outing. The well-dressed gentleman with the gold watch chain standing on the back platform of the combine is Roadmaster Jim Gallagher, and the man on the ground leaning against the end sill is Roscoe Combs. Below is the U. Ry.'s Holt caterpillar tractor at Watson about to leave with two wagonloads of freight for the Basin towns. *(Above: E. V. Earp Collection; below: F. A. Kennedy photo from W. A. Banks Collection)*

on its trial trip from Watson to Vernal and made the sixty miles on fifty gallons of gasoline. It was accompanied by optimistic predictions — the company expected to place several larger ones in use shortly and would soon do all its freight hauling in this manner, went the reports.[18] But the caterpillar didn't last long on the job and after about six months it was retired to an easier life on Captain Cooley's farm near Randlett, Utah. A year and a half later another attempt to use trucks for carrying the parcel post between Watson and Vernal was discontinued. Winter weather conditions made the roads difficult to travel for the trucks and too expensive to the company. The parcel post again moved in freight wagons behind teams and required three and four days to make the journey.[19] As late as the spring of 1918 the line was reported purchasing additional horses to add to their stables for pulling the wagons.[20]

There were also the usual rumors to the effect the Uintah would be extended or absorbed by a larger system. These, too, proved to be just rumors, despite authoritative statements from men in high positions. In 1917 it was announced by no less than Spencer Penrose, chairman of the Board of Directors of the Colorado Midland R.R., that the first extension of the Midland under its new management would be an eight-mile line from Fruita to Mack.[21] The Carlton-Penrose interests already owned the Grand River Valley R.R. Co., the electric interurban line connecting Grand Junction and Fruita, and would use this as part of their link between the Colorado Midland and the Uintah Railway. The Denver & Rio Grande, of course, already ran from Grand Junction via Fruita and Mack on its way to Salt Lake City, but talk of building a parallel line to connect the Uintah with the interurban at Fruita, and thus with the Colorado Midland, had been heard on and off since at least 1912.[22]

An interesting sidelight from this period was the long crossties. For a number of years, primarily during the 1912-1918 period, Uintah Railway section gangs used standard-gauge crossties whenever replacements were needed. This was done, of course, in anticipation of widening the Uintah to four feet eight and one half inches. The longer ties were installed as old ones were replaced between Mack and Atchee and betwen Wendella

and Watson, but not over the pass where the grades and curves were way beyond reason for any standard gauge main line. But the railway never was standard gauged and, in the line's later years, the long crossties interspersed among the shorter ones never ceased to bring a question from visitors and newcomers.

The flurry of talk about connecting with the Colorado Midland was just dying down when another statement that the Uintah would extend its line appeared in the papers. This time it was more of the old talk about building from Watson to the Uintah Basin towns of Vernal, Fort Duchesne and Roosevelt. It came from the lips of the company's assistant treasurer and secretary, W. D. Halpin of Mack. His reason for making such a statement is not hard to detect. He was in Salt Lake City at the time petitioning the Utah Public Utilities Commission for permission to raise the freight rates charged for the Watson-Vernal wagon haul from 65 cents a hundred pounds to an even $1.00. The company had been operating this wagon freight service at a loss for some time, and rising costs for labor, feed and other supplies were increasing the losses. Mr. Halpin stated the company's intention to extend its railway line to points in the Uintah Basin. He explained that it was their desire to retain their business over the wagon road until the extension might be built, but that they did not feel imposed to do so at a loss.[23] This was early in September of 1917.

A number of the merchants around Vernal were doing their own hauling, and many were not very happy with the railway's service. Management of the Acorn Mercantile Co. expressed the opinion that "the business interests would be better served if the Uintah Railway service were discontinued entirely." The Leslie Ashton Hardware Co., also of Vernal, complained that its incoming freight had been lying at Watson for months, with the railway apparently making no effort to get it delivered. As they expressed it, "the service is as poor as it could possibly be."[24]

With that atmosphere evident, hearings were held early in November in Vernal by Warren Stoutnour of the Utah P.U.C. on the wagon rate increase. Pending the investigation, permission had been granted the company to charge the higher rates as of the first of that month. The

At Carbonera, Colorado (above) many long crossties are interspersed between the more ordinary narrow-gauge ones supporting the rails. Below, an unusual three-car passenger special needs the power of two Shays to lift it up around the 65 degrees at Moro Castle. *(Top: L. W. Moody Collection, from Everett L. DeGolyer, Jr.; bottom: J. Horace Erwin photo from D. H. Gerbaz Collection)*

investigation was then made to determine whether the $1.00 rate was warranted, inasmuch as hauling was being done at the time by private teamsters for 75 cents a hundred pounds, out of which $3.50 in toll charges was paid to the railway company.[25] Apparently the P.U.C. felt the increase from 65 cents to $1.00 a hundred was excessive, since they allowed the railway to increase the Watson-Vernal rate to only 90 cents per hundred pounds on most freight.

Within just six months the company had applied for another rate increase for the wagons, this time to $1.15 a hundred. Again the Utah P.U.C. held hearings in Vernal and Duchesne, and again the opposing parties presented their arguments. The railway company was caught in a price squeeze and was still losing money providing the service. A major factor was the order, effective January 1, 1918, of Director-General of Railroads William G. McAdoo which granted large pay increases to all classes of railway labor. Technically this order had no compulsory effect on the wagon line, or even on the Uintah Railway itself, which was one of the very few railroads in the country not subject to control by the newly established United States Railroad Administration. Its practical effect, however, was to necessitate pay raises for all the company employees. Otherwise they'd soon be leaving for better paying jobs elsewhere. With many young men going off to the War the labor market was becoming tight. During the first five months of 1918, according to W. D. Halpin, the company had lost $6,500 on the wagon road operation, and this was with the increased 90-cent rate. The required wage increases for the employees would add another $600 a month to this deficit, unless the P.U.C. allowed the requested rate of $1.15 a hundred to become effective almost immediately.

Continuing, Mr. Halpin further clarified his and the company's attitude towards the wagon business:

"At the meeting held at the Commercial Club Wednesday, a number of the merchants expressed themselves as agreeable to sending private teams to Watson for their freight. Our company has no objection to this plan, in fact, we are very much in favor of it, as our wagon operations have always resulted in a very heavy loss. Owing to the shortage of labor, the high price of feed and other supplies necessary in the conduct of our business, I am afraid that our operations in the future will be even more difficult and result in a greater loss than they have in the past. I feel quite sure that the company would be very much pleased if the merchants would all go to Watson for their freight, and personally, I hope that this will prove to be the solution for our wagon line troubles."[26]

Obviously the Uintah Railway was on its way out of the wagon business!

On the railroad itself all was going smoothly. In the fall of 1917 the old Dragon mine was re-opened under the management of the American Asphalt Association. The residents there gave a dance on October 20th, and the railway ran an engine and caboose up for the accommodation of the public. Dancing was enjoyed until half past eleven when a bountiful supply of refreshments was served.[27] These dances were always welcome. Most of the miners and railroaders and their ladies didn't have an opportunity to see the bright lights of the big city (or even a small one) for many months at a time.

In August the company had purchased another locomotive, the first to be added to the roster in nearly six years. It was a third-hand Consolidation, a bit heavier than Nos. 10 and 11, and originally had been the Florence & Cripple Creek R.R.'s No. 10. The Baldwin 2-8-0 had also borne the name INDEPENDENCE when it was first placed in service in 1896, but the pleasing practice of naming its engines was discontinued by the F.&C.C. in about 1904. A surplus of railroads serving the Cripple Creek District, together with serious flood damage in July, 1912, had caused the abandonment of the F.&C.C. and left most of its roster of narrow-gauge motive power up for sale. Surplus Consolidations and Ten-Wheelers were picked up at bargain prices by roads such as the Denver & Rio Grande, Montana Southern, Nevada-California-Oregon, and Rio Grande Southern. The Uintah renumbered their purchase the No. 12 and put it to work with the other two Consolidations between Mack and Atchee.[28]

The year 1917 turned out to be a very good one for the railroad. In fact, financially it was the best year in the line's entire history. The net railway operating income, after taxes, of $180,730 was well above the previous record of $156,090 set two years earlier. The railway's operating revenues for the year came to $494,834, while the operating expenses totaled $292,737. That's an operating ratio of 59 per cent — not bad at all! The Uintah paid a dividend of $146,250 into the coffers of its parent General Asphalt Company that year, also not bad for a 68-mile railway.[29] The Great War in Europe certainly wasn't hurting the company. Demand for gilsonite was as high as ever, and practically all the country's gilsonite moved to market over the Uintah Railway.

By the time the auditor totaled the figures the following year, the profit picture was still fairly bright. The railway operating revenues were down somewhat to $452,256, and the operating expenses were up a bit at $301,650. Tax accruals had taken a big jump from $21,128 in 1917 to $34,873 for 1918. This left the net operating income, after taxes, at $115,711 and the total net income was $120,264. Again the company paid its owner a dividend, this time $151,875. Obviously some of this was paid out of surplus from previous years' earnings, but a healthy $101,250 of it was reported as resulting from the 1918 income.[30] Although no one suspected it at the time, the Uintah Railway would not declare another dividend for 17 years.

Although later brightened by the Armistice, 1918 had been marred by a tragic accident on Baxter Pass. On Sunday afternoon, September 8th, the eastbound passenger train, comprised of Baldwin tank engine No. 20 pulling its usual single combination coach-baggage car, got out of control descending the 7.5 per cent grade between Shale Tank and Moro Castle. It had been raining hard and the rails were slick. Apparently the sand pipes on the locomotive became clogged and useless. Gathering speed down the steep grade, Engineer George Lyman discovered that his brakes refused to work. He signaled for brakes, and Conductor "Patsy" Fitzpatrick rushed to the front platform of the passenger car to set the hand brake. He was thus engaged when the engine and coach, rushing down the hill at a great rate of speed, reached a sharp curve near milepost 31. By that time the momentum was too great for the engine to hold the track. It hurled off the rails and rolled over down the mountainside, tak-

ing a short cut to where the track looped back down below. The coach turned over, but stopped before it reached the bottom. Conductor Fitzpatrick had remained on the platform in a futile effort to halt the rapid speed of the train with the hand brake and was caught and crushed to death under the car.

Engineer Lyman remained in his cab trying to slow the runaway, then jumped just as the engine and coach overturned. The wreckage caught him, and both shoulders were dislocated and an elbow fractured. Fireman Roy Eno was luckier, leaping to safety just before she left the rails. Lyman had been badly injured in the washout at Bridge 2-A seven years earlier, and it was some while before he recovered from this wreck and was able to return to service.

Patrick J. Fitzpatrick whose home was at Mack had been a conductor on the Uintah for ten years. He was one of the best known and best liked railroad men on the western slope. He had been employed in train service out of Grand Junction for years before resigning to accept the position with the Uintah. There were three other men aboard his car that rainy afternoon: the company physician, Dr. Waite, lineman S. N. Shepherd (or Sheppard) and one paying passenger, Ed Janes. All three jumped and escaped with only minor injuries.[31]

Just the week before this fatal runaway, Miss Faye Wagner who worked as clerk in the Uintah Railway shops at Atchee had been injured on a push car. She was in Fruita receiving medical attention and was expected back at work before long. Business had slowed up a little, and only one freight every other day was being run. Also, some of the railroaders were away serving their country. Maurice High was in France and Roy McCoy was in training at Fort Benjamin Harrison. War bulletins were received twice daily at the shops at Atchee.[32]

And so went the life of the narrow gauge and the people who were a part of it. The Armistice a couple months later was a time of celebration for the railroaders, as it was for everyone throughout the world. But, life on the railroad went on. The only constant thing was change.

One change was in the mail business. Effective January 1, 1919, the Post Office Department did

Consolidation No. 12 (above) originally Florence & Cripple Creek No. 10 and then Cripple Creek & Colorado Springs No. 36, was purchased by the Uintah in 1917. Twenty years later she was sold again, going to the Eureka-Nevada Railway. Below, rarely photographed Shay No. 6 double-heads with older sister No. 4 pushing the snowplow uphill at Moro Castle Curve. Arriving new from Lima in 1920, the No. 6 would see little more than seven years on the line before being sold to the Feather River Lumber Company in California. *(Top: R. B. Jackson photo from Gerald M. Best Collection; bottom: James E. Boynton Collection)*

Mikado No. 40 (above) is a handsome sight as she leaves Carbonera for Atchee with two loads of coal followed by the usual empty water cars and flats. Of the nearly fifty three-foot gauge Mikes which served in Colorado, she was the only one with inside frames. Below, on the five per cent above Lake McAndrews the Mack rail motor car poses for D.&R.G. company photographer George Beam. The photo shows how narrow the car was — barely wider than the three feet between the rails it ran on. (*Above: Otto C. Perry; below: from D.&R.G.W. files, courtesy of Jackson C. Thode*)

not renew its contract with the line for hauling the mail between Watson and Vernal. Instead, they started bringing the mail into the Basin from Helper in government trucks. The situation was perplexing in December when the government first announced that a new contract had been awarded the railway, only to state within two weeks that the contract had not been signed and that trucks would start hauling the mail from Helper.[33] They picked a poor time to begin. Drifting snow and the rutted road over the West Tavaputs Plateau and Bad Land Cliffs didn't allow speedy movement of anything. By the end of March, Vernalites were wiring their protest to Washington against the "vile mail service."[34] Mr. Charles L. Davidson from the office of the fourth assistant postmaster general, investigating, found many tons of mail and parcel post piled alongside the Helper-Duchesne road at Levett, from where it could not be moved "over the hill." He promised a gathering of Grand Junction and Vernal businessmen, including Captain Cooley of the Uintah Railway, that after April 16 the government would operate its own trucks into the Basin via the easier Price-Myton road and, if this still proved impractical, would re-establish the old route via the Uintah Railway.[35] Anyway, by September the *Express* was calling "Mail service between Helper and Vernal the very best."[36]

The railway itself had some trouble with snow that winter. Ironically, the same week the government started hauling its own mail (or at least trying to), a storm which was declared to be the worst in two or three years delayed travel between Mack and Watson. The blizzard began Sunday afternoon, December 29th, and by Monday the snow was piled up as high as the coach, and travel was very slow. The train to Watson arrived at 8:00 in the evening, eight hours late. It took three locomotives to pull the coaches over the pass, and a number of times they had to go back a mile or two to get another start climbing the 7.5 per cent grade. At Watson the snow was nearly two feet deep and the thermometer registered 18 below zero![37]

Another change came with the summer. Since the early days of the Uintah, Consolidations had moved the trains between Mack and Atchee. Now

a Mikado arrived on the scene. With its two-wheel trailing truck to support its much larger firebox, and nearly sixty tons engine weight, the Mike was capable of moving a heavier train than any of the Consolidations, which weighed about 35 tons or less. Numbered 40 by the Uintah, the Baldwin-built Mike was acquired secondhand from the New York & Bermudez Company's Railroad in Venezuela. This company was also a subsidiary of General Asphalt Company. Had this not been the case, the shipment of a locomotive — even a narrow gauge — all the way from South America to western Colorado would have been an even more unlikely occurrence! One old Uintah railroader related that the Mikado, upon arriving new from the Baldwin works, was placed in service on the asphalt-hauling railroad in Venezuela and was making its very first trip when it broke through a trestle which was not strong enough to support its sixty tons. It then sat around unused for four or five years until it was sent back to the States for use on the Uintah line.

At any rate, the No. 40 was less than six years old when it came to the Uintah Railway and was a welcome addition to the motive power of the road. Not long after its arrival the Mike was hauled over Baxter Pass, as the Mikado No. 30 had been in 1911. It was used on the north end helping No. 30 move the traffic between Rainbow, Watson, Dragon and Wendella. Being lighter and less powerful than the 30, the newer Mike was rated at 500 tons from Watson to Dragon and 225 tons from Dragon to Wendella. The corresponding tonnage ratings for No. 30 were 650 and 325 tons, respectively.[38] After the first of the articulateds was purchased by the Uintah in 1926 there was no further need for two Mikados on the north end, so the 40 was brought back over the hill and thereafter used between Atchee and Mack. This rendered surplus two of the three Consolidations which had been in that service, so they were retired in 1927, leaving the No. 12 the only 2-8-0 remaining on the roster. And even No. 12 was seldom used after that. Mikado No. 40 had a tonnage rating of 175 tons from Carbonera to Atchee, compared to 150 tons for No. 12.[39]

Another locomotive was needed for Baxter Pass service, too. Not long after Mikado No. 40

At Lone Tree Curve (left) and nearby on the 7.5 per cent grade down the east side of the pass (below) the Uintah's claim agent and photographer Frank Kennedy has used the Mack car as a focal point for his views of the spectacular scenery visible from Baxter Pass. (*Left: J. L. Booth Collection; below: E. V. Earp Collection*)

arrived, an order was sent off to the Lima Locomotive Works for another Shay. Business was good, and the five Shays already on the roster were showing signs of age. The No. 6 was completed and shipped west from Lima, Ohio, in February, 1920. It arrived and added to the road's capacity for moving the gilsonite up the five per cent and down the other side to Atchee. It came just in time too, for 1920 would turn out to be the busiest year ever for the Uintah Railway.

Before 1919 was over, though, three more events occurred which deserve mention. One was the building of an extension from Rainbow to the Temple mine. This was a spur track only a few hundred feet in length to serve another gilsonite mine along the Rainbow Vein.[40] Although there was a lot of talk about building an extension, the only new trackage actually laid by the Uintah Railway after 1911 amounted to just two or three loading spurs near Rainbow.

Another occurrence was of a more serious nature. On September 10th the jury, after a week-long trial in the District Court at Grand Junction, assessed damages of $5,500.00 against the Uintah Railway in a suit brought by a former employee. The plaintiff, W. H. Holman of Atchee, had been working as a boilermaker in the shops there. His job involved using eight by sixteen-inch pieces of three-eighths-inch steel plate to repair defective places in the locomotive boilers. A steel chisel had to be used to cut and fit the plates, and Holman was holding the chisel while a co-worker struck it with a sledge hammer. While thus engaged, a piece of steel flew into Holman's left eye and damaged it so that he lost the sight. The injury to the eye affected his other eye and caused him to go totally blind. Holman charged that the company had been negligent in failing to provide proper safeguards for the protection of its employees. Apparently the jury agreed, although they were out seven hours arriving at their decision. Mr.

Holman's injury had occurred nearly three years earlier.[41]

Then, just weeks before the year end another fatal accident struck. George Rucker who had been employed as a conductor on the Uintah for just nine months met instant death about 5:00 Saturday evening, December 6, when he was caught and crushed between two engines at Carbonera. Rucker had been an engineman on the Rio Grande Western out of Grand Junction for over 17 years before taking the position with the Uintah.[42]

At the time of the accident there was a shortage of water, and the engines were not taking water at Mack before heading back to Atchee. Instead, a helper was sent down to Carbonera to meet the train. The crew would couple the helper on next to the train, and they would doublehead both engines as long as possible before the road engine on the head end would cut off and run for water, while the Shay kept dragging the train. By the time the road engine got water and backed down to meet the train, the helper would be nearly out of water, but the road engine could pull it in from there. On December 6th Engineer Roy McCoy was called at 2:00 p.m. to run Shay No. 3 down to Carbonera to help the daily train back to Atchee. One of the Consolidations, either No. 10 or 11, was the road engine. Vic Earp was at the throttle. The operation would have gone smoothly except that the front coupler on the No. 3 was not working properly. It had previously been reported defective. The Shay was coupled to the train with the Consolidation standing a short distance ahead of it, while Rucker worked to repair the coupler. Earp had set his engine air handle in lap position and had climbed down to help. With no one in the cab, and unnoticed by the men working with the Shay's coupler, the 2-8-0 started creeping backward. It made the coupling through the conductor's body.[43]

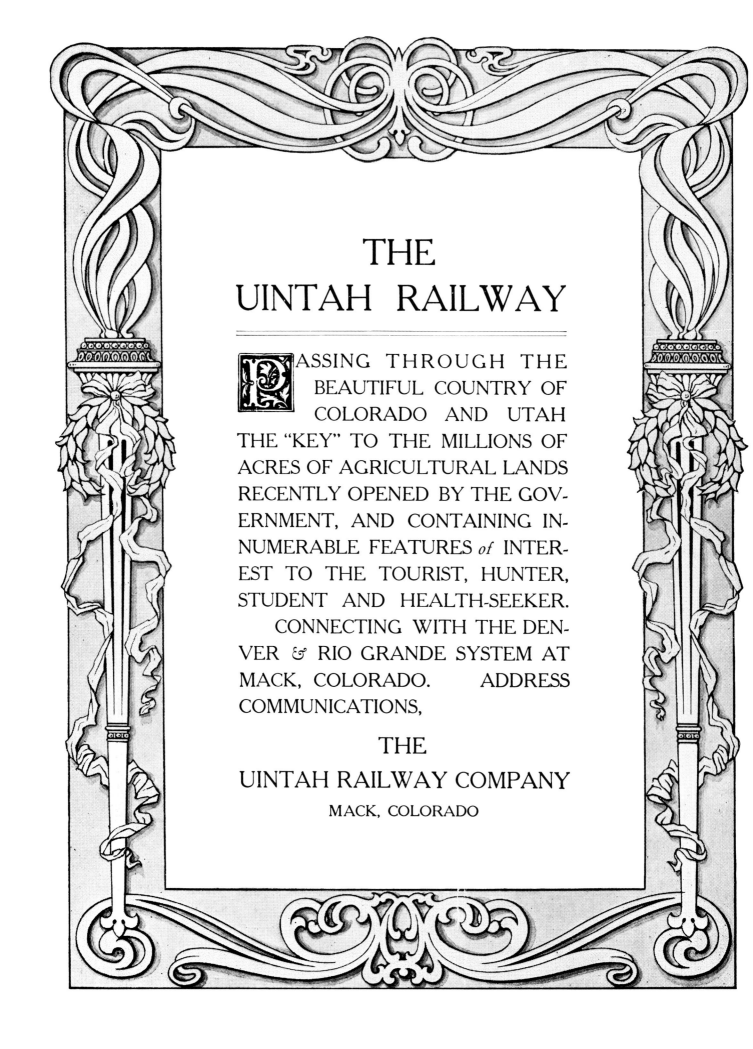

THE
UINTAH RAILWAY

PASSING THROUGH THE BEAUTIFUL COUNTRY OF COLORADO AND UTAH THE "KEY" TO THE MILLIONS OF ACRES OF AGRICULTURAL LANDS RECENTLY OPENED BY THE GOVERNMENT, AND CONTAINING INNUMERABLE FEATURES *of* INTEREST TO THE TOURIST, HUNTER, STUDENT AND HEALTH-SEEKER. CONNECTING WITH THE DENVER & RIO GRANDE SYSTEM AT MACK, COLORADO. ADDRESS COMMUNICATIONS,

THE

UINTAH RAILWAY COMPANY
MACK, COLORADO

Chapter Seven

Postwar Boom and Bust

As the new decade dawned all was going well with the gilsonite industry and the narrow-gauge railroad which served it. The arrival of spring saw the mining companies putting large forces of men to work. Both the Gilson Asphaltum Company and American Asphalt Association were finding the market for their product unusually good. Naturally they increased their production, and the railroad's traffic volume immediately reflected it. Even the passenger traffic over the Uintah was reported to be heavy, and express shipments unusually large.[1]

The traffic surge manifested itself by the time the year was over in railway operating revenues of $750,924. This was more than half again what they had ever been before. However, operating expenses climbed, too, almost keeping pace with the revenues, and also hitting an all-time high. The figure was $610,678. After subtracting these expenses and tax accruals of $35,659, the remaining net operating income came to $104,578. While this was a lower net than in two of the previous three years, it would never be this high again. After 1920 the annual net earnings would never amount to more than one half this figure.

While it was the busiest year in the Uintah's history, 1920 was not marked by any other particularly unusual events. One potential calamity was averted when lightning hit the Watson depot one evening in August during a heavy rain and electrical storm. The lightning burned out the telegraph and telephone wires in the office and set the cashier's desk on fire, burning up papers and charring the desk. The office would have burned to the ground if the clerk, Charles String, had not been occupying a room in the station. He put the blaze out with the fire extinguishers that were kept handy in the building.[2]

By the end of 1920 it was apparent that the next year would not be nearly as prosperous. Across the country businessmen were finding themselves in the throes of one of the worst recessions in many years. Traffic moving over the Uintah was suddenly as low as it had been high the year before. The operating revenues for 1921 dropped to $181,190, less than one-fourth what they had been for the previous year. The operating expenses dropped, too, but not nearly fast enough. They totaled $360,193 for the year. After deducting the taxes paid, the net railway operating income for 1921 had to be written in red ink — a tremendous loss of $208,720.

On a railroad so dependent upon a single commodity, more frequent losses might have been expected during periods when the demand for the commodity was low. This did not turn out to be the case, though. With the exception of its first and last years (1905, 1938 and 1939) the Uintah's net operating income fell below zero only one other time besides 1921 — in 1924 when the loss was a relatively insignificant $5,153. The large loss in 1921 left a lasting effect on the company's profit and loss ledger, since it left a significant indebtedness — something unknown to the Uintah before. The resulting interest charges to be paid each year thereafter frequently left the remaining net income quite small. This net income after in-

Another Kennedy photo at Lone Tree Curve (above) catches the Mack rail car hiding just behind the eastbound passenger train as both come down the hill. Below, two of the Shays have their consist well in hand as they push up the 7.5 per cent above Shale. (*Above: Margaret Romager Collection; below: Robert O. Perkins Collection*)

terest payments would be written in red in 1922, 1924 and 1927.[3] For the Uintah Railway the plush years were over.

The sudden drop in traffic and revenue affected the narrow gauge in a number of other ways, not the least of which was the company's plan to extend its rails on to Bonanza. In April, 1920, there had been a report that the line might make this extension.[4] This, of course, was nothing new, but with the war over many people had been optimistic. Anyway, the company apparently had good intentions this time. On the first of May they had sent a party of surveyors out to White River to start laying out the route.[5] Under the charge of a Mr. Morris, the crew had worked between Watson and Bonanza for over two months.[6] After that nothing more on the subject was heard for over six months. Then on January 20, 1921, the company filed an application with the Interstate Commerce Commission in Washington for the required certificate of public convenience and necessity to extend its line in Uintah County. According to the application, four connecting extensions would be built, covering a total of nearly 25 miles. Primary among these would be the Watson North Extension, 19.362 miles in length from Watson to the vicinity of the large gilsonite veins north of the White River. Connecting with this extension near its northern extremity would be three shorter branches serving various mines around Bonanza. These were designated as the Bonanza Extension, the Cowboy East Extension and the Cowboy West Extension. The Board of Directors of the railway, meeting at Philadelphia on the afternoon of January 18th, had approved the application.[7] It would appear management was ready to begin construction of the new line just as soon as the I.C.C. gave its okay. Then the sudden drop in the market for gilsonite no doubt caused them to reconsider. As things developed, the railway never laid any track north of Watson, although they did apply to the I.C.C. and the Utah Public Utilities Commission as late as July, 1922, for additional time in which to begin such construction.[8]

Other changes came with the recession of 1921. In April Captain M. W. Cooley, who had been with the railroad from its infancy, resigned his position as general manager. He said that he would in the future center all his attention on the development of the oil business in the fields of western Colorado and eastern Utah. Mr. Cooley and his associates were at the time preparing to start a well within the next few days on the Carbonera Dome, not far from the Uintah's tracks north of Mack. He was succeeded as general manager by James E. Hood, formerly with the Erie, Great Northern, and Chicago, Milwaukee & Puget Sound railways and recently returned from service in Siberia with the U. S. Army. The papers commented on Captain Cooley's decision to leave his "splendid position with the Uintah" to push development of his holdings. They observed that it was one of the greatest recommendations that the future of the oil industry in the area could have, "as those who might previously have been skeptical as to the likelihood of reaching oil may be assured that a man of Captain Cooley's capabilities would not quit a splendid position to enter the business without feeling confident that his future business is to be even more successful than his past."[9] Although not mentioned by the papers at the time, perhaps the sudden turn in the fortunes of his railroad also had some effect on his decision. Interestingly, little more than a year later Captain Cooley was again reported holding down the position of general manager, this time with the American Asphalt Association at their gilsonite mines.[10]

There was other news to mark the year 1921. Mostly it was news of the cuts in service. A few weeks after Major Hood took over as general manager, hearings were held in Vernal by Commissioner Warren Stoutnour of the Utah Public Utilities Commission on the company's application to reduce their automobile and wagon service between Watson and Vernal and Fort Duchesne. If the request was granted, the company would discontinue their daily schedule between these points and furnish service only at such times as business would warrant. There were no protests entered at the April 28th hearing, and the company showed an operating loss on the service. So by early May they were given permission to discontinue the scheduled runs, although apparently the passenger service was not actually halted until about the middle of June. After that passengers to and from the Uintah Basin had to come in by way of Price and Myton or Helper and Duchesne rather than over the Uintah Railway, unless they made arrangements privately for transportation from Watson to their destination.[11] Starting on June 24, 1921, the Uintah Railway Company advertisement in each week's Vernal *Express* offered:

PROMPT AND CAREFUL
FREIGHT SERVICE
Between
Mack, Colorado and Watson, Utah,
*Connecting With the Denver & Rio Grande
R. R. at Mack, Colorado*

Up until the previous week, the company had advertised:

PROMPT AND CAREFUL
FREIGHT *AND PASSENGER* SERVICE
Between
Mack, Colo., and Vernal, Utah,
Fort Duchesne,
and Uintah Reservation Points.

With the end of scheduled service on the toll road, the Uintah Railway office in Fort Duchesne, Utah, was no longer of much use. It was closed by company auditor W. D. Halpin on May 16th, nearly a decade after the Fort had last quartered Army troops. Mr. W. H. Allen, who had served as agent there for over 15 years, was transferred to Dragon as agent and operator for the company.[12]

By the early 1920s most of the residents of the Uintah Basin were becoming more concerned with automobiles and good highways than they were with the possibilities of a railroad ever building through their valley. Although paved roads were still a rarity outside the town limits, transportation lines were being started. In September, 1920, E. H. Abrams began operating a freight line between Price and Vernal and Duchesne and intermediate points. He commenced service with four trucks ranging from two and one half to five tons each, and ten additional trailers.[13] Of more significance, perhaps, was the inauguration of a line providing both passenger and freight service east from Vernal to Craig, Colorado, to connect with the Denver & Salt Lake R.R. With J. J. Stanton in charge, the Craig-Vernal Transportation Company started operations about a month after the Uintah Railway had discontinued its scheduled service to Vernal. Stanton expected that passenger

travel would be a big share of the business over the new line, since passengers could reach Vernal from Denver in 36 hours, 12 of which would be spent in Craig. This compared with 72 hours previously required between Denver and Vernal.[14] Within another 18 years, as things turned out, the gilsonite shipments would also be diverted over this highway to the D.&S.L. at Craig, spelling the doom of the Uintah narrow gauge.

Apparently the Uintah saw the handwriting on the wall and petitioned the P.U.C. in August for authority to reduce its existing passenger service between Mack and Watson. The company desired to establish a triweekly service, operating on Tuesdays, Thursdays and Saturdays, in place of their daily round trip over the line. The petition set forth that business was constantly declining and that with fall and winter coming on it promised to drop even further. They declared that in the six months ending June 30th they suffered a loss of $10,000 from the passenger operation.[15] So before the snow fell the little one-car passenger train was making only three trips a week to Watson. This schedule would continue until late in the 1920s, when daily except Sunday mixed train service would replace it.[16]

Even these cuts in service, though, weren't enough to pull the Uintah out of the red. The narrow gauge was just too dependent upon the gilsonite business for its livelihood, and there wasn't much of that in 1921. When the year was over and the figures were in, the road had hauled 9,359 tons of the hydrocarbon down to Mack. This was certainly quite a drop from the 56,670 tons moved the year before.[17]

There was hope in some quarters that oil could be profitably extracted from the oil shale which was so abundant in the region, but nothing commercially practical ever developed along this line. The Ute Oil Shale Company did erect a plant overlooking the White River 13 miles north of Watson, completing it in April of 1921. It had been under construction nearly three and one half years. This plant had a capacity to treat 400 tons of shale each 24 hours, and tests of the shale deposits showed the yield would be one barrel per ton. Another plant, that of the Western Shale Company located six miles east of Watson, was already in steady operation and producing from

The passenger train (above) made up of two former Pullmans and powered by Shay No. 4, is climbing the grade above Moro Castle. Below is the Cowboy Vein — one of the largest gilsonite veins and an objective of the Uintah's ill-fated plans to extend its line. The company chauffeur standing there illustrating the size of the vein is Dwight Dow. *(Both: F. A. Kennedy photos; above: from D. H. Gerbaz Collection; below: from Charles J. Neal Collection)*

There were few locations on any railroad which could equal Moro Castle. The combination of 65-degree curvature and 7.5 per cent gradient were seldom approached. Perhaps the two gandy dancers and the roadmaster (above) suspect that the curve is more suited to their push car than to the Shay and three-car train (below). *(Above: Bill Karr Collection; below: V. L. McCoy Collection)*

four to six barrels of oil a day. Although small, this plant was reported to be "operating very successfully."[18] It seems someone was exaggerating! Even today, decades later, oil shale still is not being economically processed for its oil.

Before the end of 1921 another fatal accident struck the Uintah. It was less than two years since the last one. James Callas, section foreman at Watson, was returning home from Dragon on his motor car Saturday evening, November 12th. The car turned over and Mr. Callas sustained two broken ribs. He was taken to the hospital at Fruita, a trip of over sixty miles, where upon examination the physician found that one of the ribs had punctured a lung. Mr. Callas died the following Wednesday.[19]

With the coming of the new year the gilsonite business began picking up again. A large number of men from Vernal left for the Rainbow mine, where the work force was being rapidly increased. The old employees were being put back on in the same order they had been laid off the year before.[20]

Although less significant in the long run, the bigger news of 1922 was the resurvey of the Uintah Railway with an eye toward tunneling Baxter Pass and standard gauging the line. Major Hood had big plans. Starting early in April the survey crew by mid-August had determined essentially the same thing that earlier surveys had. By drilling a tunnel through the ridge of the Book Cliffs and widening some curves, the railway could be made standard gauge and a maximum grade of three per cent maintained. The cost of this work would come to approximately $2,500,000, though, or roughly 25 per cent more than the book value of the entire line at the time! It is no wonder nothing ever came of the plans. The Moffat Tunnel bill had been passed by the Colorado legislature only weeks after the resurvey got under way, again bringing the specter of a competitive line building into northeastern Utah and the Uintah Railway's territory. It was rumored that this threatened invasion might have had something to do with the activity of the Uintah, although General Manager Hood stated that "a railroad line extended from the Moffat tunnel into the Uintah basin would be impractical . . ."[21] It seems the Major, too, was prone to occasional exaggeration,

considering his own *big plans.* Anyway, the three-foot gauge with its 7.5 per cent grades climbing over Baxter Pass remained. Despite the regulatory agencies' allowing more time that summer to start the job, the railway was never extended north from Watson to the mines at Bonanza.

After the 1921 dip, business on the railroad continued in a pretty normal fashion. Shipments of wool in May and June of 1922 added to the revenue from the gilsonite traffic.[22] Although it came only once a year, the wool business continued to be important and worthwhile for the line. Evidence of this was Major Hood's assurance the following February to John N. Davis, president of the Uintah County Woolgrowers' Association, that "the best possible care would be taken of the wool and the railway would give the very best of service in getting the wool to Mack." Major Hood had already made arrangements with the Denver & Rio Grande Western for cars to be at Mack ready for the wool so there would be no delay on its shipment east. Mr. Davis had said that practically all the Uintah County wool would be sent via Watson for shipment over the Uintah Railway.[23]

The year was rather uneventful with regard to trouble along the line. The summer rains late in August washed out some roads near White River, but apparently didn't damage the railroad grade south of Watson. That was taken care of by a minor fire which burned a trestle about four miles west of Mack the night of August 21, as a blaze spread from burning bushes nearby.[24] Compared to this, though, the next year was just the opposite!

The year 1923 was just four days old when tragedy paid its call, and before the year was out there would be more trouble.

On the afternoon of January 4th, descending the 7.5 per cent from the summit of the pass, a train of gilsonite got out of control and ran away. The speeding train left the rails when it encountered the sharp curve at Shale Tank, four miles above Atchee, the Shay locomotive rolling over onto its left side and the loads of gilsonite piling up behind it. Traveling Engineer George Lyman was killed instantly, being caught and pinned under the wreckage. His neck was broken and his body badly crushed. It was quite late in the

The morning after it's sometimes hard to tell there has been a drop of rain the day before. Only the rails and crossties hanging in mid-air and making shadows where previously there had been solid roadbed tell of the force of the water which had come roaring down the canyon. Above, August 14, 1924, sixteen men and a pair of horses take a break from repairing a washout on the Rainbow Branch. Below, Evacuation Creek has taken out a stretch of the grade under the main line about three miles from Watson. The section men with help from Shay No. 1 are busy propping up the rails with three stacks of ties. Soon the Shay will start delivering carloads of fill. (*Both: F. A. Kennedy photos; above: Bill Karr Collection; below: W. A. Banks Collection*)

evening before his body could be removed from the wreckage. The engineer in charge of the train, Richard Griffith, received serious burns and scalds and was taken to St. Mary's Hospital in Grand Junction for treatment. The fireman on the Shay, Roy Eno, and Conductor Lee Allison were more fortunate and both escaped uninjured.[25]

George Lyman was held in high esteem throughout the region, and many of his friends gathered at the Elks' Home in Grand Junction on Sunday afternoon, January 7th, for his funeral. A special train was run over the Uintah line to Mack, and the D.&R.G. ran a special from there to bring the funeral party numbering 75 or more on to Grand Junction.[26] His last accident was the third bad one for Lyman, who was about 37 years old when death came.

Engineer Richard Griffith was luckier. He recovered from the accident, although the burns on one foot never did heal completely. He had come to work for the Uintah in 1909 after 24 years service with the Colorado Midland. Quite a capable mechanic, he had served as superintendent of machinery at the Midland's shops in Colorado City, and then as both master mechanic and loco-motive engineer for the Uintah Railway. When he retired in 1928 at the age of seventy, one of his sons-in-law, Scott Shafer, was holding the position of master mechanic which Griffith had earlier filled. Griffith's son and three out of four sons-in-law, including Shafer, worked for the Uintah for a time during their railroading careers.[27]

The other accident in 1923, a derailment two and one half miles west of Mack, caused the death of General Manager James E. Hood and injured a number of other people. On Thursday morning December 13 the coach at the rear of the Watson-bound train jumped the track and, after being drawn along the ties for some 150 feet, overturned. A broken rail just east of Bridge 2-B was the cause of the accident. The engine passed over the defective rail in safety, but the rear trucks of the coach left the rails. The car was dragged entirely across the bridge, then toppled over down the embankment. It was fortunate, though, that guard rails kept the car on the trestle, or more passengers might have been killed.

Major Hood had been riding on the rear plat-form of the car and was thrown heavily when it overturned, sustaining painful injuries to his leg. Several others, including three employees of the road, were also badly hurt. Claim Agent F. A. Kennedy received a broken collar bone and other cuts and painful bruises. Superintendent L. C. Sprague had three or more ribs broken and cuts and bruises, and Brakeman Frank Wagaman was quite badly cut about the head. Two other men had ribs fractured; they were sheepman C. H. Howell of Vernal and a Mr. Moberly, agent for the Singer Sewing Machines. Mrs. Ward of Dragon suffered painful bruises about her hips, and F. A. Lowenhagen, a civil engineer from Fruita, Colorado, was badly bruised and cut. This was the first time, and it would be the only time in the railroad's history, that any passengers were seriously injured.

As soon as news of the wreck reached Mack, telephone calls were placed to Dr. Orr of Fruita and Drs. Hanson, Taylor and Reed of Grand Junction, all of whom responded. The work of returning the injured to the Uintah Railway Hotel at Mack was begun at once, and it was there they received medical attention. Hood and Kennedy were moved to St. Mary's Hospital in Grand Junction on Friday evening, Howell was in the Fruita hospital, and Messrs. Moberly and Lowenhagen were both being treated at their own homes. All were expected to recover quickly, although the physicians were unable to state just how long it would be before Major Hood was out of the hospital. He was suffering from diabetes, and his wound caused great concern to the physicians because of his general physical condition. On Saturday evening he took a turn for the worse, and the following day he died of complications caused by the diabetes. He was 56 years and 5 days old.

Major Hood was a civil engineer, starting his career with the Erie after graduation from Allegheny College. Later he became division superintendent for the Great Northern and then for the Chicago, Milwaukee & Puget Sound. He rose to the rank of Major during the war, serving the Army in an executive capacity in the management of the Russian railroads in Siberia. After special funeral services in Grand Junction, Mrs. Hood and Mr. Halpin of the railway accompanied the Major's remains to his birthplace, Cambridge Springs, Pennsylvania, for burial.[28]

The bottom side of a Shay and a jumble of five or six flat cars in a space not long enough for two (above) is what can be seen after the January, 1923, runaway in which George Lyman was killed. The Shay is believed to have been the nearly-new No. 6. (*Margaret Romager Collection*)

Action photos of pile drivers (below) were not common, but here "Judge" Kennedy has snapped a perfect one of Uintah Ry. No. 001 with its hammer falling. (*V. L. McCoy Collection*)

Over a year and a half later Charles H. Howell of Vernal, one of the injured passengers, filed suit against the railway in federal court for damages of $15,007. The case had first been brought in a state court, but was later ordered transferred to the federal court because the parties to the suit were of different states. Howell claimed that four ribs broken in the accident and other bodily hurts and injuries to his eyes had made it almost impossible for him to earn a living. He further charged that the wreck was due to negligence on the part of the railroad company and that the latter was therefore responsible for the injuries received by the passengers.[29] The outcome of the suit is uncertain at this late date, since available reports neglect this important detail. It is interesting to conjecture, however, in light of the times, how favorably the courts would have looked upon Mr. Howell's claims.

With Major Hood's passing, a new general manager was needed. After a suitable interval, Superintendent L. C. Sprague was chosen for the job.[30] A native of Illinois, Lucian Charles Sprague was born September 29, 1885, in Serena, a small town on the Chicago, Burlington & Quincy. For a young boy, the lure of the rails was too much to resist. At the age of 14 he hired out as a call-boy for the Burlington. After a spell as machinist helper and a few years firing a locomotive, he was promoted to the right-hand side of the cab. From the Burlington, Sprague went into engineering and to the Great Northern as their superintendent of air brakes for the system. Not satisfied in one place, he continued to build his knowledge of railroading. Railway equipment sales work, responsible positions in the mechanical departments of the Baltimore & Ohio and the Great Northern, and consulting work for the D.&R.G.W. broadened his horizons.[31] He came to the Uintah Railway in 1923 as superintendent, and was promoted to general manager the following February. Although far shorter and a bit narrower, the Uintah could equal any of its bigger brothers when it came to operating problems!

Just a few days prior to Lucian Sprague's appointment, word came from Washington that the Interstate Commerce Commission had reached its decision on the complaint of Utah Gilsonite Company v. Atchison, Topeka & Santa Fe Railway

Company et al. In reality, the Utah Gilsonite Company's major gripe was with the $10.35 rate charged them by one of the "and others," the Uintah Railway, for hauling their product from their loading point, American, Utah, to Mack, Colorado, but the complaint also requested that the I.C.C. establish joint rates on gilsonite from American to destinations east of Mack. This the Commission denied, finding that division of joint rates on a mileage basis, as ordinarily employed by connecting carriers, would be inequitable to the Uintah. It said that maintenance of joint rates would, in any case, mean merely the imposition of additional accounting on connecting lines with no gainful result. But the I.C.C. did find that the Uintah's local rate of $10.35 per net ton was unreasonable and ordered it lowered to $9.75, and also ordered reparation be paid the complainant for shipments made since May, 1920. This decision, though, did not stand for long.

The Utah Gilsonite Company was a newcomer in the field, having been organized in May, 1920. It began shipping that month from some claims it had procured, trucking the ore about four miles from its mine to the loading spur at American, less than a mile north of Rainbow. Although definitely in third place, the company quickly became significant in the business. Of the 30,265 tons of gilsonite shipped over the Uintah Railway in 1922, the Gilson Asphaltum Company loaded 18,979 tons, American Asphalt Association shipped 7,114 tons and Utah Gilsonite, 4,172 tons. The new firm went on to increase its proportion of the total somewhat in the following years.

Utah Gilsonite was quick to perceive that its railroad outlet was owned by the same combine as its major competitor and that excessive rates which the railroad might charge would thus be an unjust burden on its profitability. And the Uintah Railway's rates were, without a doubt, rather high. So, just as American Asphalt Association had done some fourteen years earlier, Utah Gilsonite Co. entered the aforementioned complaint before the I.C.C. on April 18, 1921.

The basic decision reached by the I.C.C. in the American Asphalt Association v. Uintah Railway Company case, decided in 1908, still held — that the rates charged by a railroad which had been built for a special purpose need not be compared

The entire Uintah Railway office staff (above) had their picture taken in front of the office on an autumn day in the 1920s. From left to right, standing, are Accountant W. R. Lockett, Claim Agent Frank A. Kennedy, Engineer and Purchasing Agent F. G. Morss, Chief Dispatcher J. L. Booth, Superintendent Walter L. Rader, Assistant Dispatcher H. M. Phillips, and General Manager L. C. Sprague. Seated are Eunice Newton, Hotel Superintendent Maud Levi, Freida Grieser, and Assistant Secretary & Treasurer Fred Baird. Just a short distance away in the Mack yard were the parallel tracks (below) where the gilsonite was transferred from the narrow-gauge to the adjacent standard-gauge cars. *(Top: J. L. Booth Collection; bottom: Margaret Romager Collection)*

with rates in effect elsewhere, but must be determined by the financial returns which they produced. A reasonable rate could thus be determined from an analysis of the Uintah's initial cost and its operating revenues and expenses. The I.C.C. and the opposing lawyers spent considerable time at this. Over two years elapsed before the examiner submitted his report to the Commission, and the Commission then took another seven months to reach its decision. Nor was this the end of the matter. Little more than two months later, on March 11, 1924, the Uintah Railway asked that the case be reopened. Thirteen additional months passed. Then, after further hearing the I.C.C. saw fit to reverse its previous decision and dismissed Utah Gilsonite's complaint. Just five days shy of four years had elapsed since the original complaint was filed, and once again the rate on gilsonite from American to Mack stood at $10.35 per net ton.[32]

The transcript of the case is rather interesting, though not included here. The published record occupies 46 pages in two volumes of the *Interstate Commerce Commission Reports.* Leaving most of the details to the lawyers, a few do deserve mention, however. Besides the request for joint rates, which was denied, and the complaint that the rate from American to Mack was unreasonable, which was upheld and then later dismissed upon rehearing, Utah Gilsonite made certain other allegations. As summed up in the *Reports,* these allegations were:

(1) the operation by the Uintah of an unprofitable wagon road between Watson and Fort Duchesne and Vernal, Utah, is detrimental to complainant by reason of its effect on the rail rates through increase of the Uintah's operating expenses; (2) the use of this wagon road by the Gilson Company to transport gilsonite from its mines at Bonanza or Little Bonanza, Utah, while complainant must haul its product by wagon or truck at its own expense 4 miles from its mine to the American station, is unduly prejudicial to complainant in favor of the Gilson Company; (3) track extensions were made from Rainbow to the Gilson Company's mine and the Rainbow rate applied without tariff authority, while the Uintah refuses to provide complainant adequate sidetrack facilities at American to properly handle its shipments; (4) complainant fails to receive a sufficient number or an equitable proportion of narrow-

gauge and standard-gauge empty cars, to its disadvantage and in preference of the Gilson Company; (5) the Uintah prefers the Gilson Company to complainant's disadvantage in extending financial credit, furnishing telephone service, transferring the shipments from narrow-gauge to standard-gauge cars at Mack, and in the use of its cars at Mack for temporary storage purposes; and (6) the tariff provision that cars containing sacks of gilsonite weighing in excess of 225 pounds shall be transferred at Mack at shipper's expense is unjust, unreasonable, and unjustly discriminatory.

It reflects favorably upon the Uintah Railway management that the I.C.C. found each of these allegations unjustified and the complainant not subjected to any undue prejudice because of them. For example, with regard to that last allegation, it was found that if the sacks of gilsonite were very much in excess of the 225 pound weight there would be serious objections from the transfer men at Mack. The sacks were loaded into the standard gauge cars in tiers, and only two men at a time could conveniently handle a sack. Any charge for handling overweight sacks went directly to the transfer men anyway, and not to the Uintah Railway. No particular difficulty had been found in keeping the sacks within the prescribed weight, and the complainant had never been called upon to pay any additional charges under the regulation. Since the rule was designed to facilitate the transfer at Mack, and was apparently applied alike to all shippers, there were no grounds to find it imposed any burden on the complainant.[33]

When, upon petition of the defendant Uintah Railway, the case was reopened in March, 1924, the railway's attorney Henry McAllister directed his evidence toward showing that the I.C.C. had erred in estimating the normal annual average railway operating revenues and expenses. He claimed the reduced rate from American to Mack, which would require a downward readjustment of gilsonite rates from other points on the line, was arrived at through overestimating the revenues and underestimating expenses. These lower rates, McAllister argued, would result in the confiscation of the property.

The Uintah took no exception to the I.C.C. estimate of the average annual gilsonite movement. The estimate was 34,000 tons, and the

The job of transferring the sacks of gilsonite, weighing up to 225 pounds each, from the Uintah Railway flats to the standard-gauge boxcars at Mack required an able-bodied crew (above). Their pay, figured on a piecework basis, was fairly good for the time, and often they moved on to less strenuous work after a few months of moving gilsonite. The unique caboose (below) on the rear end of a westbound freight, was rebuilt from the remains of unsuccessful and short-lived rail motor car No. 31. *(Both: F. A. Kennedy photos from Margaret Romager Collection)*

movement during 1923 turned out to be just higher — 34,461 tons. At the rates then in effect this estimated tonnage would produce an annual revenue from gilsonite traffic of $337,140. If the former rate of $10.35 from American still applied, this estimated revenue would be increased to $338,940. What McAllister did object to was the I.C.C.'s estimated annual revenue from all other sources. They had judged that $50,000 per year would be fairly representative of revenue from all freight other than gilsonite, and $40,000 would approximate operating revenue from all other sources. These figures were reasonably close to the average for the period from 1909 through 1921. However, revenue from these sources had been shrinking, and for the three years 1921, 1922 and 1923, the annual averages were $35,593 for freight other than gilsonite, and $31,732 for revenues other than freight. It was the Uintah's contention that this decline was not temporary but was due to reasonably permanent conditions. For example, much of the miscellaneous traffic formerly moved to points tributary to the Uintah's wagon road was now being sent by parcel post, and the Post Office Department had in 1918 shifted this chunk of business from the railway to its own mail route from Price into the Basin. Other traffic had been lost to trucks. Passenger revenue had declined chiefly due to the increase of travel by automobile and the curtailment of the Uintah's wagon-line service. As a result of these arguments, the I.C.C. saw fit to reduce its former estimate of $90,000 annual revenue from sources other than gilsonite to $67,000. From this latter figure it deducted $11,000 (rather than the previous $22,000) as representative of the revenue that would not accrue but for the operation of the stage lines.

In a like manner, the litigants presented evidence and the Commission re-evaluated the annual operating expenses. Wages had been rising, worn rail and ties needed replacement, 75 per cent of the freight cars were stated to be in bad condition, and so on. After all the figuring the new estimate of operating expenses for a normal year totaled up to $289,500. The previous total, for comparison, had been $280,000. The increase was in the allowances for maintenance of way and structures and maintenance of equipment, al-though the I.C.C. saw fit to decrease by $4,500 the amount allowed for transportation expenses.

Based on these recalculated revenue and expense figures, application of the $9.75 rate from American and corresponding downward adjustment of the other gilsonite rates would result in a railway operating income of less than $63,000 a year. If a return to the former $10.35 rate were allowed, the operating income would rise to $75,715. The former would be equivalent to a return of 5.75 per cent on $1,095,652, while the latter income would yield a return of 5.75 per cent on $1,316,783. The record did not include sufficient data to accurately determine the valuation of the property, but the Commission found no evidence that it would be lower than the latter figure, so the original $10.35 rate from American to Mack was judged to be the lawful rate.[34] Ratemaking gets rather complicated!

One unusual item of expense which affected the outcome of the rate case was a landslide. Sometime during March of 1923, at a point about a mile below Baxter Pass and just above Shale Tank, a tremendous mass of earth and rock broke away from the mountainside above the tracks and slowly started moving downward. The slide was about 1000 feet in length and began some 400 feet above the tracks. It applied a pressure beneath and to the side of the track, causing it to rise above its normal level and at the same time to be pushed out of alignment horizontally. Dirt and rocks also slid down onto the track upon breaking free. The company found it necessary to keep a force of men and a steam shovel at work constantly except during the winter, and the track past the slide area had to be relaid almost daily. The steam ditcher was, in fact, purchased new from the American Hoist & Derrick Co. of St. Paul, Minn., in 1923 or early 1924 primarily because of the near impossibility of fighting the "big slide" economically with teams and scrapers.[35] The actual operating expense in combating the slide totaled up to $13,125 by the end of 1923 and was $6,526 for the first six months of 1924. Nearly all of this cost was for labor. What was worse, though, was that no one could say for sure how long the slide might continue. Engineers called as witnesses could do little more than speculate. One engineer thought it might continue indefinitely, another

A derailment near milepost 6 in 1924 reduced the stock car at the left practically to kindling wood. Too much speed on the desert run is said to have been the cause. *(Margaret Romager Collection)*

The bands have broken on one of the two water tanks at Atchee (above), scattering staves toward all points of the compass. The commodious house at the left was for many years the residence of John McAndrews and his family in Vernal, and also served as headquarters for C. O. Baxter and other officials of the Uintah Railway when they visited Vernal. Today most of the poplars are gone but the house still is in use — as the Vernal Funeral Home. *(Above: Margaret Romager Collection; left: J. L. Booth Collection)*

said that it would continue for several years, and another thought that it would probably become stabilized in 1925. The passage of time certainly proved this last man wrong.

Prior to 1923 the most serious slide to trouble the Uintah was one at Moro Castle two or three years earlier, which had cost approximately $15,000 to fight.[36] At that point seepage of water had made the roadbed unstable and was causing it to slide out from under the track at the sharp horseshoe curve.

Except for the big slide, 1924 and 1925 were rather quiet years for the Gilsonite Route. The year 1924 opened on a sad note with the death of Chief Dispatcher R. D. Clark at Mack. Mr. Clark had put in a full day of work on January 2nd before succumbing to a sudden heart attack that night.[37] Then in March, Uintah people shared the nation's shock and sorrow at the news of the tragic explosions at the Castle Gate No. 2 mine of the Utah Fuel Company which took the lives of over 170 miners.[38] There was an accompanying feeling of thankfulness that the gilsonite mines had never witnessed a disaster of this magnitude. But then, they weren't nearly as large-scale operations, and extraordinary care was taken to avoid any possible sparks or flames which might ignite the gilsonite dust.

On August 19, 1924, tragedy paid another call on the Uintah. The scene was the big slide above Shale Tank, and the victim was Roy Wagaman, 18-year-old son of Mr. and Mrs. Frank Wagaman of Mack. The young man was employed as fireman on the new American ditcher, which was hard at work on the slide. The ditcher had just been moved and blocked up in a new position on freshly-moved ground. As the big machine, steaming away, raised a scoopful of earth, the blocking sank into the soft earth and the ditcher turned over on its side. It all happened so quickly that young Wagaman had no chance to save himself, and he was crushed under the rig. Engineer Roy McCoy and another employee on the shovel escaped without injury. There was practically no damage to the equipment.

The boy's father had been employed as a trainman on the line for a number of years and was braking on the southbound passenger train, which

was but a mile away when the accident occurred. He arrived at the slide a few minutes later. The other employees of the work gang had rapidly pried up the ditcher and extricated his son's body, and it was taken into Mack on the train, and later to a Grand Junction funeral home before burial at Fruita, Colorado. The young man, who was not quite 19 at the time of his death, had been honor man in his graduating class at Fruita High School the year before and had been employed by the railway company on and off for several years.[39]

With the autumn came a happier occurrence. On November 1st, just three days before the G.O.P. landslide in the national elections swept Cal Coolidge back in for four more years as president, Miss Mary McAndrews and General Manager Lucian C. Sprague were united in marriage. The bride was a daughter of Uintah Railway Superintendent John McAndrews and had worked for the company in the office at Mack. After their wedding at Oakland, California, the couple spent their honeymoon in the east before returning to make their home at Mack.[40]

Early in 1925 there was more news from the I.C.C. offices in the nation's capital. A tentative valuation, as of June 30, 1919, of the property of the Uintah Railway Company was completed and made public on January 19, 1925. For rate-making purposes, the examiner estimated the property to be worth $1,012,000. Quite naturally, the railway company filed a protest against this tentative valuation. Their own figure for the book value of the railway was $2,091,670 — more than double the I.C.C. valuation![41] Interestingly, it was just four days after the I.C.C. disclosed the tentative valuation when the Uintah Railway filed its appeal to the first decision in the *Utah Gilsonite Company* v. *A.T.&S.F. Ry. Co. et al* case. Perhaps this was just coincidence, perhaps not. Anyway, the tentative valuation didn't have any effect on the outcome of that case, and it would be April, 1928, before the Commission reached its final decision on the valuation case. At that date the value of the property owned and used for common-carrier purposes, as of 1919, was found to be $1,035,200.

With the spring of 1925 another flurry of railroad building talk again raised false hopes in the Uintah Basin. The headlines on the front page of the Vernal *Express* read "UINTAH BASIN IS NOW

The size and extent of the landslide at milepost 33 is shown vividly in the photograph above. Below is the American steam ditcher which was purchased to help fight the slide. It is picking up a large rock with a chain attached to the dipper tooth. This photo is one of a series taken by American Hoist & Derrick Co. and published in the November, 1924, issue of their bimonthly *American Ditcher Scoopings* for distribution to railroad officials and ditcher operators everywhere. *(Top: E. V. Earp Collection; bottom: courtesy of William F. Karr)*

ASSURED RAILROAD TRANSPORTATION." This time it was the D.&R.G.W. spreading the talk, and their plans were to build a line from Soldier Summit to Vernal. President J. S. Pyeatt of the Rio Grande, together with his general counselor Henry McAllister and chief engineer O. E. Ridgway, and L. C. Sprague of the Uintah Railway, visited Vernal in April. They came on special invitation of Mr. Sprague that they might get firsthand knowledge of the resources of the Basin and the probable tonnage which could be developed for rail transportation. Mr. Pyeatt told a group of Vernal businessmen that the Rio Grande's Board of Directors was unanimous in the proposed expenditure of $7,000,000 to construct the line to Vernal "providing the Interstate Commerce Commission granted the franchise and the construction of the Dotsero cutoff necessary for the shortening of the distance between Denver and Salt Lake."[42] Obviously the Rio Grande management was much more interested in the completion of the Moffat Tunnel, already well under way, and I.C.C. permission to build the Dotsero Cutoff than it was with any branch line into the Basin. It didn't want to take any chances, however, that former Governor Bamberger's proposed Salt Lake & Denver might be built into and through the Basin to connect with the Moffat Road at Craig. It would appear the talk about building to Vernal was purely a diversionary tactic.

Less than two weeks later another party of railroad officials toured the area — this time the Uintah's own officers from Philadelphia. President Arthur W. Sewall, together with Charles W. Bayless, A. L. Robinson, Charles H. Schlacks, Frank Seamans, E. L. Riter and several other officials of the road spent several days in Colorado and eastern Utah inspecting the gilsonite mines and oil shale properties around Watson. Although officers and directors of the railway and the Gilson Asphaltum Company, most of these men seldom ventured more than a few miles west of Philadelphia. The affairs of the parent company, General Asphalt, occupied most of their time. They were ac-

Here's a close-up of the ditcher, newly arrived at Mack from the builder. The siderods on the trucks are proof that it was self-propelled, and the gears, cables and vertical boiler behind the railroaders actuated the important parts — the boom and scoop. (*William F. Karr Collection*)

Mack, Colorado, was a welcome oasis where travelers could stop and rest before continuing their journey. Not all the travelers arrived in Mack by train. Above, in front of the Uintah Railway office is an Austrian who was *walking* around the world. The fellow next to him, in the derby, is Joe Perry. In another of "Judge" Kennedy's photographs, at the bottom of the page, three young men with a newer form of transportation pause briefly next to the wye, on their long trip from Death Valley, California, to Boston, Massachusetts. The center photo taken in the late 1920s at Atchee shows, from left to right, Car Foreman E. C. "Doc" Dunlap, Gilbert Miller, Master Mechanic Scott Shafer and Jim Findley. Mr. Findley was a Civil War veteran without a pension — the official Army records showed him legally dead! *(Top: J. V. Kelly Collection; center: Margaret Romager Collection; bottom: J. L. Booth Collection)*

companied on their tour by General Manager L. C. Sprague, Superintendent John McAndrews and Roadmaster E. S. Gurr, and Homer D. Ford, superintendent of the gilsonite mines at Rainbow.[43]

There was another visit of top D.&R.G.W. officials to Vernal early in June, and rumors of new railroad construction continued to circulate.[44] But the days of major railroad-building projects in the United States were pretty much past by the mid-1920s. Besides, all this activity didn't mean too much to the Uintah Railway, anyway, except an occasional special train to accommodate the big shots.

Of more significance was the establishment in Craig that October of another truck line to haul freight to and from Basin points. Four of the five large trucks which initiated the service were assigned to haul gilsonite from Dragon to Craig, while the fifth would make regular runs between Craig and Vernal. The Denver & Salt Lake was naturally co-operating with the truck line operators and planned to build a warehouse for the truck line adjacent to its freight house in Craig.[45] Thus came the first noticeable diversion of the Uintah's life-blood traffic away from the narrow gauge, and the start of a trend which would become inexorable during the coming decade.

Besides the persistent slide above Shale Tank, the only out-of-the-ordinary thing to hinder the line's operations during 1925 was an abnormally heavy rainstorm in mid-July. The floodwaters roaring down the washes took out five bridges along the line and damaged the roadbed in a number of places. Passengers and some freight were moved over the line in a gasoline-powered railcar for a few days while repair work was in progress.[46]

The big slide was responsible for more trouble the next year when another young railroader met his death fighting it. The accident occurred just at quitting time Friday afternoon, August 6th. George C. Winder, a 19-year-old from Vernal, planned to work just one more day for the Uintah before collecting his pay and returning home to get ready for college. He no doubt had other thoughts on his mind, and as he went to place his tools aboard the American steam ditcher he walked directly under the shovel which was suspended over the track. The engineer and fireman were at the time adjusting the machinery and oiling it to get ready for the next day's work, and in doing so accidently released the lever which lowers the shovel. As it fell the heavy scoop struck with a slanting blow and pinned the young man between the rails inflicting mortal wounds in the region of his abdomen. He was given immediate first aid and rushed to Mack, where he was placed in an ambulance and taken to the hospital at Fruita. Despite the most skillful medical attention he died within a few hours.[47]

Railroading could be a dangerous business at times. The slide had claimed two young lives in as many years. Happily, though, there would be no more. George Winder's was the last fatal accident to mar the history of the Gilsonite Route.

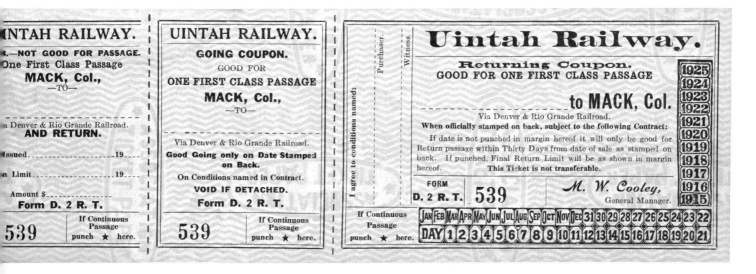

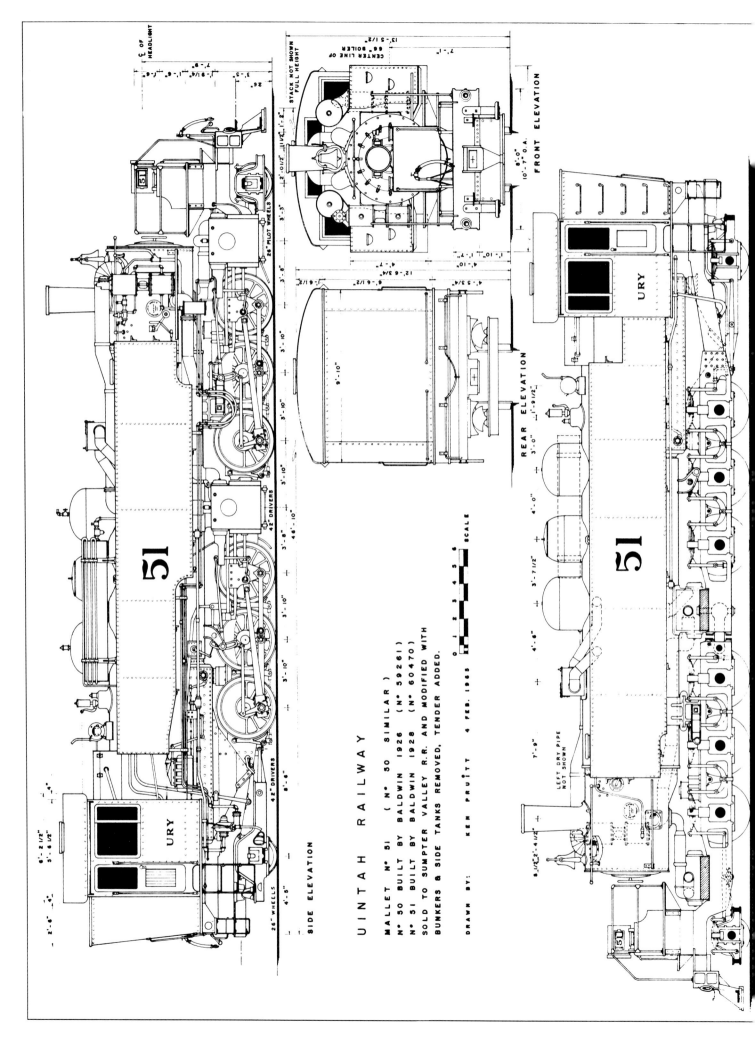

UINTAH RAILWAY

SIDE ELEVATION

MALLET N° 51   (N° 50 SIMILAR)

N° 50 BUILT BY BALDWIN 1926 (N° 59261)
N° 51 BUILT BY BALDWIN 1928 (N° 60470)
SOLD TO SUMPTER VALLEY R.R. AND MODIFIED WITH
BUNKERS & SIDE TANKS REMOVED, TENDER ADDED.

DRAWN BY: KEN PRUITT   4 FEB. 1965

SCALE

FRONT ELEVATION

REAR ELEVATION

Chapter Eight

The Articulateds Arrive

A new era dawned in 1926 for the Uintah Railway. The new articulated which arrived in July that year from Baldwin's Eddystone plant was more than just another new locomotive for the road — it represented a major advance in narrow-gauge motive power and, more important, a great increase in hauling capacity over any locomotive previously used on the line. This, of course, was the reason for its coming.

Financially the early 1920s had not proven quite so lucrative for the Gilsonite Route as the plush years of the previous decade. Following right on the heels of the massive losses in 1921, the net income again came out in the red (although by much smaller amounts, happily) for the years 1922 and 1924. Only the receipt of a federal payment covering losses of the railroad while under U. S. Railroad Administration operation kept the 1923 net from going below zero.[1] Even the net railway operating income, before interest payments, was written in red ink for 1924, as Lucian Sprague completed his first full year with the company. Higher operating costs were largely to blame. Both wages and maintenance costs had been climbing since the Great War, and among the higher expenses were those for keeping the all important motive power in good operating condition. The Shays and other engines seemed to require more time in the shops at Atchee as they grew older. Confronted with this situation, Mr. Sprague made up his mind that new power was in order. But, for a road like the Uintah, not just *any* new motive power would do. Something

special was called for. So one afternoon Mr. Sprague disappeared into Master Mechanic H. S. "Scott" Shafer's office behind the enginehouse at Atchee, and the two of them came up with the rough plans and specifications for an articulated. Baldwin Locomotive Works, the firm which had produced all of the Uintah's previous rod engines, was the natural choice to complete the plans and build the new design. Only after a special representative from Baldwin made a trip to Mack, and traveled over the entire Uintah line to ascertain that such an engine could be operated successfully on the steep grades and sharp curves, did Baldwin go ahead and tackle the job.

In keeping with their tradition of quality workmanship, the Baldwin people built a fine engine. When it arrived at Mack aboard a large artillery flat car belonging to the Erie R.R., the new locomotive was reported to be the largest ever built for use on three-foot track.[2] Numbered 50 on the Uintah's roster, it was a high pressure articulated with a 2-6-6-2T wheel arrangement. Many of the mechanical details of the design were unique at the time and are worth noting. Justifiably proud, the builder's *Baldwin Locomotives* magazine featured an article titled "Narrow Gauge Articulated Locomotive for the Uintah Railway" not long after the No. 50 was placed in service, and included the following description:

> This locomotive develops a tractive force of 42,100 pounds; and with 194,500 pounds on driving wheels, the ratio of adhesion is 4.62. The average load per driving axle is approxi-

The articulateds were impressive, coming or going. Even the cab was that of a modern engine. The photo below shows the way articulated No. 50 looked rounding the curve at Moro Castle. *(Top two photos: Baldwin Locomotive Works, from H. L. Broadbelt Collection; below: L. C. Sprague, courtesy of Paul D. Howard)*

Many of the changes made to the No. 50 during her thirteen-year active life on the Uintah are apparent in these photos. The back views at the left and right were taken eleven or twelve years apart. During those years the backup light atop the cab roof disappeared. It was subject to damage while coaling the engine and was of practically no use. The seven wyes along the railway eliminated the need for nearly all backing movements, and the trains seldom ran after dark. The rear footboards were removed and replaced with steps and side grab irons at each corner. The coal bunker was extended outward and upward, and five pipes placed through it to provide ventilation into the cab. The air hose position was moved immediately when the Mallet arrived on the Uintah. The most notable front-end changes were the big sandbox under the headlight which added weight as well as sand to prevent slipping, and the steel boxes full of scrap behind the air pumps which were for added weight. The enginemen, below, are Seth S. Starbuck, left, and V. L. "Roy" McCoy. (*Top: J. L. Booth Collection; center: Lawrie Brown Collection; below: Roy F. Blackburn photo from W. O. Gibson*)

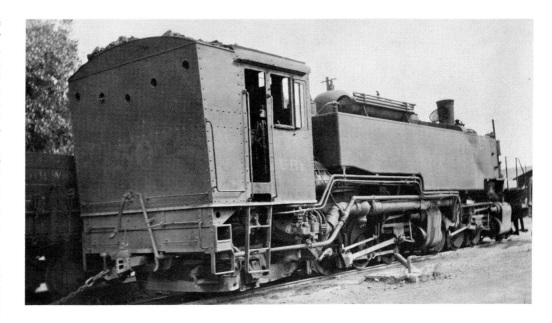

B. H. Cox (right) was a D.&R.G.W. brakeman when he posed for this portrait at Mack in 1938, but he had formerly been a Uintah railroader. He is credited with the idea of raising the brakeline so that the air hoses mated above the couplers, as seen at the left. This prevented moisture in the line from freezing during the winter months. *(Both: Roy F. Blackburn photos; right: from V. L. McCoy Collection)*

At the left is Al Green, the I.C.C. boiler inspector, standing in front of Mikado No. 40 at Atchee with Master Mechanic Scott Shafer. Below, articulated No. 50 pauses for a drink of water at Columbine. *(Both: Margaret Romager Collection)*

mately 32,400 pounds; and 82 per cent of the total weight, including the supply of fuel and water, is carried on the drivers.

In view of the excessive curvature on the line, the design of the running gear of this locomotive was given most careful consideration. The arrangement of the frames is in all respects similar to that used on Baldwin Mallet compound locomotives. The radius bar connecting the front and rear frames is attached to the former by a horizontal pin, and at its rear end has a ball jointed connection with a vertical pin which is seated in the back cylinder saddle. This construction provides ample flexibility in both a horizontal and vertical direction.

The leading truck is of the Economy constant resistance type, with cast steel frame and outside journals. The load carried by the forward equalizer is transferred to the truck frame through a single rocker placed on the center line. This truck is designed to swing 6¾ inches on each side, and is equalized with the driving wheels of the front unit.

The back truck is of the Delta type and is equalized with the rear group of drivers. The locomotive frames are supported on the truck frame through two constant resistance rockers, whose centers are 9 feet 6 inches apart transversely. There is practically no overhang at the rear end, so that, while ample flexibility is provided, the frames are very stably supported. The driving wheels of the middle pair in each group have plain tires.

The boiler is supported on the front frames by a single sliding bearing placed between the second and third pairs of driving wheels, and designed to permit a rocking movement in a vertical plane. There is a rigid support at the cylinder saddle of the rear engine, and the firebox is supported on sliding shoes at the front and back.

The boiler itself requires no special comment. It is of the straight-top type, with a sloping back head and roof sheet. The firebox extends over the rear driving wheels and contains a Gaines bridge wall. The fuel used is a good grade of bituminous coal, and the grates rock in four sections, and have drop-plates at the back.

The dome is centrally located on the barrel, and an internal dry pipe leads forward from the throttle to the smokebox. The superheater is a type "A," with 24 elements. Live steam is conveyed from the header to the rear cylinders through two external pipes which pass out through the top of the smokebox, and are heavily lagged. Just above the steam chest these pipes branch, and the branches unite in a single flexible pipe placed on the center line, which conveys live steam to the cylinders of the front unit. The exhaust from the rear cylinders is conveyed forward to the smokebox through external, rigid pipes; while the exhaust from the front cylinders passes through a flexible pipe, which is placed on the center line. The nozzle in the smokebox has a central circular tip through which the front exhaust is discharged, and two semi-annular tips for the exhaust from the rear engine.

The steam distribution to all the cylinders is controlled by 8-inch piston valves, which are set with a travel of 5 inches and a lead of 1/8-inch. The steam lap is 13/16-inch, and the exhaust lap zero.

The valve gears are of the Walschaerts type, and are controlled by a power reverse mechanism. The front and back reverse shafts are connected by a jointed reach rod, which is placed on the center line of the locomotive.

The boiler is fed by one non-lifting and one exhaust steam injector, the latter being placed on the right-hand side and receiving its steam supply from the exhaust of the rear cylinders. The fuel supply is carried in a box placed back of the cab, and the water in two rectangular side tanks, which are placed as low as possible. The tanks are connected by a transverse equalizing pipe, placed at approximately mid-length. The rear end of the locomotive is so constructed that a separate tender can subsequently be used, should this prove desirable.

Combined automatic and straight air brakes are applied to all the driving wheels, and the Le Chatelier brake is applied to the cylinders of the rear engine. Air is supplied by two 9½-inch pumps which are mounted on the forward deck plate; and there are two air-drums, placed right and left on top of the water tanks.

Sand is delivered in front of the leading drivers from a rectangular sandbox placed on the forward deck plate; while a box placed over the boiler supplies sand to the front and rear drivers of the back engine.

Each unit is equipped with a mechanical force feed lubricator, having four feeds which lead to the cylinders and steam chests. The air pump cylinders are lubricated by a single-feed bull's eye lubricator.

Owing to the swing of the front cylinders when traversing sharp curves, it was found impracticable to apply a manually operated cylinder cock rigging; and the cylinder cocks, therefore, are operated by air.

This locomotive has a height over all of 14 feet 2½ inches, and an extreme width of 10 feet 1 inch; while the length over the outside

No. 51 (above) fresh from the erecting floor in 1928, poses on the special curved track that was laid at Baldwin's Eddystone plant. They wanted to show the sharp curve the articulated could handle. Below, climbing Baxter Pass less than six months later, she's doing the job she was designed to do. *(Above: H. L. Broadbelt Collection; below: E. V. Earp Collection)*

faces of the front and rear bumpers is 45 feet 8 inches. These are very liberal dimensions for a locomotive of only three feet gauge, but in service the locomotive has proved more stable on the track than any of the smaller locomotives in use on the road.[3]

Despite the considerable engineering know-how which obviously went into the design of the No. 50, there were a few bugs, as there often are with any new product. The first of them came to light on the initial trial run from Atchee up Baxter Pass. Sam High, who was firing, recalls the chagrined expression which passed over Mr. Sprague's face as the lead truck derailed when it encountered the 66 degree curvature at Moro Castle. This particular problem was remedied in short order by the Atchee shops, but before many months had passed another rather serious design oversight became apparent to the engine crews. It seems that as soon as the articulated started downhill from the crest of Baxter Pass the water in its boiler would run towards the front end, and on the 7.5 per cent grade this effect was so great that it usually left the water glass in the cab entirely empty! Of more concern was the likelihood that the crown sheet would be left high and dry — a sure invitation to a boiler explosion. After bringing the No. 50 down off the Pass one afternoon, Engineer Sam High exclaimed, "I'm quitting, before I get myself killed," and immediately turned in his resignation and left the Uintah for a safer job elsewhere. Sam had not suffered a serious accident in over 14 years of Uintah Railway service and did not want to spoil his record now! General Manager Sprague was away on business at the time, and Sam High had left before he returned. Sprague was sorry to lose one of his best employees but at the same time was forced to think about his new engine and the safety of his men. He quickly called the I.C.C. boiler inspector, Al Green, in Grand Junction and requested he come up to Atchee and investigate the situation. Inspector Green was even quicker, as soon as he confirmed the potential danger, in slapping an embargo on the engine. The Uintah could not even fire it up again until the defect was cured! So Master Mechanic Scott Shafer and his men got busy on the job. On an elevation drawing of the boiler Shafer plotted the highest water level

possible when descending the 7.5 per cent grade. This line from the base of the steam dome, located midway along the boiler shell, intersected the backhead very near the lower water glass connection and not far above the top surface of the crown sheet. A major redesign was called for, it seemed, but the two-part solution decided upon was relatively simple. A second steam dome was installed back closer to the firebox, and the crown sheet itself was lowered somewhat. This did the trick. The two steam domes, placed close in front and back of the single sand dome, show clearly in most later photographs of the articulateds and were especially obvious after the Sumpter Valley Railway removed the side tanks from the engine and relocated the air reservoirs.

Other modifications to the Mallet, as it came to be called, were of a more minor nature. Immediately upon arrival from the builder the air hoses at either end were raised to the Uintah's unique above-the-coupler position. Apparently the original specifications to Baldwin had neglected this detail. Later changes included installation of a transverse filler pipe above the boiler so that both side tanks could be filled more conveniently from a waterspout in the normal position over the centerline of the engine. There was also a modification of the trailing-truck rigging to eliminate a tendency to derail when backing, and removal of the two single-lung air pumps from the front deck plate to positions on each side of the smokebox. The latter alteration resulted in better weight distribution and left room for placement of a larger sandbox on the front deck. The capacity of the coal bunker was found to be less than desired, so it was increased by moving the inward-sloping sides at the top outward until they were flush with the sides of the cab. This allowed room for an additional half ton of fuel. Five cylindrical air ducts were also built through the coal bunker to provide better ventilation for the men working in the cab; this was especially welcome when the locomotive was backing. Finally, later in the 1930s, rectangular steel boxes filled with assorted chunks of scrap iron were added on each side of No. 50's smokebox just ahead of the side tanks. They supplied additional weight on the drivers of the front engine, which had shown more tendency towards slipping than the rear unit.

No. 51 (above) is easing across bridge 28-A into Atchee, where she will stop her train to take on water and let the brake shoes cool. *(Linwood W. Moody Collection, from Everett L. DeGolyer, Jr.)*

Sitting under the water spout at Dragon (center) Mallet No. 51 gets ready for the climb of 2,649 feet — more than a half mile — in the next 19.1 track miles. *(E. Victor Earp Collection)*

No. 51 (bottom) fired up for the first time after unloading at Mack. The man in the right-hand seat is E. V. Earp — a cousin, a few times removed, of the famous Wyatt Earp.

(E. Victor Earp Collection)

	1929 ENGINE RATING		1931 ENGINE RATING	

1929 ENGINE RATING

WESTBOUND

From Mack, Colo., to Carbonera, Colo.:

Class Eng. 12	180 tons
Class Eng. 20 and 21...........	125 tons
Class Eng. 40	225 tons
Class Eng. 50	525 tons
Class Eng. 51	525 tons

From Carbonera, Colo., to Atchee, Colo.:

Class Eng. 12	150 tons
Class Eng. 20 and 21...........	90 tons
Class Eng. 40	175 tons
Class Eng. 50	525 tons
Class Eng. 51	525 tons

From Atchee, Colo., to Baxter Pass, Colo.:

Shay Class Eng. 2, 3 and 5........	60 tons
Class Eng. 20 and 21...........	35 tons
Class Eng. 50	145 tons
Class Eng. 51	145 tons

From Rainbow Junction, Utah, to Rainbow, Utah:

Shay Class Eng. 2, 3 and 5........	105 tons
Class Eng. 30	110 tons
Class Eng. 50	240 tons
Class Eng. 51	240 tons

EASTBOUND

From Watson, Utah, to Dragon, Utah:

Class Eng. 20 and 21...........	250 tons
Class Eng. 30	650 tons
Class Eng. 50	1150 tons
Class Eng. 51	1150 tons

From Dragon, Utah, to Wendella, Colo.:

Class Eng. 20 and 21...........	100 tons
Class Eng. 30	325 tons
Class Eng. 50	525 tons
Class Eng. 51	525 tons

From Wendella, Colo., to Baxter Pass, Colo.:

Shay Class Eng. 2, 3 and 5........	105 tons
Class Eng. 20 and 21...........	50 tons
Class Eng. 50	240 tons
Class Eng. 51	240 tons

1931 ENGINE RATING

WESTBOUND

From Mack, Colo., to Carbonera, Colo.:

Class Eng. 12	210 tons
Class Eng. 20 and 21...........	125 tons
Class Eng. 40	300 tons
Class Eng. 50	525 tons
Class Eng. 51	525 tons

From Carbonera, Colo., to Atchee, Colo.:

Class Eng. 12	175 tons
Class Eng. 20 and 21...........	90 tons
Class Eng. 40	225 tons
Class Eng. 50	525 tons
Class Eng. 51	525 tons

From Atchee, Colo., to Baxter Pass, Colo.:

Shay Class Eng. 2, 3 and 5........	60 tons
Class Eng. 20 and 21...........	35 tons
Class Eng. 50	90 tons
Class Eng. 51	90 tons

From Rainbow Junction, Utah, to Rainbow, Utah:

Shay Class Eng. 2, 3 and 5........	105 tons
Class Eng. 30	110 tons
Class Eng. 50	200 tons
Class Eng. 51	200 tons

EASTBOUND

From Watson, Utah, to Dragon, Utah:

Class Eng. 20 and 21...........	250 tons
Class Eng. 30	650 tons
Class Eng. 50	1150 tons
Class Eng. 51	1150 tons

From Dragon, Utah, to Wendella, Colo.:

Class Eng. 20 and 21...........	100 tons
Class Eng. 30	325 tons
Class Eng. 50	525 tons
Class Eng. 51	525 tons

From Wendella, Colo., to Baxter Pass, Colo.:

Shay Class Eng. 2, 3 and 5........	105 tons
Class Eng. 20 and 21...........	50 tons
Class Eng. 50	185 tons
Class Eng. 51	185 tons

All of the modifications, though, were only of secondary importance. The big articulated was designed and built to do a job, and she did it well. That's what counted. Initially, she was put to work on the northern section of the line, between the summit at Baxter Pass and the mines near Rainbow, doing a job previously assigned to three locomotives. Cars loaded with gilsonite were made up into trains at Rainbow for the movement down to Rainbow Junction and from there up to the Pass. From Wendella to Baxter Pass, against the steadily ascending five per cent grade, the new locomotive handled as much tonnage per train as *two* of the Shay geared locomotives and made the run in a little more than half the time. It was evident from the start that this represented a very significant reduction in the operating expense per train mile, as well as increasing the track capacity of the line. Furthermore, the maintenance expense for the No. 50 was expected to be less than for *one* of the Shays it replaced.[4]

With this sort of performance the articulated proved to be just what the Uintah needed. The next step was obvious. Before many months had passed Mr. Sprague placed an order for a sister engine. Outshopped by Baldwin in April of 1928,

Twenty-two months separated the builder's photographs of the two articulateds (above) and a number of details were different. The large sandbox on the front deck took the place of smaller ones behind No. 50's air pumps. The pumps themselves were relocated so they'd be less in danger when bucking snow and the main reservoir air line wouldn't need that damage-prone flexible connection. The backup light and rear footboards were omitted. A heftier pilot beam and a solid pilot replaced the more traditional but less substantial boiler-tube pilot. The larger bunker behind the cab could hold about a half ton more coal.

A different injector arrangement, with the injector drawing its water supply from ahead of the center of the side tank, left more of the water available when going downhill. Even the shape of the left side tank was changed, and the filler hole moved to the forward end, away from the pop valves. A second steam dome was installed on each engine at the Atchee shops, just behind the two domes shown in these photos. Below, No. 51 rolls north toward Watson in 1928 with a long train including well over half of the road's stock cars. *(Top: H. L. Broadbelt Collection; center and bottom: E. V. Earp Collection)*

the No. 51 was nearly five tons heavier, with a total engine weight of 246,000 pounds, and took the honor of being the world's largest and heaviest three-foot gauge locomotive away from the No. 50.[5] The No. 51 also embodied many of the design refinements such as the air pumps on each side of the smokebox and the larger coal bunker, which had been worked out for her older sister.

The tonnage rating of the articulateds on the various sections of the line was approximately double that of the heaviest locomotives they replaced. Interestingly, however, on the steeper and more difficult parts of the line their rating was apparently overestimated at first. At least by August, 1931, it had been lowered by a noticeable amount. Perhaps Mr. Sprague was too optimistic and expected too much of his Mallets on the hill. A quick comparison of the preceding tables shows what happened. The first table of engine ratings is from The Uintah Railway Company *Employees' Time Table No. 24*, which went into effect Sunday, July 21, 1929. The second table comes from *Employees' Time Table No. 25*, of August 23, 1931. The 7.5 per cent up from Atchee and the five per cent grade from Wendella to Baxter Pass were a proving ground for any engine!

A few more changes may also be noted in comparing the above tables. Engines No. 12 and No. 40, assigned to the less torturous line between Mack and Atchee, were allowed to handle heavier trains. The No. 12 had received a new boiler from Baldwin in 1924, and the tonnage rating of Mikado No. 40 was increased three years later when the shopmen at Atchee equipped her with a superheater.

Although strictly speaking they were not Mallets, the No. 50 and No. 51 came to be called by that name. Technically, a Mallet (usually pronounced Mal'-lee) is a compound locomotive — one which uses steam twice, first in the rear or high-pressure cylinders and then in the larger low-pressure cylinders, before exhausting it to the atmosphere. The Uintah's articulateds were simple locomotives, utilizing high pressure steam in all four cylinders, and thus not true Mallets. But, unless you noticed that the cylinders were all the same size, they looked like Mallets. They bent in the middle like Mallets. So, to the men who ran them, they were "Mallets." Even the official Uin-

tah Railway locomotive roster stated, "Engines #50 and 51 are Mallet single expansion."

The "Mallets" brought a number of changes to the Uintah, not the least of which was a surplus of the older motive power sitting unneeded at Atchee. Up until this time the line had scrapped only one engine, and that was over 15 years earlier when the Consolidation numbered second No. 11 arrived to replace first No. 11 on the roster. Now it was the second No. 11's turn! She was retired and scrapped in 1927. During the same year buyers were found for two more locomotives. Seven-year-old Shay No. 6 went to Feather River Lumber Co. at Delleker, California, and Consolidation No. 10 was sold to the Eureka-Nevada Ry. and delivered to them at Palisade, Nevada. Then in 1928, practically coincident with the construction and delivery of No. 51, two of the older Shays were scrapped. These were Nos. 1 and 4.

While the new motive power was certainly the big news on the Uintah during those pre-depression years, other events were taking place which would have their effect on the Gilsonite Route during the coming decade. Over 200 miles to the east the Moffat Tunnel was opened for traffic in February, 1928, bypassing the tough climb over Rollins Pass and giving the Denver & Salt Lake a shorter and easier route from northwestern Colorado to Denver.[6] As we've noted, some of the gilsonite traffic was already moving east from Craig over the D.&S.L. Joe Stanton of that city had a fleet of White trucks busy carrying the hydrocarbon from the Little Emma mine near Watson to that railroad.[7] But for the present the Uintah Railway was still hauling the greatest part of the ore, and the railway's operating revenues and net income for 1928 and 1929 were higher than they had been since 1920. There was even new track being laid!

A new loading spur constructed during the summer of 1927 facilitated the opening of new workings along the Rainbow Vein. Nile Hughel, a civil engineer from Vernal, completed the survey for the extension by the middle of June, and the contractor had crews and 16 teams at work and expected to finish the new trackage in four weeks. Two miles in length, the new spur ran northwesterly from Rainbow following the vein.[8] Built and paid for by the Gilson Asphaltum Com-

This was the big slide that tied up the railway for over seven weeks in the spring of 1929. The same slide had blocked the line at other times since it started in March of 1923, including once for about three weeks in 1927. *(Left: Margaret Romager Collection; center, J. L. Booth Collection; bottom: E. V. Earp Collection)*

pany, this new track was not actually owned by the Uintah Railway, but was operated by them. So in effect it was an extension — the last one for the Uintah.

Later in 1927 the railroaders were saddened at the news that John McAndrews had succumbed to a sudden heart attack. Although nearly 72 years of age, he had been in good health and had returned from a duck hunting trip just hours before the seizure. One of the pioneers in the Uintah Basin, Mr. McAndrews had been appointed chief herder at the Ouray Indian Reservation in 1884. He resigned from the Indian Service to accept a position with the Uintah Railway when the road was built and had served the company as superintendent since that time.[9]

Other railroaders, too, made the news on occasion, but frequently it was not good news. All too often the frailties of human beings make front-page copy, as when William H. Allen, station agent for nearly twenty years for the Uintah Railway at Fort Duchesne and later Dragon, committed suicide. He had been suffering from heart disease and shot himself one night after writing a note stating that he was about to end his suffering.[10] The very next week former Uintah Railway auditor W. D. Halpin was found guilty by a Grand Junction jury of alienating the affections of a married woman.[11]

A scarcity of newspaper articles mentioning the narrow gauge became increasingly evident, too, as the 1920s continued. There probably were two major reasons for this. First, the local editors no longer had any illusions that the Uintah would ever be anything more than a short line, and one serving a very thinly populated region at that. Besides, their readers were more interested in other things now. Highways were being built and improved, and people traveling to and from the Uintah Basin seldom rode the railroad any more. There were even plans for starting an air line to fly passengers and mail between Salt Lake City and the Basin.[12] Secondly, not very much that was newsworthy happened along the Gilsonite Route after the mid-1920s. For example, when a blizzard in February, 1929, tied up the line for four or five days, it rated just a few lines on page 3 of the next week's Vernal *Express*.[13] Twenty years earlier such a storm would have delayed travelers and

the mail, and would have been assured a front page spread!

The next news important enough to make the front page concerned the resignation of General Manager L. C. Sprague during the spring of 1929. He left the Uintah for a job as president and general manager of the Carrier Holding Corporation, with principal offices in New York City. Within six more years he would become receiver and later president of the Minneapolis & St. Louis Railway.[14] Back in western Colorado Walter L. Rader, who had been in the service of the Uintah Railway for 18 years, was picked in May to replace Sprague as general manager.[15] At about the same date Homer D. Ford, who had been superintendent of the mines at Rainbow, was promoted to general manager of all the Gilson Asphaltum Company operations, with his headquarters remaining at Rainbow.[16]

Walt Rader, Homer Ford and their men were immediately faced with a problem of major proportions — perhaps the most serious the Gilsonite Route had ever encountered. The big slide above Shale Tank had slid! A large portion of the mountainside undermined by spring thaws and subsequent rains had broken off and started for the valley below, taking over 1000 feet of the railroad's main line with it. By the end of May the caving had grown to a width considerably in excess of a half mile, and it was still sliding. Enormous masses of dirt and rocks, 100 feet deep in places, covered the tracks and accumulated faster than the crew of workers could remove them.

The slide occurred during the night of May 1st. Within days the gilsonite mines were forced to suspend operations due to the lack of empty flat cars and sacks for the ore. About 150 miners and other men employed in the diggings at the Rector, Country Boy and Rainbow mines were laid off by May 25th. Large quantities of ore had accumulated at Watson and the mines, and arrangements were immediately made to get this ore to eastern markets by trucking it to Craig, as one gilsonite company had been doing for several years. By early June, nine trucks were hauling gilsonite from Rainbow to Craig, making the trip in 24 hours.[17] In addition, more than 180,000 pounds of wool was at Watson, and a smaller quantity at Ute Switch, five miles south of Watson, awaiting ship-

At the left is the crawler shovel which was brought in to help clean up the big slide. The frame of water car No. 023 sags noticeably under the weight of the big shovel. The center photo is at Atchee, looking toward the shops and enginehouse. Below is Carbonera, with props for the coal mine stacked near the tipple. (*Left: E. V. Earp Collection; center: R. B. Jackson photo from Gerald M. Best Collection; bottom: Linwood W. Moody Collection, from E. L. DeGolyer, Jr.*)

ment when the slide occurred. Because it was under contract for delivery at definite dates, this wool also had to be trucked to Craig.

It was ascertained that a spring issuing from the mountain at the site of the slide was the principal cause of the trouble. The water flowing from the spring steadily undermined the rocks and surface soil. The sliding at this location had been going on for over six years now, and no doubt the amount of material already removed by the Uintah's men and ditcher had not made the remaining mountainside above the grade any more stable. But now that the location of the spring was known, draining it would help stabilize the slide in the future.

All the while the Uintah's men were hard at work attempting to reopen the line. Another big shovel, on caterpillar treads, was brought in to supplement the steam ditcher and the men with teams and scrapers. At one point the flow of the slide halted for a time and the roadbed was quickly leveled off and track laid. Sixteen carloads of gilsonite were hurried over the uncertain rails before the mountain gathered itself for another attack and let go again, all but wiping out the old landscape. It was only by heroic efforts that the newly laid rails and ties were saved as the roadbed moved off downhill. But the Uintah Railway was not about to be beaten by a mountain! Finally the slide was stabilized and a new grade, hugging closer to the rocky innards of the mountain, was finished. The first train for some weeks arrived in Watson on Saturday, June 22nd.[18]

After the excitement of the landslide, the next few years for the Uintah tend to seem anticlimactic. In some ways they were. They were years of belt tightening. The market crash and the great depression following it slowed down the whole country. Actually, the gilsonite industry and the railroad weathered the depression years in much better shape than much of the nation's business community. The bottom didn't drop out of the gilsonite market as it did in so many other industries. There was still a demand for the unique hydrocarbon, although not quite in the same quantities as before. Production from the mines had reached an eight-year high in 1928. It then declined steadily until 1932 before bouncing back

a bit. The following production figures show the pattern for the industry:[19]

Year	Gilsonite Mined
1924	35,907 tons
1925	39,520 tons
1926	42,190 tons
1927	42,580 tons
1928	47,023 tons
1929	42,580 tons
1930	37,684 tons
1931	32,763 tons
1932	25,955 tons
1933	28,029 tons
1934	30,355 tons
1935	35,768 tons
1936	33,654 tons

As would be expected, with most of the gilsonite still going to market over its line, the Uintah's railway operating revenues followed a similar pattern. They dropped from a high of $487,830 in 1929 to $232,649 three years later, then recovered slowly, reaching $266,638 by 1935. The operating expenses dropped from $408,683 in 1929 to $296,796 the next year and $240,749 in 1931.[20] Fortunately the company was able to keep its expenses in line as the revenues fell, so that there was not a year between 1928 and 1937 that the net income went into the red.

The big slide had accounted for a considerable portion of those 1929 expenses. The declining traffic in the early 1930s required fewer trains, and the two articulateds further reduced motive power and crew costs. Other economies were of a more minor nature. One attempt to cut costs backfired, however, when the railway gave notice in November, 1930, that its telegraph office in Vernal was being closed. There was so much protest from the businessmen and the Vernal Lions Club that the order was rescinded, and the telegraph line to Watson and Mack remained open.[21] Five months later the telegraph office was moved from the railway's own brick building to the Calder Motor Building, and by the following November the former Uintah Railway office had been secured by the Eastern Utah Transportation Co. and the Sterling Transportation Co. for a freight and express depot for their trucks.[22]

Next, in June, 1931, General Manager Rader applied to the Utah Public Utilities Commission for permission to discontinue the station agency

In August, 1937, Consolidation No. 12 (above) made a final trip to Mack and back to Atchee — a test run — before returning to Mack to be loaded and shipped west to Palisade, Nevada, and her new owner, the Eureka-Nevada Railway. The same month another photographer found former Uintah Ry. Shay No. 6 (center) sold to Feather River Lumber Co. ten years earlier as their second No. 3, sitting partly stripped near the mill at Delleker, California. Shay No. 5 (below) would see only infrequent service after 1936, when the picture below was taken at Atchee, despite her near-perfect condition. (*Top: R. B. Jackson photo from Gerald M. Best Collection; center: James E. Boynton Collection; bottom: L. W. Moody Collection, from E. L. DeGolyer, Jr.*)

at Dragon. Passenger business to and from Dragon by that date was practically nonexistent, and the freight business during the first five months of 1931 totaled only about $1200, while the expense of the agency for the same period was $1250. Mr. Rader claimed that most of the freight shipments could be handled as conveniently from the Watson agency as they had been from Dragon.[23] Another cut in service came just a few weeks later when the scheduled mixed train over the line went from a daily except Sunday operation to triweekly. After August it ran westbound on Mondays, Wednesdays and Fridays and returned to Mack the next day.[24]

There still was the surplus of motive power that resulted when the Mallets replaced some five or six of the older engines, and the declining traffic volume didn't help the matter. Here was another place for economizing. So in April, 1933, Walt Rader made a visit to Ridgway, Colorado, to see Superintendent Forest White of the Rio Grande Southern to persuade him to lease engines No. 12 and No. 30. The No. 12 was slightly larger than any of the Consolidations then pulling R.G.S. freights, and Mikado No. 30 a little bigger than D.&R.G.W.'s K-27 class engines. The two engines were in first class condition, and Mr. Rader offered to lease them for less than the R.G.S. would have to pay the Rio Grande for similar engines. He did not care to sell them for what they would bring since he would have to take too much loss. The Uintah was carrying the No. 12 on their books at $12,000 and the No. 30 at $14,000. The next day Superintendent White wrote the R.G.S. receiver's office in Denver about the offer, stating that if business picked up he would need more power and that it looked as though they could get some mighty good engines very reasonably.[25] But nothing further ever came of this interchange — Mr. White's railroad came to be better known for traffic in quantities that a Galloping Goose or two could handle. Finally, in 1937 Walter Rader was able to sell the No. 12. She went to the Eureka-Nevada Ry., little more than a year before that once-prosperous narrow gauge was abandoned. The No. 30 would still be sitting at Dragon when the Uintah itself ran its last train.

Probably the most extraordinary event of the depression years was the construction of a brand new Shay locomotive, the No. 7, by the Uintah Railway men at the Atchee shops. It seems there was quite a supply of spare Shay parts on hand there, so in 1933 a new boiler was ordered from the Lima Locomotive Works and a new Shay was built. No doubt Lima was happy to get the order, even for just a boiler — they had sold their last Shay two years earlier and would not sell another until 1936.[26]

Under the direction of Master Mechanic Scott Shafer, the men at Atchee put together a fine machine. They *had* had some practice for the job. Since 1924 they had rebuilt every engine on the roster, with the exception of the pair of still-almost-new articulateds. Most recent had been Shay No. 5, which was rebuilt in 1930 with a new and noticeably bigger boiler from Lima. Prior to that the men had reboilered Consolidation No. 12, relocated the main drivers of No. 10 from their position as second pair to a new location as the third pair of drivers, applied syphons to improve the water circulation in the boilers of tank engines No. 20 and No. 21, and superheated Mikado No. 40. But building a new locomotive, even from spare parts and a new boiler, was something else again. When the No. 7 was finished in December and rolled out into the bright Colorado sunlight for the first time, the men were pretty pleased and proud of her. It showed on their faces as they lined up, 18 strong, in front of the shiny new Shay for the "builder's photo," recording the event for posterity. None of them could have expected that warm December afternoon that their new No. 7 would have an active life of less than six years.

Even then the shadows were lengthening for the Uintah Railway. It was becoming apparent to the management, and to the men, that the end was drawing near. If the signs had been rather dim and hard to read before, they became clear in 1935 when General Asphalt Company published its *Annual Report* for the preceding year. After 14 years without a single mention of its railway subsidiary in its *Report,* the parent corporation inserted the following paragraph in the 1934 *Annual Report:*

Transportation of Gilsonite: The tonnage now being mined is transported over a wholly-owned railroad subsidiary. Government improvement of highways in Utah in recent years

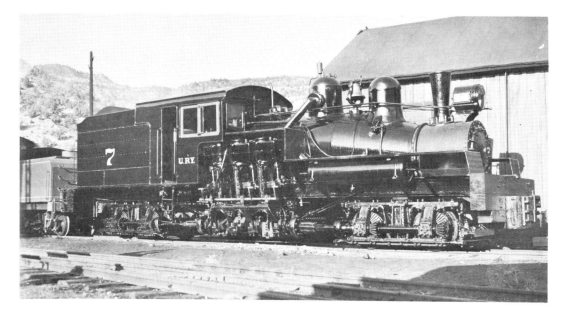

Shay locomotive No. 7 (left) looked handsome when she rolled out of the shops at Atchee in December, 1933, to pose for her builder's photo. The men who built her look proud, too. From left to right, they are Doc Dunlap, William Karr, Robert Wilson, Billy Mort, Roy McCoy (in the cab gangway), Floyd Kendall, Bud Karn, Glenn Griffin, Joe Zellers, and Robert Hester. Next a young man identified only as "Ted," followed by a Seventh-day Adventist whose name is not remembered. Then come Bruce Angus, Morris High with his son Johnny, Tom Bird, Jimmy Gold, Walter Rader and Scott Shafer. General Manager Rader also appears in the picture below, standing second from the right, on the front porch of the office in Mack. At the right is Assistant Secretary and Treasurer J. I. McClain and on the other side of Mr. Rader is Superintendent E. V. Earp. Chief Dispatcher J. L. Booth stands at the left. (*Two builder's photos: E. V. Earp Collection; below: L. W. Moody Collection, from Everett L. DeGolyer, Jr.*)

has made transport by truck more economical. When the Company's mining conditions can be advantageously adapted to truck transport, the railroad property now owned and used will become obsolete. The Directors have, therefore, authorized the creation of a reserve of $1,325,000 against this contingency.

The reserve, equal to the corporation's investment in the railway, was established as of January 1, 1935.[27]

But the Uintah wasn't quite dead yet, although some of the railroaders who had been with the line since the early years were passing on. In June, 1931, Mrs. Sarah M. Logan, who for many years had been manager and telegraph operator at the company's Vernal office, succumbed after a lingering illness.[28] Nearly two years later, on May 18, 1933, death claimed the man who had, perhaps more than any other, been responsible for the development of northeastern Utah's gilsonite deposits and the building of the Uintah Railway — Charles O. Baxter. His brother, Frank, who had surveyed the route for the railway over the pass which bore their name, had died several years earlier.[29] Another old-timer, who had assisted in filing on most of the gilsonite claims in Uintah County, died the following June. He was E. S. Gurr, well known as road superintendent of the Uintah Railway for some thirty years. Living first at Dragon, then at Kennedy Station for a few years and later at Vernal, Mr. Gurr had kept the toll roads maintained and open, even during the most inclement weather.[30]

Less than two years after Mr. Gurr's death the Uintah Toll Road Company went out of business. As we have noted, the road north from Watson had seen little traffic since the early 1920s. Occasionally some of the miners would drive up to Vernal for a Fourth of July baseball game or to visit with their folks, but even then some of them would drive the long way around from Dragon via Rangely, Colorado, to avoid paying the toll at the White River bridge. Since at least 1928 people had been urging the road be made public. A petition was circulated that February asking the Uintah County commissioners to negotiate the purchase of the White River bridge from the railway. There was a payroll of $11,000 per month at the mining

camps, and Vernal businessmen were aware that the toll of $3.00 a round trip for cars was keeping a large part of the miners' trade away from their stores.[31] But nothing much happened until June of 1929, when General Manager Rader met with the County commissioners to request an extension of the franchise entitling the Uintah Toll Road Company, as successor and assignee of C. O. Baxter, to operate the 45 miles of toll road between Watson and Jensen. Mr. Rader told them that whenever Uintah County was ready to take over the maintenance of the road and the bridge the railway company would surrender both bridge and franchise. But the county had no spare cash in its road fund, so the commissioners extended the company's franchise for another ten years. They did ask, however, that the toll rate over the White River bridge for wagons and touring cars be reduced to $1.00 each way. This was agreed to. The franchise extension also contained the provision that the Uintah Toll Road Company, upon six months' written notice from the county, would convey without charge the road, bridges and right of way to Uintah County on the first of January following.[32]

Thus the maintenance of the road remained the company's responsibility for the next six years, and primarily E. S. Gurr's responsibility until he died. There was no stinting on the job. Early in 1930 four bridges were replaced, including the one crossing Evacuation Creek, south of White River. This one, with steel plates covering the floor boards, cost about $3,000 to put in, and Mr. Gurr predicted it would last indefinitely.[33] Finally, in November, 1935, after some pressure from county residents who were separated from the county seat by the toll station, the board of commissioners voted unanimously to take over the road and White River bridge. Shortly thereafter, however, someone read the fine print and discovered that it was necessary to give six months' written notice. But the company quickly came to the rescue. Paul Brinton of the Gilson Asphaltum Company, together with Mrs. Edith R. Lawrence Cooper, their attorney, appeared at the regular December meeting of the commissioners and agreed to waive the requirement for six months' notice, provided the county would give an assur-

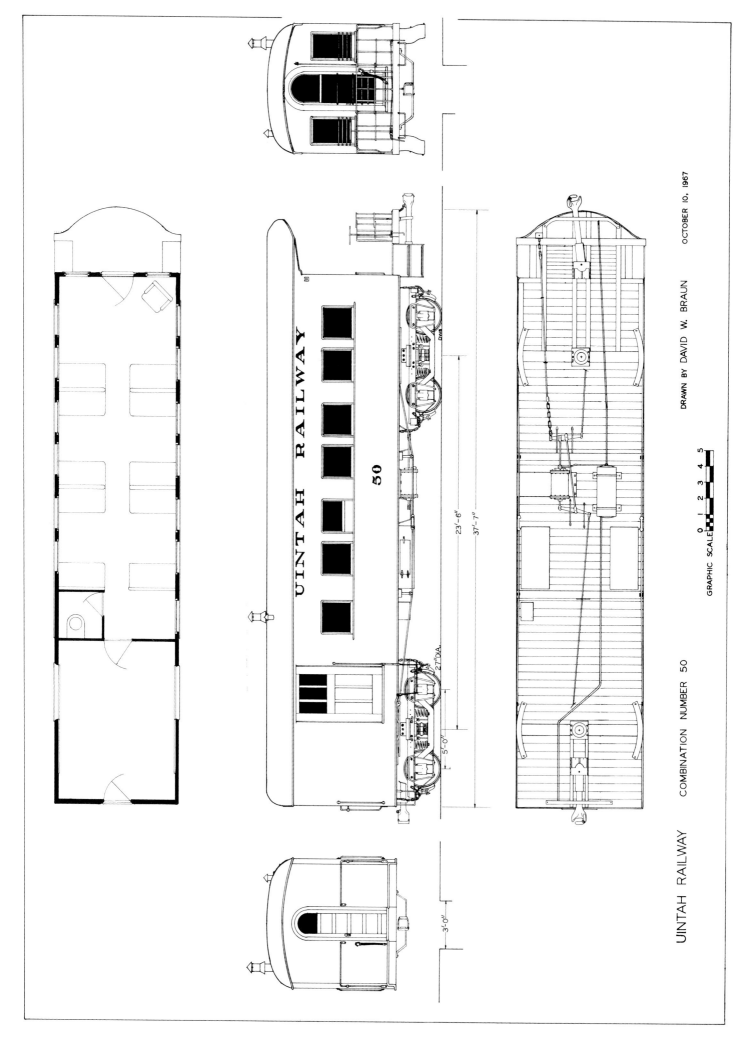

UINTAH RAILWAY

23'-6"

37'-7"

27"DIA.

5'-0"

3'-0"

50

UINTAH RAILWAY   COMBINATION NUMBER 50

DRAWN BY DAVID W. BRAUN   OCTOBER 10, 1967

GRAPHIC SCALE
0 1 2 3 4 5

Combination baggage-coach No. 50 (above) was finished and rolled outside the Atchee shops. Looking like an entirely new car, it was actually rebuilt from an old wooden combine also numbered 50. Master Mechanic Scott Shafer stands in for the builder's photo. Also a rebuild is rail car No. 52 (below). Basically a Model "T" Ford coupe, it had a Chevrolet transmission and a universal joint to the four-wheel power truck. Special wheels with wooden spokes were installed so it wouldn't make so much noise. A ten-gallon tank was located in the dovetail behind the seat and connected through a water pump to the radiator so the car never ran out of water and couldn't run hot climbing Baxter Pass. It was used almost exclusively by Superintendent Vic Earp, shown in the driver's seat, and could haul two motor cars loaded with section men and their tools up the 5 per cent from Wendella to Baxter Pass — in low gear, no faster than a walk. (*Above: William F. Karr Collection; below: L. W. Moody Collection, from E. L. DeGolyer, Jr.*)

A single-stall enginehouse (left) at the tail of the wye in Mack provided protection for the one engine that usually spent the night there. By this wintry gray February day in 1939, the Barber Asphalt name had been lettered on the side of the big steel water tank behind the enginehouse. Below is the steel bridge crossing the White River at Ignatio (also called White River Station). *(Left: Robert M. Hanft; below: F. A. Kennedy photo, from Charles I. Neal Collection)*

ance in writing that the road would be maintained. A contract was drawn up and sent back to company headquarters for approval. After a short delay, everything was ready. On April 15th Homer D. Ford, general manager of the Gilson Asphaltum Company, met with Commissioners Willis L. Johnson, John G. Bolton and John B. Weaver and officially transferred the property to Uintah County. The only technicality then remaining was taken care of soon afterward, with the filing by The Uintah Toll Road Company of an "Application to Voluntarily Withdraw from the State of Utah." Thus, with the final hearing on Tuesday, July 14, 1936, at the Uintah County Courthouse, the history of one of the West's last toll road companies came to an end.[34]

Another change in the corporate structure came later that year. On November 1, 1936, the parent firm changed its name from General Asphalt Company to Barber Company, Incorporated. At the same time its gilsonite-mining subsidiary, Gilson Asphaltum Company, was merged into the Barber Company.[35] Even the old names were becoming history! The new name itself didn't last very long. At their annual meeting in 1938 the stockholders voted to change it again, to "Barber Asphalt Corporation."[36]

Whatever its name, the company had a more than passing interest in letting the county take over the toll road. Plans were to transfer the mining operations from Rainbow to Bonanza, Utah, and to truck the ore from there to the Moffat Road at Craig. Good roads were a necessary part of the plan. The paving of U. S. 40, the "Victory Highway," between Vernal and Craig was started in 1937 and practically completed by the end of the year.[37] With the link from Bonanza

north to U. S. 40 now in the county's hands, everything was ready.

Late in September, 1937, Homer Ford, whose title was now superintendent of the Barber Company, disclosed the plans to shift operations to Bonanza. By December the work was already well under way and, according to Mr. Ford who was supervising the operations, the old mining camp was becoming one of the most modern mining communities in the West. Sixteen cottages were being erected to accommodate the single workers and workers with their families. Much of the material for them was being salvaged from the Rainbow camp, but no expense was being spared to make the homes modern and comfortable. Each family cottage would be equipped with living rooms, basement and screened porch, and double insulation on all buildings would protect the workers from excessive heat or cold. The famous Gemasco shingles, manufactured by the Barber Company, were being used on all the buildings. (Homer Ford couldn't pass up a chance for a plug like that for his employer.) Five garages to accommodate four cars each, a community hall where employees and their families might "enjoy supervised recreation" and a modern school for the boys and girls would round out the building program. As a finishing touch the streets would be landscaped, and more than a dozen fine Siberian Elms had already been brought in and planted in imported mountain soil. More than a little pleased, Homer Ford stated, "We plan to make the Bonanza camp so desirable a place to live that our employees will always be contented here."[38]

For the Uintah Railway, though, the move to Bonanza meant one thing. The stage was set for the final chapter.

Business car B-8 at Mack in 1938. *Roy F. Blackburn photo from Ray Buhrmaster Collection*

Atchee-built Shay No. 7 and Lima-built No. 5 (above) catch their breath at the summit of Baxter Pass before starting down the west side with the plow. The light snow should be little trouble for them. Below it was just a little patch of ice between the rails that did the plow in. (*Above: E. V. Earp Collection; below: William F. Karr photo from his Collection*)

At times there was a bit more snow and there were drifts to contend with. The snowplow and two of the Shays (above) are almost hidden. At the right, the retainers are all set up and No. 50's engineer is oiling around before starting his train of gilsonite down the long hill. In just an hour the Mallet will be rolling to a stop under the tank in Atchee (below) next to the icicle-draped enginehouse. (*Top and right: E. V. Earp Collection; below: Margaret Romager Collection*)

The Baldwin 0-6-2 side-tanker with its one-car train announces its coming with a plume of smoke. Within minutes it will be climbing the second level of track heading for Moro Castle, only to reappear moments later around the hill on the third level. (*George L. Beam photo, from D.&R.G.W. files courtesy of Jackson C. Thode*)

Chapter Nine

The End of the Line

By the summer of 1938 the end of the line for the Uintah Railway was clearly in sight. A new operating time table, destined to be the next to the last, went into effect on the last day of July, and train service was reduced to two round trips per week between Mack and Watson.[1] Previously three trains a week had run to Watson and back, with an additional daily except Sunday turn scheduled up the hill from Atchee to Baxter Pass.[2] Thus, it came as no surprise when the Interstate Commerce Commission announced, on August 26, 1938, that the Uintah Railway had filed an application for abandonment.[3]

The economic facts of life were such that the Uintah management had no other choice but to abandon the line. As early as 1930 the Gilson Asphaltum Company had begun to shift its operations from the Rainbow to the Bonanza Mine, located some 15 miles northwest of the railway's terminus at Watson. By 1938 mining at Rainbow had come to a halt. Thus, at the time of the abandonment hearing there were no commercial deposits of gilsonite known to be available adjacent to the railroad. The Barber Company, successor in 1936 to the General Asphalt Company, had been trucking their gilsonite from Bonanza, to the railway at Watson, at a cost of $1.80 per ton. On top of this, the railroad rate from Watson to Mack was $9.95 a ton. In 1938 the Barber interests entered into a contract with a truck operator for the hauling of their ore from Bonanza over 22 miles of dirt road to U. S. Highway 40, and thence to the Denver & Salt Lake Railway at Craig, a total distance of about 122 miles, at a rate of $5 a ton.[4] With the resulting savings in transportation costs amounting to $6.75 for every ton of gilsonite they shipped, it was only logical that the Barber Company should switch to trucks. The Uintah was, by its very nature, an expensive railroad to operate.

Both the Barber interests and the American Asphalt Association discontinued use of the railroad in December, 1938. The other major company mining gilsonite in the area, the Utah Gilsonite Company, had ceased using the line in 1929, after which time its output was trucked to Hebron, Utah [sic], and Craig.[5] The Barber Company had been planning this switch to trucks for some time. The management was aware the Uintah Railway was nearing the end of its economic usefulness, as indicated by the following quote taken from the Grand Junction *Daily Sentinel's* account of the abandonment hearing before the I.C.C. examiner:

> Frank Seamans, vice president of the Uintah line and also the Barber Asphalt company, told the examiner that for the past four years the abandonment of the line had been contemplated, but that the completion of highway 40 had been awaited in order to insure a cheap truck haul. Fifty per cent can be saved by the truck haul, and the Barber company was forced to adopt this method to meet competitive prices of other companies. The Stanton Transportation company of Craig has a five-year contract for the gilsonite haul by truck.
>
> Mr. Seamans stated that before a decision to abandon the road was finally reached, efforts were made to interest the D.&R.G.W. in its operation as a feeder line, but this failed.[6]

179

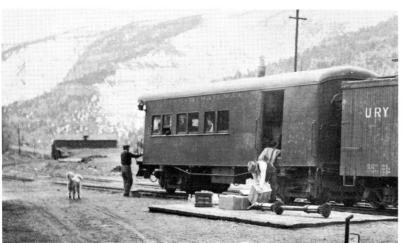

By the 1930s the nation's network of paved roads had expanded to touch nearly every town of any size in the country. But the paved highway never reached Atchee, Colorado. The everyday needs of the town continued to arrive, as they had for years, in the baggage compartment of the train. At the left, a new drive shaft for one of the Shays was delivered along with the bottles of milk and boxes of groceries in April, 1937. By this time the depot at Mack (below) was quietly slipping into the slumber of old age. (*Top: Roy F. Blackburn; left: Lawrie Brown Collection; bottom: R. B. Jackson photo, from Gerald M. Best Collection*)

The attempt to interest the Rio Grande in taking over the Uintah Railway is rather an interesting story in itself. Mrs. J. L. Booth, wife of the Uintah's Chief Dispatcher, in reporting the local news from Mack to the *Daily Sentinel* for their issue of July 22, 1938, wrote: "President Auten of the Barber Asphalt corporation, Philadelphia, Pa., paid Mack an official visit Friday. He, with General Manager A. L. Rader [sic] and a party of Denver and Rio Grande Western railroad officials made the trip over the Uintah railway." Former Uintah engineer William F. Karr recalls that the Rio Grande officials were interested in taking over the operation of the line, provided it wouldn't cost too much to put the railway back in good operating condition. But they found that the costs would be excessive, due to rather large amounts of deferred maintenance, primarily in the form of crossties which were past due for replacement. So the men from the Rio Grande refused to buy the line, and, quoting Bill Karr, "Walter Rader was fired that day, and he immediately moved out of the hotel at Mack where he'd been living for years."[7] In the very same column of news from Mack which is quoted above, Mrs. Booth reported, "J. I. McClain was notified this week of his appointment as general manager of the Uintah Railway Co., succeeding W. L. Rader who resigned after a long term of service with the company." Mr. McClain served in the capacity of acting general manager until the last train ran, some ten months later.

The D.&R.G.W. officials who inspected the Uintah Railway in July, 1938, could not have been unaware of that line's almost total dependence on the gilsonite mines for revenue traffic. It is also likely that they were aware of the transfer of the mining operations from Rainbow and Dragon to Bonanza, and of the anticipated switch to trucks for hauling the ore. Thus it must have been pretty obvious to them that the Rio Grande would not have found the Uintah very profitable as a feeder line, even if it had been in first class condition and standard gauge. The "Grande" already had too many branch lines with relatively high operating costs and declining traffic.

The sparsity of traffic, other than gilsonite, in the territory served by the Uintah would have been obvious to anyone glancing at the region's population statistics. Mack, of course, was the only

station on the Uintah line which was served by another railroad. At the time of the abandonment hearing, in January, 1939, it had a population of 159, about half of whom were employees of the Uintah Railway and their families. The only other agency station on the line, Watson, Utah, had ten residents at the time. The population of Carbonera, the coal-mining camp eight miles south of Atchee which furnished coal exclusively for railroad use, was variously reported by the Grand Junction *Daily Sentinel* and the Interstate Commerce Commission as being either ten or twenty. Other locations along the railway were Atchee, with a population of twelve as of January, 1939; Baxter Pass, with two residents; Wendella, at the foot of the heavy grade on the north side of the pass, with a single inhabitant; and Dragon, Utah, boasting a population of 72, of whom 13 were employees of the railroad and their families, and 39 were employees of the American Asphalt Association and their families. It was estimated that there were probably 100 other families residing in the territory, engaged principally in cattle and sheep raising.[8]

These population figures, of course, show a significant decline from those of a few months earlier, much less those during the railroad's heydays a decade or two previously. During the 1920s as many as 46 pupils had been enrolled in the school at Atchee. By the end of December of 1938, Atchee had become almost a ghost town as the Uintah's railroaders and their wives and children left for greener pastures. A year later the town was entirely abandoned.

It is interesting to note that the Uintah's gilsonite traffic did not show a significant decrease in volume until the last full year of the line's operation, 1938, and also that the company operated at a profit each year prior to 1938. In its report authorizing abandonment, the Interstate Commerce Commission recorded the following details, which also reiterate how highly dependent the Uintah was on the gilsonite mines for its traffic:

Carloads of local freight handled on the line during the years 1933-38 are shown, in order, as 110, 89, 69, 52, 45, and 30, consisting principally, and in the latter years almost entirely, of water hauled in tank cars to gilsonite mines.

From Rainbow and Watson, from Dragon and Atchee and Mack, as the fall of 1938 turned to winter the people began packing up and moving away. By the time the westbound train (below) was photographed leaving Baxter Pass on November 7, 1938, the towns along the line were already beginning to look a little like the ghost towns they would become within a few months. *(Left and above: F. A. Kennedy photos, from J. L. Booth Collection; below: Roy F. Blackburn)*

Carloads of traffic moving between points on the line and points beyond during the same years were, in order, 1,456, 1,606, 1,670, 1,398, 1,693, and 1,020. Of those carloads outbound gilsonite shipments were 1,187, 1,342, 1,404, 1,229, 1,461, and 876. Local less-than-carload traffic varied from a high of 373 tons in 1933 to a low of 163 tons in 1938. Less-than-carload traffic between points on the line and points beyond it varied from a high of 52 tons in 1933 to a low of 35 tons in 1938.

The applicant's net railway operating incomes for the years 1933-37 were, in order, $33,363, $26,598, $49,961, $23,227, and $31,332. In the first 11 months of 1938 it had a net railway operating deficit of $13,321. Its gross revenues for the six years 1933-38 were, in order, $239,710, $259,965, $266,638, $232,119, $271,195, and $162,386, a total of $1,432,013, of which $1,381,497 was freight revenue, and the remaining $50,516 passenger, mail, and other revenue. Less than 4 percent of the freight revenue was derived from traffic handled for shippers other than the gilsonite operators.[9]

As mentioned, the Uintah Railway reduced their operating schedule to two round trips per week, northbound on Mondays and Fridays, returning the next day, effective July 31, 1938. It had been just about two weeks since the D.&R.G.W. men had made their inspection trip over the road in the company of President Auten and General Manager Rader. On August 24, 1938, less than four weeks later, the Uintah had filed application for abandonment with the Interstate Commerce Commission in Washington, although this filing was not announced to the public for another two days. The following week, on August 30, an application was filed with the Colorado Public Utilities Commission for abandonment of the portion of the railway within that state. Presumably a similar application was also made in Salt Lake City. The company then gave the public official notice of its plans with the following brief announcement in the Grand Junction *Daily Sentinel* of Friday evening, September 9, 1938:

NOTICE

THE UINTAH RAILWAY COMPANY hereby gives notice that on the 24th day of August, 1938, it filed with the Interstate Commerce Commission at Washington, D. C., an application for a certificate of public convenience and necessity permitting abandonment of its entire line of railroad extending from a connection with the railroad of The Denver and Rio Grande Western Railroad Co. at Mack, in Mesa County, northerly thru Garfield and Rio Blanco Counties, Colorado, to Watson, Uintah County, Utah, a distance of approximately 63.0 miles; with branches extending from Dragon to Dragon Mine, approximately 1.14 miles, and from Rainbow Junction to Rainbow, approximately 4.23 miles, both in Uintah County, Utah.

THE UINTAH RAILWAY
COMPANY   9-8-38

Meanwhile the Craig *Empire-Courier,* observing that the Uintah had made application for abandonment, anticipated the gilsonite traffic that would be transported to Craig by truck and shipped out from there over the Moffat Road, should the abandonment be approved.[10]

The wheels grind slowly in Washington. While waiting for the I.C.C. to schedule a hearing on the abandonment application, the management of the Uintah Railway proceeded to cut their operations back to a bare minimum. Both the Barber Company and the American Asphalt Association made their last use of the railway for shipping gilsonite during the month of December, 1938. As of December 11, no date had yet been set for the I.C.C. hearing, and officials of the railway made public the fact that business was continuing to decline. After Christmas, they informed the *Daily Sentinel,* only one train would be operated over the line each week.[11]

As a result of the diminished business over the road, the town of Atchee was to be virtually abandoned by the road after the holidays. The *Daily Sentinel* noted that much of the business had already moved out of Atchee. The force of employees had been reduced, and with the reduction to one train a week, much more of it was scheduled to go. The second week in January of 1939 brought the population figures quoted earlier. The mining camp of Rainbow had already been entirely abandoned by that time.

The Uintah Railway's 27th and last employees' time table went into effect on Christmas day, Sunday, December 25, 1938, at 12:01 a.m. Mountain Standard Time. The train ran only on Tuesdays, leaving Mack at 8:10 a.m. and taking five hours

Eight miles from the station and the hotel at Mack was the location named Rader — named for the former superintendent and general manager, Walt Rader. It was just a signboard and a telephone box on a pole near the end of the Uintah's longest tangent. Below, Shay No. 7 churns its way up the 7.5 per cent above Shale. The day is Tuesday, May 9, 1939 — one week before the last train ran. (*Top: F. A. Kennedy photo, from J. L. Booth Collection; left: Roy F. Blackburn; bottom: Otto C. Perry*)

and five minutes to get to Watson, with stops scheduled at Atchee, Baxter Pass, Wendella and Dragon. Returning, they left Watson at 1:40 p.m. and were scheduled to cover the 62.8 miles back to Mack by 6:30 p.m.[12] This once-a-week schedule remained in effect until the last train ran on May 16, 1939.

The abandonment hearing was held before I.C.C. Examiner Sullivan on Thursday, January 12, 1939, in Grand Junction. Henry McAllister, a Denver attorney, represented the applicant, the Uintah Railway Company, as well as the D.&R.G.W. E. B. Adams was attorney for the protestants, which included the Chamber of Commerce and City of Grand Junction, Mesa County and others. With the transportation picture in the gilsonite industry being such as it was, there was really very little the protestants could do to prevent the junking of the railroad. They did succeed in delaying the inevitable for forty days.[13]

The Mesa County authorities were apparently quite worried about the loss in tax revenues which would result if the Uintah were abandoned. Attorney Adams sought to introduce evidence of the tax losses to three Mesa County school districts, but was told by Examiner Sullivan that tax payments were no reason for maintaining a utility, if it was a losing venture, and were not admissible as evidence. The railway company had paid into Mesa County a total tax of $4,718.85 on an assessed valuation of $128,634 during the year 1938. This valuation amounted to $10,049 for each of the railway's 12.80 miles of mainline track in that county. Three school districts, those of Fruita, Mack and New Liberty, stood to suffer from the tax loss, with District No. 44 at Mack being hardest hit. The Uintah Railway had accounted for over 21 per cent of the district's total assessed valuation, with property of the Barber Asphalt Company representing another three per cent of the total. Operating in four counties, in two states, the Uintah's total tax bill in 1937 had been $34,376.95, the highest figure in the history of the road.[14]

Only one individual, a Mr. Lafe Bown of Provo, Utah, showed up at the hearing with what seemed, at first glance, to be a valid reason for protesting the abandonment of the railway. He owned the hotel at Watson, and, through ownership or lease, controlled about 100,000 acres of

land near Watson, using these lands as winter range for some 16,000 sheep. He stated that abandonment of the road would seriously affect his business. Further testimony, however, revealed that Bown brought the sheep to Mack on the Denver & Rio Grande Western and then "trailed" them to winter range. After shearing at the public corral at Watson each spring, they would be driven back to Mack and loaded on the Rio Grande for shipment to the protestant's summer range in Eagle County, Colorado. He used the Uintah Railway only to ship bucks to and from the winter range, to return to Mack such sheep as he believed were not strong enough to stand the long trail drive and to ship his wool. During 1938, the railway's records revealed, they had handled 15 carloads of sheep, one carload of horses, and ten carloads of wool for the protestant. Total loads of sheep handled by the line amounted to 156 cars in 1935, and 67 cars in 1938. Each car had a capacity of about 160 sheep. Total carloads of wool handled on the line decreased from 65 in 1933, yielding $3,503 in revenue, to 31 in 1937, yielding $1,423. In 1938 there were 37 carloads, of which the witness shipped about ten carloads. Clearly, although the sheepmen furnished the Uintah Railway's second largest source of freight traffic, that traffic would not, alone, justify the continued operation of the road. During the last years, in fact, mail revenues were somewhat higher than revenue received from wool shipments.[15]

Examiner Sullivan filed his report with the Interstate Commerce Commission early in March of 1939. He recommended abandonment. There were no exceptions to the report, and the commissioners decided the case on April 8th. Their decision, which was published in Volume 233 of the *Interstate Commerce Commission Reports*, pretty well wrote finis for the Uintah. The next to the last paragraph of their report sums it up:

The record shows that the gilsonite shippers, one of whom owns all the capital stock of the applicant, have abandoned use of the railroad; that they have adopted trucks for hauling their gilsonite from points considerably beyond the line as a more economical means of transportation to meet competition; that there are no commercial deposits along the line; and that the line has served the purpose for which it was built. There is no prospect of traffic or revenue from any source sufficient to warrant the retention of the line. Its continued operation would impose an unnecessary and undue burden on interstate commerce.[16]

Thus the Commission permitted "the abandonment by The Uintah Railway Company of its entire line of railroad." Their permission was, however, subject to one condition: that within forty days from the date of their certificate "the applicant shall sell all or any part of its line of railroad to any person, firm, or corporation offering to purchase same for continued operation and offering to pay therefor not less than the fair salvage value thereof." The Grand Junction Chamber of Commerce had requested this last provision, in order that they might have ample time to search for a buyer for the property. But one wonders if they really had any hopes that such a search might be successful.

The I.C.C. announced its decision to authorize abandonment of the Uintah Railway on April 14, and, out in western Colorado, plans were made to end the already-abbreviated service on the line. Notices and embargoes were issued to all agents of the connecting D.&R.G.W. advising that the last train would leave Mack the morning of May 16th and that, therefore, any shipments enroute to the Uintah be moved promptly so they could be delivered before the last train was operated. People who had never before witnessed the glories of Baxter Pass purchased tickets for the final trip.[17]

Mallet No. 50 pulled that last train leaving Mack on schedule at 8:10 a.m. Tuesday, May 16, 1939, with a consist of one box car, two flats and the usual combination car. Some twenty persons were aboard, mainly those interested in railroading or in making the last trip over the scenic line. At Wendella, on the western side of Baxter Pass, water cars were filled and taken to Dragon and Watson to furnish the last water supply for those two dying towns. At Watson, the end of the line, there was a carload of furniture consigned to Grand Junction. The few remaining residents of Watson planned to be gone within a few days. The telegraph operator stepped onto the rear platform as the train pulled out, his telegraph key in hand and his office closed. Baggage was taken aboard at stations along the line, and passengers climbed on, leaving behind them towns boarded up and empty. Aboard the train there was a funeral-like atmosphere.[18]

Crew members for the last run, all veterans on the Uintah, were Roy Eno, engineer; George Lohman, fireman; and John Beaslin, conductor. Superintendent E. V. Earp, who had first hired on in the shops at Atchee nearly 27 years earlier, also made the last trip. The reporter for the Grand Junction *Daily Sentinel*, making his first trip over the Uintah aboard the last train, noted that Vic Earp did much toward making the run "an interesting and delightful one so far as the passengers were concerned."[19]

Thus the Uintah Railway made its exit from the ranks of companies in the business of providing transportation for the world's people and commodities. Indeed, the Uintah transported very little of anything during 1939. Graphic proof of this is provided by the financial statement which formed a part of the final annual report of The Uintah Railway Company to the Public Utilities Commission of the State of Colorado, covering the 1939 period ended May 17, 1939. Observe the excess of red ink:

Railway operating revenues	$ 4,686
Railway operating expenses	37,667
Net revenue	$32,981 (in red)
Railway tax accruals	8,173
Railway operating income	$41,154 (in red)
Other income:	
Miscellaneous rent income	$ 364
Interest	1
Total, other income	365
Total income	$40,789 (in red)
Interest on funded debt	2.295
Interest on unfunded debt	12
Total fixed charges	2,307
Income after fixed charges	$43,096 (in red)

In these last few months of its operation the Uintah Railway achieved the rather fantastic figure of 803.84 per cent as its operating ratio (the ratio of operating expenses to operating revenues). Certainly far from profitable! The few employees who remained with the Uintah these last months spent their days waiting for the end, winding up the affairs of the company and looking for new jobs for themselves.

The next to the last scheduled weekly train out of Mack, on May 9, 1939, was a long one of fifteen cars behind 2-6-6-2T No. 50. Colorado rail photographer Otto Perry recorded its passage in the rugged canyon north of Cooley that day. Articulated No. 50 had received new flues and heavy repairs in April of 1938 and was in good condition. In September, 1938, Vice-President and General Manager Robert Rice of the Colorado & Southern had suggested to his motive-power men that they investigate the purchase of one or both of the Uintah Mallets for use on their nar-row-gauge Clear Creek District. The Uintah offered both for sale at $28,750 each, F.O.B. Mack. The C.&S. found, though, that it would have to spend $12,150 to reinforce bridges and another $60,000 to recondition the track on its Clear Creek line before the heavy Mallets could be used; and service on that line was down to twice-a-week, and someone estimated that one of the Mallets would cost nearly as much to operate as two of the existing Consolidations, so the matter was dropped. *(Top: Otto C. Perry; bottom: Everett L. DeGolyer, Jr.)*

Mikado No. 40 (above) noses an empty water car back toward Atchee to get more domestic water for Mack in August of 1939, some three months after the last scheduled train ran. The flats behind the Mike will be used to bring back scrap rail. The location is in the canyon south of Carbonera. During that same week, Shay No. 7 (below) spots a car of coal on the trestle at Atchee for use in fueling the wrecking trains. Still less than six years old, she would soon be scrapped, too. (Both: Everett L. DeGolyer, Jr. photos)

Someone added the Baxter Pass sign to the top of a load of scrap rail and here it sits in Mack — a definite comedown! Also at Mack, the remains of Mikado No. 30 (below) sit on another flat car. She had been cut up at Dragon and her pieces hauled back over the mountain when this picture was snapped on November 1, 1939. Below, the No. 50 has just been loaded on a heavy-duty Erie flat and is ready for the trip to Oregon and the Sumpter Valley Railway. (Top: J. L. Booth Collection; middle: Roy F. Blackburn; bottom: Paul Garde Collection)

The last rail to be taken up was that in the yards at Mack (above). There's not much left except two pair of trucks, a few other pieces of scrap, and old crossties. Within four years, though, gilsonite was again rolling over parts of the former Uintah Railway line. Below, on a planked-over railway trestle north of Dragon are three of Charles J. Neal's trucks hauling the hydrocarbon from his operation at the reopened Dragon Mine. (*Above: J. L. Booth Collection; below: Charles J. Neal photo*)

The entire railway, including locomotives, rolling stock, shop equipment, electric plant and other equipment, was offered for sale as scrap, and bids from a number of scrap dealers were opened on Monday, June 12, in the company offices at Mack. The successful bidders, as reported by the Grand Junction *Daily Sentinel*, were Meyer Goodstein and Arthur T. Herr of Denver. They operated under the name "The G. & H. Supply Co.," which was a subsidiary of A. T. Herr Supply Co. and American Iron & Metal Co. of Denver. The conclusion of the sale of the railway property, with the exception of real estate holdings, was announced by Acting General Manager J. I. McClain (incorrectly referred to as superintendent by the *Daily Sentinel*) at the office at Mack on the afternoon of June 26. McClain had been in Denver for a number of days in connection with the sale of the property. Officially, the sale had taken place on June 23rd. The *Daily Sentinel* noted that, at the request of the purchasers, the consideration in the transaction was not announced. Dismantling operations were the responsibility of the purchasers, and were expected to begin "in the very near future."[20]

On August 1st the *Sentinel* revealed that John W. Moore of Price, Utah, had recently been awarded the contract for the dismantling of the railway, and that he was expected to arrive in Mack that same week to organize a wrecking crew. Moore had successfully bid on Herr and Goodstein's request for a wrecking contractor. By September 10th the *Sentinel* reported that dismantling was progressing nicely. A force of 25 men including two engine and train crews, was busy at the work. They had already removed the branch lines near Watson and were tearing up the main line, from the Watson end, at the rate of about a half mile a day. It was hoped they would reach Baxter Pass before winter weather halted operations. Then the work on the eastern slope could proceed during the winter months. Daily shipments of salvaged material were being made to Mack, and from there the steel was being transshipped to the Colorado Fuel & Iron mills at Minnequa, near Pueblo, Colorado. None of the motive power or rolling stock had then been disposed of, since they were needed in the wrecking operation.[21]

As the rails were being taken up, the grade below Atchee was the scene of one last runaway. Almost child's play when compared with the "Big Hill," the 2.9 per cent out of Atchee towards Carbonera and Mack was still nothing to be sneezed at. Fortunately, though, this last wreck had more of a humorous quality about it than anything else, as related by the following account in the Grand Junction paper:[22]

FREIGHT CARS RUN WILD; NOW KINDLING WOOD
(Special to The Sentinel.)

———

ATCHEE, Sept. 20 — The Uintah Railroad, in the process of dismantling its line, won't have to worry about junking 23 cars. They junked themselves Tuesday afternoon.

Ten flat cars, 11 stock cars, a car loaded with coal and a freight caboose were standing peacefully in the Uintah yards at Atchee. Suddenly, they started to roll down the grade toward Mack.

No one was close enough at the time to stop them, and they bid a rushing farewell to Atchee and tore wildly down the canyon toward Mack. But they didn't get far.

One car on the tail end decided it had gone far enough and left the rails a short distance out of town. The others took a suicidal plunge on a curve three miles south of Atchee.

When the dust settled, all that was left was kindling wood, railroad wheels, trucks and other metal parts, and the coal that took the unsupervised ride.

Part of the wreckage was piled up in a heap, and the other was scattered in a wide radius. The door of the caboose flew 50 feet from the main pile and landed without even cracking the glass in it.

The reason for the A.W.O.L. trip of the cars that ended in the junk heap was not known today.

While the salvagers were systematically stripping the rail from the ridges and canyons of the Book Cliffs, The Uintah Railway Company quietly brought its corporate existence to an end. A brief article in Denver's *Rocky Mountain News* on November 1, 1939, served as the obituary, informing the public that the company had filed a notice of dissolution the previous day with Colorado Secretary of State George E. Saunders. Stockholders had approved the dissolution and debts had been paid, according to this notice. Not mentioned was the

The Sumpter Valley got the two Uintah Mallets for a bargain price of $20,000 F.O.B. Mack, Colorado, under a sales contract from American Iron & Metal Co. of Denver dated November 16, 1939. But by the time they had them running the two engines had cost the S.V. a total of $38,547.88. Freight on the locomotives was $2,561.96, and other material furnished from the Uintah came to $5,096.98. Tenders from two Sumpter Valley Mikes had an estimated value of $2,000.00. The shop labor, overhaul and conversion, and store and machine shop expenses totaled $8,298.54. The remainder of $590.40 was for miscellaneous freight, express and postage, unloading, and casualty insurance. Here they are in service, both photographed at Whitney, Oregon, on the same day — September 27, 1940. No. 250 still was wearing her side tanks and her old number on the headlight. Both were removed soon afterward. (*Both photos: Henry R. Griffiths, Jr.*)

rather pertinent fact that 22,495 shares of capital stock out of a total issue of 22,500 shares were owned by the Barber Asphalt Corporation — the remaining five shares were voting shares held by each of the five directors of the railway, all of whom were also officers of the parent corporation. The narrow gauge had served the purpose for which it was built some three and a half decades earlier.

By the middle of February, 1940, all of the rail had been taken up except for that in the yards at Mack. More than 10,000 tons of scrap steel had been shipped to Pueblo to be consumed by C.F.&I.'s furnaces. The two articulateds, both less than 14 years distant from Baldwin's erecting floor, were sold to the Sumpter Valley Railway and had been shipped, one at a time aboard the same Erie depressed-center flat car, to Baker, Oregon. Like other Uintah towns, much of Mack, previously owned by the railway, had been sold and moved. Several homes were relocated in Grand Junction.[23]

Thus the little railroad died, and the scrap merchants picked its bones clean. The right of way was converted into a trucking road during the summer and fall of 1943, through the cooperation of the U. S. Bureau of Mines, the Grazing Service, the Public Roads Department and the War Production Board.[24] Today, driving along that old grade past the remnants of Carbonera and Atchee, up the seven and a half per cent of Baxter Pass, around Lone Tree Curve high up on the side of the mountain, memories of the old Uintah Railway return. The Shays and "Mallets" may work the hill no more, but they live on in the memories of the men who ran them, and in the thoughts of those fortunate enough to have stood at the summit of Baxter Pass admiring the men who built and operated a railroad such as the Uintah.

This was all that remained of Atchee twenty years afterward — the concrete shell of the machine shop, some pieces of rotting wood and bridge 28-A. Up the valley, though, the 7.5 per cent grade still climbs up around Moro Castle Curve and the distant mountainside to reach Baxter Pass. *(James Ozment photo)*

193

The Mallets finally reached the end of their line. No. 251 had been supplying parts to keep her sister running, but by March of 1965 they were both out of service and derelict at Escuintla. In Colorado, the old Uintah Railway office building at Mack burned down on the afternoon of April 1, 1960. It had been in use as a rock shop, as well as for storage of household goods, and the losses were estimated to be more than $50,000. There was no insurance. The fire started in the roof, apparently from a defective flue. *(Top: Robert W. Richardson photo, Colorado Railroad Museum Collection; bottom: James Ozment photo)*

After their service in Oregon the two articulateds, rather famous by this time, went south to Guatemala and a new career on the International Railways of Central America. At first they were assigned to Palín Hill — sixteen miles of 3.0 to 3.7 per cent grade winding up the slopes of the Volcán Agua from Escuintla to the central plateau at Palín — but they proved rather slippery there. They had been more sure-footed before they lost their side tanks. Here No. 250 (opposite page) works a northbound Mazatenango-to-Escuintla local freight across the Rio Coyolate bridge in March, 1962, after being reassigned to that run. *(Frank Barry photo)*

By 1965 the old grade heading for the Book Cliffs (above) was becoming almost in-
distinguishable. Here it is not far from the location of the siding called Sprague. At
the ghost town of Atchee (below) the trestle over West Salt Wash seemed to be in
reasonably good shape when photographed in 1960. By 1965 it had developed a definite sag in the middle and was closed to vehicle traffic. *(Photo above by the author;
below: James Ozment)*

The faded remains of Shale (left) in 1960. Below, we see that the many years of Colorado sun and rain had not been particularly kind to business car B-8, as this 1957 photo shows. In 1959 this car body was purchased for $800 by the Colorado Railroad Museum and hauled over from Grand Junction to Golden. There it was restored and put on display, equipped with trucks from R.G.S. coach No. 260 bought at a sheriff's sale at Ouray in 1962. *(Left: James Ozment; below: Del H. Gerbaz)*

Pictured above is the catalytic reformer section of American Gilsonite Company's refinery at Gilsonite, Colorado, in 1957 when the refinery and pipeline were new. (*Courtesy of American Gilsonite Company*)

Chapter Ten

Gilsonite Up To Date

Although the gilsonite railroad was gone, the gilsonite industry was far from dead. In fact, it had never looked more alive. The year 1946 brought the establishment of the American Gilsonite Company, which acquired the properties and operations of the Gilson Asphaltum Company. Jointly owned by Barber Oil Corporation and Standard Oil Company of California, it had sufficient financial backing to undertake a major research program to investigate the profitable commercial production of increasing numbers of petroleum products from gilsonite. This new organization would bring about a revolution in the industry within the next eleven years.

During the years following 1946 a million dollars went into laboratory research, operation of a pilot production plant and into product testing. Research facilities of Standard Oil of California, the University of Utah and other institutions and American Gilsonite's own newly built laboratory were used during this time. The pilot plant was built near the mines at Bonanza to process 100 tons of gilsonite daily. The plant produced high-octane gasoline, which was tested under laboratory and highway conditions, and a metallurgical coke, which was sent to various aluminum refineries for testing. The results of the product tests were excellent, and it was evident that the investment of time and money had paid off.

Happy with the success of this pilot program, American Gilsonite went ahead with a new method of mining the gilsonite, and constructed a pipeline to transport the mineral and a refinery

to process it. The engineering "firsts" were many, and the operation differed considerably from the gilsonite industry of the early years.

Hydraulic mining was begun in 1957 and is constantly being improved. Today's modern method involves the sinking of a shaft from the surface, usually to a depth of more than 850 feet. Then a drift, or tunnel, is driven from the side of the shaft into the gilsonite vein, using modern tunnel boring equipment. Afterward a rotary drill on the surface sinks a six-inch hole down through the vein to tunnel level. A special bit shooting powerful high-pressure jets of water is installed on a rotary drill, and it rotates and cuts the gilsonite to the width of the vein and to a distance of eight to twelve feet laterally on each side of the drill hole. As the cutting proceeds, the bit is moved slowly upward. The gilsonite falls to the tunnel level and is washed to a sump at the bottom of the shaft, where it is pumped to the surface by special pumps. Using this method, most of the work is done on the surface with few men underground.

The material mined using this effective method is almost pure gilsonite, but minor amounts of sand and rock are loosened in the cutting operation and must be removed. To do this, as the mixture of water and gilsonite flows along the tunnel bottom to the sump it is routed over riffles or sand dams, where the sand and rocks, being heavier than the gilsonite, settle out.

When it reaches the surface, the gilsonite is routed to the slurry preparation plant. Here it is

Above, the pipeline carrying the gilsonite slurry spans the White River near Bonanza, Utah, on the 700-foot long suspension bridge in the distance. About a mile away a similar 625-foot bridge carries the line over Evacuation Creek Canyon. Below is a view of the refinery where coke and gasoline are made from the gilsonite. Not far away, across the Colorado River in the background, is Colorado National Monument. *(Both photos: American Gilsonite Company)*

crushed to the proper size and mixed with water in the proportion necessary for transportation through a pipeline. The slurry then goes to holding tanks and is later pumped into the pipeline which carries it to the refinery 72 miles away, near Grand Junction. Another function of the slurry preparation plant is to cleanse the surplus water pumped up from the mine. When this has been done the water is recirculated to the mine and is used to carry more gilsonite to the surface.

Some gilsonite is routed from the slurry preparation plant to a storage stockpile room with more than 2,000 tons capacity. This ore is used to feed the pipeline when mining is shut down for maintenance or during periods when the mine cannot meet its scheduled output. This supply is also used to produce several packaged gilsonite products. Although much of the gilsonite goes to feed the pipeline, a substantial tonnage is diverted at Bonanza to prepare these products for direct sale. After it is dried, crushed and blended, as required, this gilsonite is packaged in multi-wall paper bags for delivery in trucks to customers, or it is hauled in bulk by truck to the rail connection at Craig, Colorado. The company maintains a second packaging and shipping terminal at Craig where various of the gilsonite products are bagged and shipped via rail or truck to customers. European customers are supplied from stocks maintained at a warehouse in Antwerp, Belgium, as well as by direct shipments.

As the Uintah Railway had replaced horse-drawn wagons for hauling gilsonite over a half-century earlier, the pipeline replaced the motor trucks in 1957. The reason was essentially the same: the earlier transportation could not economically move the gilsonite in the quantities required. But a pipeline? No one had ever used a pipeline to transport a *solid* material over long distances before. And these distances were tough — 72 miles of desert and mountains, an 8,500-foot mountain pass, subzero winter temperatures, and the necessity of moving over 1,000 tons of gilsonite daily, and doing it reliably and at low cost. The "solids pipeline" presented many new problems: Would the gilsonite settle out and gradually plug the line? Would it slide down to low places if the line were shut down, and thus plug it? The answers to these and other operating questions

had to be found. Tests sponsored at the Colorado School of Mines Research Foundation and by the Wilson-Snyder Manufacturing Company at Braddock, Pennsylvania, confirmed earlier evaluations that the idea was feasible. And so the pipeline was built. Much of its route is on the roadbed of the old Uintah Railway.

Safeguards against plugging of the line were carefully provided. The pipeline is designed for continuous flow and is shut down only after all slurry is flushed out. Three electric-driven slurry pumps are situated at the Bonanza pump station with two being used in normal operation to provide the 2,300 pounds per square inch pressure necessary. One pump unit remains as a spare. In the event of a power failure a diesel-driven pump is automatically cut into the line to flush it with water. Baxter Pass, long an obstacle to moving gilsonite, provides another safeguard. A reservoir at the Pass can flush the line by gravity in both directions if needed. Further protection is provided by a high pressure pump at the refinery which can backflush the line. Precautionary measures were wise, but operating experience has demonstrated that so long as adequate velocities are maintained through the pipeline there is no settling of gilsonite particles inside the pipe.

At any time when the pipeline is in operation, there are about 1,500 tons of gilsonite in the line. This material moves in the pipe with 240,000 gallons of water at a speed of about three miles per hour and takes about 24 hours after leaving the mines to reach the refinery.

Like the pipeline, the refinery also was a first — the first privately financed processing plant in the United States to produce petroleum products from a solid raw material. Located at Gilsonite, Colorado, about twelve miles west of Grand Junction on U. S. Highway 50 and the Denver & Rio Grande Western, the refinery manufactures electrode grade coke and conventional petroleum products such as gasoline, special industrial fuels and road oils. It is a combination of several plants, each with complex equipment and processes.

First is the filter-flotation plant. The gilsonite slurry upon reaching the refinery is fed from the pipeline into a 5,000 barrel tank and then routed over screens which separate and wash the coarse particles of gilsonite. These coarse particles are

The coking tanks and furnaces at the refinery are shown at the left. They are also visible just above the center in the aerial photo below. The towers are sixteen stories high and house high-pressure hoses to cut the coke out from the tanks below when they are full. In the lower part of the aerial view are the kiln and the storage bin from which the calcined coke is loaded into railroad cars. Marketed as Gilsocarbon, its major uses are in the electrolytic reduction of aluminum and the alloying of steel. (*Both photos: American Gilsonite Company*)

then sent through a centrifuge which almost completely removes the water. The fine particles are routed through a two-stage flotation plant to remove any remaining quantity of sand and silt. In the flotation process a reagent is added which causes small air bubbles to attach themselves to the gilsonite but not to the sand particles. The gilsonite floats as a thick froth which is raked from the top of the flotation cells while the sand settles and leaves through the bottom of the cells with relatively little loss of gilsonite. The froth is then filtered with a conventional vacuum filter.

The filter cake from the filter and the coarse particles from the centrifuge are then routed by conveyor belts either to the melt plant as feed for the refinery or to a stockpile adjacent to the filter plant. The refinery can be fed from the stockpile by means of self-propelled front-end loaders and automatically controlled conveyor belts.

Next comes the melt plant. There the damp gilsonite is fed into the top of an agitated hot tank where it is mixed with hot oil recycled back from the coker plant. This oil at a temperature of about 450°F. melts the gilsonite and drives off the remaining water in the form of steam. This steam and the oils carried with it are condensed and recovered in an adjacent processing unit. The 1,000 tons per day feed rate of the refinery is equivalent to 5,600 barrels per day of liquid crude oil.

Part of the mixture of melted gilsonite and recycle oil is used to make road paving products. The remainder is fed to the next process, the delayed coker plant. This plant performs the first major step in processing. It generates the raw feed stocks for other sections of the refinery where, through reprocessing and purification, desired product specifications are achieved.

The first step in the coking process consists of the formation of "green" coke in two large vertical drums. The feed enroute to these drums is heated to 900°F. at which temperature it is largely a vapor. This vapor enters one of the two drums at the bottom. The heavier components stay behind to form coke which grows in successive layers from the bottom upward. The capacity of each drum is about 475 tons of green coke — one day's production. When the drum is almost full, the feed is switched to the other and removal of the coke from the first drum is begun. This switching is usually done on a 24-hour cycle.

After the coke in the drum has been cooled by flooding with water, it is removed by cutting with a water jet, very similar to the method used in the mines. The water jet apparatus is mounted in derricks on top of the drums. The tops of the derricks are 200 feet above ground level. The mixture of water and coke flows through the bottom opening of the drum into a crushing mechanism which breaks the larger lumps of coke into pieces about three inches in size. These pieces, plus fine material and water, fall into a sluice and then go to an especially designed pump which moves them to a settling tank. The larger pieces of coke settle to the bottom of the tank and the fine material and water overflow the top lip of the tank to a clarifier. When the coke has been removed from the drum, the settling tank is drained and the coke is moved by a conveyor to coke storage. Meanwhile the clarifier has separated the fines from the water and the water is then re-used.

The next step for the coke is the calciner-boiler plant. The green coke is fed from a large storage silo to a kiln, which is a sloping, rotating, brick-lined cylinder in which the coke is heated to about 2400°F. In this process, known as calcining, the water and heavy oil present in the green coke are vaporized and the final product, "calcined coke," is formed. It is cooled by a water spray, screened and stored in a large bin over the railroad siding serving the plant. From there it is loaded by gravity into covered hopper cars for shipment.

While all this has been going on, the vapors leaving the top of the drum at the coker plant have been routed to the fractionating column, where the various liquid products and oils are separated by their boiling point ranges. Some of these products are gases at ordinary temperatures and pressures. These gases contain liquids which are recovered in the gas recovery section of the coker. The lightest liquid recovered is naphtha, the feed stock for gasoline production. The next lightest is the feed stock for industrial fuel oils. Heavier oils are withdrawn for refinery fuel, blending stocks for road oils and asphalts, or they are recycled to the melt plant.

The naphtha is fed to the catalytic reformer, called the "cat reformer," and through its feed preparation section, where the portion that is too heavy for gasoline production is removed and recycled back to the coker. A light portion which does not require the complicated processing of the cat reformer is also separated and sent through a treating section directly to tankage where it is held for gasoline blending. The major portion of the naphtha is processed through the remaining two stages of the plant.

The first stage is a process known as hydrogenation which removes contaminants by the use of hydrogen at high temperature and pressure in the presence of a catalyst. This purified product is then processed through the platformer section, where characteristics important in gasoline are improved. The final product, called "platformate," is routed to the tank field where it is blended with the light fraction mentioned above to make gasoline.

The final step in gasoline manufacture is the addition of antiknock and other compounds to give the finished product superior performance. A dye is also added to distinguish easily between the two grades of gasoline — premium and regular. Both grades are shipped to customers in the western Colorado area. Prior to the establishment of American Gilsonite Company's refinery, the nearest oil refinery was about 300 miles distant, and the need for a closer source of gasoline for the area was a key point in the decision to locate the refinery near Grand Junction.

Besides the gasoline, several grades of road oils and paving asphalts are produced. These oils are accumulated in tanks in the tank field and are blended in the correct proportions by a special proportional blender directly into tank trucks. Like most road paving work, this is a seasonal operation — mainly between April and October.

Finally, specialty products and industrial fuel oils complete the spectrum of products from the refinery. These are produced to meet customer requirements, by methods including acid and caustic treatment, redistillation, and stripping to remove volatile fractions.

The gilsonite diverted at the mines for direct sale to customers has already been mentioned. Among the products marketed by American Gilsonite Co. are Gilsulate®, Gilso-Gard® and Gilso-Therm® — especially ground and graded gilsonites used for insulation and corrosion protection of buried piping in the temperature ranges of below 60°F. to 520°F.; Gilsabind® — an asphalt pavement sealer which binds, weatherproofs, rejuvenates and beautifies paved surfaces; and an ingot mold coating which prevents steel ingots from sticking to their molds after pouring. Other uses for gilsonite, including that mined by the handful of other companies in the business, are many and varied. A partial list of the products manufactured with this versatile material would include: asphalt floor tile, coated building papers, roofing materials, felt-base floor covering, sound-proofing and insulating compounds for the automotive industry, electrical insulating varnish, acid and alkali resisting paints and other types of protective coatings, battery boxes, brake and clutch linings, tubing, rotogravure and printing inks, rope and cable lubricants, mineral wool binder, military flares, fingerprint powders and oil well cement and drilling muds.

All in all it's quite an industry these days. The annual gilsonite production figures are on the order of ten times what they were during the years that the versatile hydrocarbon was hauled over the narrow-gauge rails of the Uintah Railway. The industry has come a long way since the first few sacks of ore were brought out of the Basin in horse-drawn wagons.

Notes

CHAPTER ONE
Gilsonite — The Reason for a Railroad

1. Daughters of the Utah Pioneers of Uintah County, Utah, *Builders of Uintah; A Centennial History of Uintah County, 1872 to 1947* (Springville, Utah: Art City Publishing Co., 1947), p. 199.
2. G. E. Untermann and B. R. Untermann, "Dinosaur Country," *Utah Historical Quarterly,* 26 (July, 1958), p. 256.
3. John B. Brebner, *The Explorers of North America, 1492-1806* (Garden City, N.Y.; Doubleday Anchor Books, 1955), pp. 355-57.
4. *The Vernal Express,* July 6, 1928, p. 1.
5. *Ibid.,* April 16, 1926, p. 1.
6. *Ibid.,* April 16, 1926, p. 1; and January 15, 1931, p. 2.
7. Herbert Abraham, *Asphalts and Allied Substances* (6th ed.; Princeton, N.J.: Van Nostrand, 1960), I, pp. 224, 228, 229.
8. *Ibid.,* p. 57.
9. *Ibid.,* p. 220.
10. American Gilsonite Company, *Gilsonite Guidebook* (Salt Lake City: By the author, 1963), pp. 17-20.
11. Herbert F. Kretchman, *The Story of Gilsonite* (Salt Lake City: American Gilsonite Co., 1957).
12. Statement by Charles Hoel, personal interview by Newell C. Remington, July, 1952, as cited by Remington, *A History of the Gilsonite Industry* (lithographed Master's thesis; Salt Lake City: Dept. of History, University of Utah, 1959), p. 31. Remington notes that Hoel was an intimate acquaintance of Kelly, Blankenship, Dodds and others of the agency, and that this incident of the agency is reported by another source to have occurred in 1876. He believes, however, that 1868 or 1869 is the most realistic date.
13. *Ibid.,* p. 35.
14. F. M. Endlich, "Report of F. M. Endlich, S.N.D., Geologist of the White River Division," *United States Geological and Geographical Survey of the Territories, 10th Annual Report (Hayden),* (Washington: Government Printing office, 1878), pp. 85-86, as cited by Remington, *op. cit.,* p. 33.
15. A. C. Peale, "Report of A. C. Peale, M.D., Geologist of the Grand River District, 1876," *United States Geological and Geographical Survey of the Territories, 10th Annual Report (Hayden),* (Washington: Government Printing Office, 1878), p. 175, as cited by Remington, *op. cit.,* pp. 33-34.
16. W. P. Blake, "Uintahite — A New Variety of Asphaltum from the Uintah Mountains, Utah." *The Engineering and Mining Journal,* XL, No. 26 (December 26, 1885), p. 431.
17. See, for example, Newton I. Sax, *Dangerous Properties of Industrial Materials* (2d ed.; New York: Reinhold, 1963), p. 857.
18. Remington, *op. cit.* p. 36.
19. Harold A. Bezzant, "The Chromatographic Separation of Gilsonite," (unpublished Master's thesis, Brigham Young University, Provo, 1949), p. 3, as cited by Remington, *op. cit.,* pp. 37-38.
20. "The Gilson Hydraulic Concentrator," *Salt Lake Mining Review,* II, No. 5 (June 15, 1900), p. 10, as cited by Remington, *op. cit.,* p. 37.
21. Kretchman, *op. cit.,* p. 27.
22. E. W. Harmer, "Gilsonite Mining in Utah Expands," *The Mining Journal* (Arizona), XXIII, No. 7, (August 30, 1939), p. 6, as cited by Remington, *op. cit.,* p. 38.
23. U.S. Patents 361347 of April 19, 1887 to C. T. Crowell, 361759 of April 26, 1887 to S. H. Gilson, 362076 of May 3, 1887 to S. H. Gilson, and 415864 of November 26, 1889 to S. H. Gilson, as cited by Abraham, *op. cit.,* p. 319.
24. Harmer, *loc. cit.*

25. Statement by Charles Hoel, personal interview by Remington, July, 1952, as cited by Remington, *op. cit.*, p. 42.

26. Letter from Seaboldt to A. L. Crawford, May 20, 1946, as cited by Remington, *op. cit.*, p. 44.

27. *Ibid.*

28. *Ibid.*, p. 45.

29. "Uintah County," *The Engineering and Mining Journal*, XLVII, No. 2 (January 12, 1889), p. 52, as cited by Remington, *op. cit.*, p. 47.

30. Statement by Charles Hoel, interview cited by Remington, *op. cit.*, p. 39. "Hoel said that C. O. Baxter, who attended the meeting, reported this incident to him personally."

31. The $150,000 price is from a letter by Bert Seaboldt to A. L. Crawford, May 31, 1946, while *The Vernal Express* of May 6, 1897, p. 1, reported a sale price of $185,000. Both cited by Remington, *op. cit.*, p. 48.

32. Letter from Seaboldt to A. L. Crawford, Remington, *loc. cit.*

33. Herbert Tyzack, "Hydro-Carbons of Uintah County," *Salt Lake Mining Review*, II, No. 19, (January 15, 1901), p. 11, as cited by Remington, *op. cit.*, pp. 56-57.

34. Statement by Charles Hoel, interview cited by Remington, *op. cit.*, p. 50.

CHAPTER II
The Coming of the Railway

1. U.S. Interstate Commerce Commission, *Reports*, Vol. 13, pp. 196-97.

2. "Amzi Lorenzo Barber," *Dictionary of American Biography*, I (New York: Scribner, 1928), pp. 586-87.

3. John Moody, *Moody's Industrials*, 1928, pp. 1281-82, as cited by Remintgon, *op. cit.*, p. 130.

4. Remington, *op. cit.*, pp. 135-36.

5. *The Vernal Express*, December 20, 1907, p. 6.

6. U.S. Interstate Commerce Commission, *op. cit.*, p. 198.

7. *Ibid.*

8. Remington, *op. cit.*, pp. 133-34.

9. Charles O. Baxter and others, "Articles of Incorporation of The Uintah Railway Company: Filed in the office of the Secretary of State, of the State of Colorado, on the 4th day of Nov., A.D. 1903 . . ." (in the files of the Colorado State Archives), p. 3.

10. *The Vernal Express*, January 9, 1896, p. 2.

11. U.S. Interstate Commerce Commission, *op. cit.*, p. 199.

12. Linwood W. Moody, "The Big Hill," *Railroad Magazine*, 28, No. 2 (July, 1940) pp. 74-75.

13. As quoted in *The Vernal Express*, February 12, 1909, p. 4.

14. Denver & Rio Grande Western R.R., "Condensed Profile of the D. & R.G.W.R.R. System" (Office of Chief Engineer, Denver, Jan. 1, 1962), p. 11.

15. Randolph L. Kulp (ed.), *History of Mack Rail Motor Cars and Locomotives* (Allentown, Pa.: Lehigh Valley Chapter, National Railway Historical Society, Inc., 1959), pp. 4-5.

16. U.S. Interstate Commerce Commission, *Reports*, Vol. 141, p. 282.

17. Colorado Writers' Project, "The Names of Colorado Towns," *The Colorado Magazine*, XVII (January, 1940), pp. 28-36.

18. The Uintah Railway Company, *The Uintah Railway* (Mack, Colo.: By the author, printed by The Holmes Press, Philadelphia, [no date, probably 1905]), pp. 4-5.

19. *The Vernal Express*, October 14, 1927, p. 1.

20. Daughters of the Utah Pioneers of Uintah County, Utah, *op. cit.*, p. 152.

CHAPTER III
Stage Road Operations and Storms on the Pass

1. Baxter, *loc. cit.*

2. The Uintah Railway Company, "Certificate of Amendments of Articles of Incorporation: Filed in the office of the Secretary of State, of the State of Colorado, on the 24th day of September, A.D. 1904 . . ." (in the files of the Colorado State Archives), pp. 4-5.

3. Remington, *op. cit.*, pp. 261-62.

4. U.S. Commissioner of Indian Affairs, "Report of the Commissioner of Indian Affairs, 1905," in *Annual Report of the Secretary of Interior; 1905* (Washington: U.S. Government Printing Office, 1906), p. 95.

5. *The Vernal Express*, December 29, 1906, p. 3.

6. "Uintah Toll Road Company," Corporation Files, Office of Utah Secretary of State, as cited by Remington, *op. cit.*, p. 262.

7. See, for instance, *The Vernal Express*, February 3, 1906, p. 5.

8. *Ibid.*, January 20, 1906, p. 2.

9. *Ibid.*, February 10, 1906, p. 2.

10. *Ibid.*, March 17, 1906, p. 3.

11. *Ibid.*, March 24, 1906, p. 3.

12. *Ibid.*, April 14, 1906, p. 1.

13. *Ibid.*, p. 2.

14. *Ibid.*, May 12, 1906, p. 2.

15. *Ibid.*, May 26, 1906, p. 3.

16. *Ibid.*, July 14, 1906, p. 2.

17. *Ibid.*, November 3, 1906, p. 2.

18. General Asphalt Company, *Annual Report to the Stockholders of the General Asphalt Company for the fiscal year ending April 30, 1909* (and for following years, through 1917; Philadelphia: By the author, 1910-18).
19. *The Vernal Express*, January 12, 1907, p. 1.
20. *Ibid.*, January 26, 1907, p. 1.
21. *Ibid.*, October 30, 1908, p. 5.
22. *Ibid.*, December 18, 1908, p. 1.
23. *Ibid.*, p. 5.
24. *Ibid.*, January 8, 1909, p. 5.
25. *Ibid.*, January 15, 1909, p. 1.
26. *Ibid.*, January 29, 1909, p. 6.
27. *Ibid.*, February 12, 1909, p. 1.
28. Statement by William Cook, personal interview by Newell C. Remington, as cited by Remington, *op. cit.*, p. 257.
29. *The Vernal Express*, February 26, 1909, p. 5.
30. *Ibid.*, March 5, 1909, p. 4.
31. *Ibid.*, March 12, 1909, p. 4.
32. *Ibid.*, April 2, 1909, p. 5.
33. *Ibid.*, July 2, 1909, p. 2, and July 9, 1909, p.6.

CHAPTER IV
High Freight Rates and the First Complaints

1. *The Vernal Express*, April 27, 1907, p. 2.
2. *Ibid.*, November 15, 1907, p. 1.
3. U.S. Interstate Commerce Commission, *Reports*, Vol. 13, p. 205.
4. *Ibid.*, p. 207.
5. *Ibid.*, p. 209.
6. *Ibid.*, p. 210.
7. *Ibid.*, p. 211.
8. *The Vernal Express*, February 14, 1908, p. 4.
9. *Ibid.*
10. *Ibid.*, April 16, 1909, p. 1.
11. *Ibid.*, November 11, 1910, p. 8.
12. *Ibid.*, March 13, 1908, p. 1; February 21, 1908, p. 5; and September 27, 1907, p. 3.
13. *Ibid.*, November 8, 1928, p. 1.
14. *Ibid.*, August 20, 1909, p. 2.
15. *Ibid.*, August 27, 1909, p. 4.
16. *Ibid.*, January 7, 1910, p. 1.
17. *Grand Junction Daily Sentinel*, January 8, 1910, p. 6.
18. *The Vernal Express*, January 14, 1910, p. 3.
19. *Ibid.*, February 4, 1910, p. 2.
20. *Ibid.*, February 11, 1910, p. 6.
21. *Ibid.*, January 28, 1910, p. 1; February 11, 1910, p. 6; and March 4, 1910, p. 5.
22. *Ibid.*, February 18, 1910, p. 2.
23. *Ibid.*, April 15, 1910, p. 1.
24. *Ibid.*, May 13, 1910, p. 1.

25 *Ibid.*, June 24, 1910, p. 1.
26. *Ibid.*, May 20, 1910, p. 1; and May 27, 1910, p. 1.
27. *Ibid.*, June 10, 1910, p. 1.
28. *Ibid.*, August 12, 1910, p. 1; August 26, 1910, p. 1; and September 2, 1910, p. 1.
29. *Ibid.*, September 30, 1910, p. 1.
30. General Asphalt Company, *Annual Report to the Stockholders of the General Asphalt Company for the fiscal year ending April 30, 1911* (Philadelphia: By the author, 1911).
31. Frank R. Hollenback, *The Argentine Central; A Colorado narrow-gauge* (Denver: Sage Books, 1959).
32. *The Vernal Express*, November 18, 1910, p. 8; and November 25, 1910, p. 1.
33. *Ibid.*, November 25, 1910, p. 10; December 9, 1910, p. 14; and January 6, 1911, p. 8.

CHAPTER V
Extension to Watson and Rainbow

1. *The Vernal Express*, February 3, 1911, p. 1, (Quoting the *Denver News*, of unspecified date).
2. *The Vernal Express*, September 25, 1908, p. 1.
3. *The Vernal Express*, March 26, 1909, p. 6, (Quotting the *Grand Junction Daily Sentinel*, of unspecified date). In introducing this story, the editor of the *Express* observed that, "The season for building railroads on paper is just about over as the snow is fast disappearing from the ground." He went on to state that the *Sentinel* had "full charge of the construction gang" for this particular paper railroad!
4. *The Vernal Express*, February 17, 1911, p. 1.
5. *Ibid.*, April 14, 1911, p. 3.
6. *Ibid.*, July 21, 1911, pp. 1, 3.
7. *Ibid.*, August 18, 1911, p. 1.
8. Linwood W. Moody, "The Big Hill," *Railroad Magazine*, 28, No. 2 (July, 1940), p. 75.
9. "Uintah Ry.," *Poor's Manual of the Railroads of the United States*, 1906, 1907, and 1908 issues.
10. General Asphalt Company, *Annual Report to the Stockholders of the General Asphalt Company for the fiscal year ending April 30, 1913* (Philadelphia: By the author, 1913).
11. *The Vernal Express*, September 15, 1911, p. 1.
12. *Ibid.*, February 9, 1912, p. 1.
13. *The Daily News* (Grand Junction, Colo.), October 3, 1911, p. 3; and October 4, 1911, p. 8; and *The Vernal Express*, October 6, 1911, p. 1. The accounts of the wreck in these two papers differ in only one or two details, mainly the time at which the accident occurred. The *Express* says it was Saturday evening, September 30th, at 6 o'clock.
14. *The Daily News* (Grand Junction, Colo.), October 7, 1911, p. 3.

15. *The Vernal Express,* September 12, 1913, pp. 1, 4; and September 19, 1913, pp. 1, 3.
16. "Extension of Uintah Railway," *Rio Grande Service Gazette,* Vol. I, No. 10 (October, 1911), p. 3.
17. *The Vernal Express,* November 17, 1911, p. 1.
18. *Ibid.,* April 5, 1912, p. 1.
19. *Ibid.,* November 1, 1912, p. 1.
20. *Ibid.,* December 20, 1912, p. 2; and December 17, 1913, pp. 1, 3.
21. *Ibid.,* August 9, 1912, p. 2.
22. *Ibid.,* March 22, 1912, p. 3.
23. *Ibid.,* April 5, 1912, p. 1.
24. *Ibid.,* August 2, 1912, p. 1.
25. *Ibid.,* June 20, 1913, pp. 1-2.
26. *Ibid.,* December 10, 1915, p. 1.

CHAPTER VI
Bricks by Parcel Post

1. *The Vernal Express,* January 30, 1914, pp. 1, 3.
2. *Ibid.,* June 2, 1916, p. 1
3. *Ibid.,* January 30, 1914, pp. 1, 6.
4. *Ibid.,* May 7, 1915, p. 3.
5. *Ibid.,* June 2, 1916, p. 1.
6. *Ibid.,* January 30, 1914, pp. 1, 3.
7. *Ibid.,* May 12, 1916, p. 1; and August 25, 1916, p. 1.
8. *Ibid.,* July 14, 1916, p. 1.
9. *Ibid.,* November 17, 1916, p. 1.
10. *Ibid.,* November 23, 1917, p. 4.
11. Interview with E. Victor Earp, July 17, 1965. It should be noted that, since he was employed by the Uintah Ry. on September 13, 1912, Mr. Earp did not witness the blizzards and blockades of 1907 and 1909, each of which tied up the line for about a week.
12. *The Vernal Express,* January 30, 1914, p. 1.
13. *Grand Junction Daily Sentinel,* December 30, 1915, p. 1; and December 31, 1915, p. 1.
14. *The Vernal Express,* January 28, 1916, p. 3.
15. *Ibid.,* February 4, 1916, p. 1.
16. *Ibid.,* March 10, 1916, p. 1.
17. *Ibid.,* August 18, 1916, p. 1.
18. *Ibid.,* May 19, 1916, p. 1; and June 30, 1916, p. 1.
19. *Ibid.,* November 23, 1917, p. 8.
20. *Ibid.,* May 3, 1918, p. 10.
21. *Ibid.,* June 22, 1917, p. 3.
22. See, for example, *The Vernal Express,* June 7, 1912, p. 1; also *Engineering And Contracting,* October 30, 1912 issue.
23. *The Vernal Express,* September 14, 1917, p. 1.
24. *Ibid.,* September 21, 1917, p. 2.
25. *Ibid.,* November 9, 1917, p. 5.
26. *Ibid.,* June 28, 1918, p. 1.
27. *Ibid.,* November 9, 1917, p. 4.
28. Morris Cafky, *Rails Around Gold Hill* (Denver: Rocky Mountain Railroad Club, 1955), pp. 140-151, 414, 422, 450.
29. U.S. Interstate Commerce Commission. *Annual Report on the Statistics of Railways in the United States for the Year 1917* (Washington: U. S. Government Printing Office, 1918); also, *The Vernal Express,* July 26, 1918, p. 10.
30. U.S. Interstate Commerce Commission, *Annual Report on the Statistics of Railways in the United States for the Year 1918* (Washington: U. S. Government Printing Office, 1919); also, *The Vernal Express,* June 13, 1919, p. 1.
31. *Grand Junction Daily Sentinel,* September 9, 1918, p. 1; *The Vernal Express,* September 13, 1918, p. 1, and December 5, 1929, p. 2; and *Grand Junction Daily Sentinel,* October 8, 1939.
32. *Grand Junction Daily Sentinel,* September 10, 1918, p. 5.
33. *The Vernal Express,* December 6, 1918, p. 12; and December 20, 1918, p. 1.
34. *Ibid.,* March 28, 1919, p. 1.
35. *Ibid.,* April 18, 1919, p. 1; and April 25, 1919, p. 3.
36. *Ibid.,* September 19, 1919, p. 1.
37. *Ibid.,* January 3, 1919, p. 8.
38. "The Uintah Railway," *Baldwin Locomotives,* 2, No. 1 (July, 1923), p. 22.
39. The Uintah Railway Company, *Employees' Time Table No. 24; To take effect Sunday, July 21, 1929, at 12:01 a.m.*
40. *The Vernal Express,* September 5, 1919, p. 1.
41. *Ibid.,* September 12, 1919, p. 8.
42. *Grand Junction Daily Sentinel,* December 8, 1919.
43. Correspondence from V. L. "Roy" McCoy (via Roy Blackburn), July 18, 1969; and interview with Sam High at Glenn, California, July 5, 1969.

CHAPTER VII
Postwar Boom and Bust

1. *The Vernal Express,* March 12, 1920, p. 1.
2. *Ibid.,* August 13, 1920, p. 1.
3. U.S. Interstate Commerce Commission. *Annual Report on the Statistics of Railways in the United States for the Year [indicated]* (Washington: U.S. Government Printing Office, 1906- 1940). The table in the appendix of this volume on p. 211 shows more completely the Uintah Railway's annual revenues, expenses, and resulting income.
4. *The Vernal Express,* April 23, 1920, p. 4.
5. *Ibid.,* May 7, 1920, p. 4.
6. *Ibid.,* June 11, 1920, p. 1; and July 9, 1920, p. 8.
7. *Ibid.,* February 11, 1921, p. 1 and p. 2.
8. *Ibid.,* July 21, 1922, p. 1.
9. *Ibid.,* April 15, 1921, p. 1.
10. *Ibid.,* August 25, 1922, p. 2.
11. *Ibid.,* April 29, 1921, p. 8; and May 13, 1921, p. 1; and Denver & Rio Grande Railroad Co., Passenger Traffic Dept., *General Letter No. 98-1921* (Denver: June 18, 1921). The latter is in the collection of the Colorado Railroad Museum at Golden.

12. *The Vernal Express,* May 20, 1921, p. 8.
13. *Ibid.,* September 24, 1920, p. 1.
14. *Ibid.,* July 22, 1921, p. 1; and July 29, 1921, p. 1.
15. *Ibid.,* August 19, 1921, p. 1.
16. "The Uintah Railway," *The Railroad Red Book* (August, 1924), p. 763; and The Uintah Railway Company, *Employees' Time Table No. 24; To take effect Sunday, July 21, 1929,* at *12:01 a.m.*
17. *The Vernal Express,* November 23, 1923, p. 2. Also, *The Vernal Express* for July 21, 1922, p. 1, incorrectly states that 8,359 tons of gilsonite were moved over the Uintah Ry. in 1921. According to 85 I.C.C. 563 the gilsonite movement during 1920 was 56,189 tons, and in 1921 it dropped to 9,323 tons.
18. *The Vernal Express,* April 29, 1921, p. 1. For more on this subject, see also *The Vernal Express,* November 30, 1917, p. 1; December 28, 1917, p. 1; May 10, 1918, p. 1; and March 25, 1921, p. 1. The name of the company building the plant near the White River north of Watson is variously reported as Utah Shale & Oil Corporation, Ute Oil Co., and Ute Oil Shale Co., and the cost of the plant was to be variously $100,000 or $800,000.
19. *Ibid.,* November 18, 1921, p. 8.
20. *Ibid.,* January 13, 1922, p. 6.
21. *Ibid.,* August 18, 1922, p. 1. Also, *Ibid.,* April 7, 1922, p. 8; and May 5, 1922, p. 1.
22. *Ibid.,* May 26, 1922, p. 8; June 2, 1922, p. 8; and June 30, 1922, p. 8.
23. *Ibid.,* March 2, 1923, p. 1.
24. *Ibid.,* August 25, 1922, p. 6.
25. *Grand Junction Daily Sentinel,* January 5, 1923, p. 3; and *The Vernal Express,* January 5, 1923, p. 1.
26. *Grand Junction Daily Sentinel,* January 8, 1923, p. 3.
27. Correspondence from Mrs. Beverly G. Whyler of Glenn, California, January 23, 1969, and March 7, 1969; and interview with Mrs. Whyler and Mr. Sam High at Glenn, July 5, 1969.
28. *Grand Junction Daily Sentinel,* December 13, 1923, p. 1; December 14, 1923; and December 17, 1923, p. 1; and *The Vernal Express,* December 21, 1923, p. 1.
29. *The Vernal Express,* September 4, 1925, p. 1. Also, *Ibid.,* December 14, 1923, states that Howell first reported three ribs broken.
30. *Ibid.,* February 22, 1924, p. 1. The Uintah Ry. advertisements in *The Express* carried Major Hood's name through February 8, 1924; in the next issue Sprague's name appeared as General Manager.
31. Frank P. Donovan, Jr., *Mileposts On the Prairie; The Story of the Minneapolis & St. Louis Railway* (New York: Simmons-Boardman Publishing Corp., 1950), p. 188.
32. U.S. Interstate Commerce Commission, *Reports,* Vol. 85, pp. 557-577; and Vol. 96, pp. 653-677.
33. *Ibid.,* Vol. 85, pp. 571-577.
34. *Ibid.,* Vol. 96, pp. 676-677.
35. "Narrow Gauge Railway Sixty-Eight Miles Long Penetrates Basin Rich In Mineral Deposits,"*American Ditcher Scoopings* (published every other month by the American Hoist & Derrick Co., St. Paul, Minnesota) 5, No. 4 (November, 1924), pp. 1, 3-4.
36. U.S. Interstate Commerce Commission, *Reports,* Vol. 96, pp. 661-662.
37. *The Vernal Express,* January 4, 1924, p. 1.
38. *Ibid.,* March 14, 1924, p. 1.
39. *Grand Junction Daily Sentinel,* August 20, 1924, p. 1.
40. *The Vernal Express,* November 7, 1924, p. 8.
41. *Ibid.,* January 23, 1925, p. 1; and U.S. Interstate Commerce Commission, *Reports,* Vol. 141, p. 259.
42. *The Vernal Express,* April 24, 1925, p. 1.
43. *Ibid.,* May 1, 1925, p. 1.
44. *Ibid.,* June 12, 1925, p. 1.
45. *Ibid.,* October 16, 1925, p. 2-1.
46. *Ibid.,* July 24, 1925, p. 1.
47. *Ibid.,* August 13, 1926, p. 1.

CHAPTER VIII
The Articulateds Arrive

1. *The Vernal Express,* March 21, 1924, p. 8.
2. *Ibid,* August 27, 1926, p. 1.
3. "Narrow Gauge Articulated Locomotive for the Uintah Railway," *Baldwin Locomotives,* 5, No. 3 (January, 1927), pp. 47-50.
4. *Ibid.,* p. 50.
5. *Denver Post,* June 13, 1928, p. 19.
6. *The Vernal Express,* February 17, 1928, p. 1.
7. *Ibid.,* September 3, 1926, p. 4; and December 3, 1926, p. 1.
8. *Ibid.,* June 17, 1927, p. 4.
9. *Ibid.,* October 7, 1927, p. 1; and October 14, 1927, p. 1.
10. *Ibid.,* November 25, 1927, p. 1.
11. *Ibid.,* December 2, 1927, p. 1.
12. *Ibid.,* November 25, 1927, p. 1. See also, *Ibid.,* October 3, 1929, p. 1.
13. *Ibid.,* February 21, 1929, p. 3.
14. Donovan, *op. cit.,* pp. 189, 193.
15. *The Vernal Express,* May 23, 1929, p. 1.
16. *Ibid.,* April 25, 1929, p. 3; and May 23, 1929, p. 1.
17. *Ibid.,* June 13, 1929, p. 3.
18. *Ibid.,* May 2, 1929, p. 7; May 30, 1929, p. 1; May 30, 1929, p. 3; June 6, 1929, p. 1; June 20, 1929, p. 1; and June 29, 1929, p. 3.
19. *Ibid.,* October 21, 1937, p. 1.

20. See the table in the Appendix to this Volume, on page 211.
21. *The Vernal Express*, November 27, 1930, p. 8; and December 4, 1930, p. 1.
22. *Ibid.*, April 2, 1931, p. 1; and November 12, 1931. p. 1.
23. *Ibid.*, July 2, 1931, p. 1.
24. *Ibid.*, December 10, 1931, p. 3.
25. Rio Grande Southern R.R., letter dated April 27, 1933 from Supt. Forest White to Mr. F. C. Krauser, Assistant to Receiver, Denver; in collection of the Colorado Railroad Museum at Golden.
26. Ralph D. Ranger, Jr., "Shay: The Folly that was Worth a Fortune," *Trains*, 27, No. 10 (August, 1967), pp. 32-49. See, especially, p. 41 and p. 49.
27. Barber Asphalt Corporation, *Thirty-Sixth Annual Report of Barber Asphalt Corporation, 1938* (Barber, N.J.: By the author, 1939), p. 8.
28. *The Vernal Express*, June 18, 1931, p. 1.
29. *Ibid.*, May 25, 1933, p. 1.
30. *Ibid.*, June 21, 1934, p. 1; and June 28, 1934, p. 1.
31. *Ibid.*, February 24, 1928, p. 1; April 27, 1928, p. 1; and May 4, 1928, p. 1.
32. *Ibid.*, July 4, 1929, p. 1; and January 2, 1930, p. 7.
33. *Ibid.*, March 6, 1930, p. 8; and March 13, 1930, p. 8.
34. *Ibid.*, December 5, 1935, p. 1; December 19, 1935, p.1; January 2, 1936, p. 1; January 23, 1936, p. 1; April 16, 1936, p. 1; and June 4, 1936, p. 6.
35. *Ibid.*, December 17, 1936, p. 3.
36. Barber Asphalt Corporation, *op. cit.*, p. 8.
37. *The Vernal Express*, May 6, 1937, p. 1; May 13, 1937, p. 1; and November 18, 1937, p. 1.
38. *Ibid.*, December 9, 1937, p. 1.

CHAPTER IX
The End of the Line

1. The Uintah Railway Company, *Employees' Time Table No. 26; To take effect Sunday, July 31, 1938, at 12:01 a.m.*
2. "Uintah Railway," *Official Guide*, LXXI, No. 2 (July, 1938), p. 1169.
3. *Rocky Mountain News*, August 27, 1938. Also *Grand Junction Daily Sentinel*, August 28, 1938.
4. U.S. Interstate Commerce Commission, *Reports*, Vol. 233, p. 44.
5. *Ibid.*
6. *Grand Junction Daily Sentinel*, January 13, 1939, p. 1.
7. Statement by William F. Karr, personal interview, July 9, 1965.
8. U.S. Interstate Commerce Commission, *Reports*, Vol. 233, p. 43.
9. *Ibid.*, pp. 43-44.
10. *Craig Empire-Courier*, September 19, 1938.
11. *Grand Junction Daily Sentinel*, December 11, 1938.
12. The Uintah Railway Company, *Employees' Time Table No. 27; To take effect Sunday, December 25, 1938, at 12:01 a.m.* (Reprinted 1959 by the Colorado Railroad Museum, Golden).
13. *Grand Junction Daily Sentinel*, January 12, 1939, p. 1.
14. *Ibid.*, January 13, 1939; and January 12, 1939, p. 11.
15. U.S. Interstate Commerce Commission, *Reports*, Vol. 233, pp. 45-46; and *Grand Junction Daily Sentinel*, January 13, 1939.
16. U.S. Interstate Commerce Commission, *Reports* Vol. 233, p. 46.
17. *Grand Junction Daily Sentinel*, April 14, 1939; and Denver & Rio Grande Western Railroad, Notice to "All Agents," dated May 8, 1939 (in collection of Colorado Railroad Museum, Golden).
18. *Grand Junction Daily Sentinel*, May 17, 1939.
19. *Ibid.*
20. *Ibid.*, June 9, 1939; and June 26, 1939; and The G. & H. Supply Co., *We Offer for Sale This Equipment and Property at a . . . Great Reduction!* (Denver: the author, 1939). The original of this latter item is in the collection of Jackson C. Thode.
21. *Grand Junction Daily Sentinel*, August 1, 1939; and September 10, 1939.
22. *Ibid.*, probably September 21, 1939. (Clipping in collection of Roy Eno, Salem, Ore.).
23. *Denver Post*, February 18, 1940.
24. *Grand Junction Daily Sentinel*, September 8, 1943.

CHAPTER X
Gilsonite Up To Date

1. The material in Chapter X is taken, verbatim to a large extent, from the 1963 and 1969 editions of American Gilsonite Company, *Gilsonite Guidebook* (Salt Lake City: By the author, 1963 and 1969), with the permission of the Company. These editions reflect a couple of significant changes in the operations which have occurred since the early 1960's. The first is in the mining techniques. When hydraulic mining commenced in 1957 the gilsonite was being taken from veins of very brittle ore which was under pressure from the sidewalls, and thus fractured easily. More recently, other ores which are tougher and often in narrower veins have required the development of other mining methods to meet the characteristics of the ore involved. Several jet cutting methods are now in use, each of them employing high pressure water jets in generous quantities to break the gilsonite and carry it to the pump station.

Secondly, a Liquid Petroleum Gas (LPG) plant at the refinery is no longer in use and thus is not mentioned in the 1969 *Gilsonite Guidebook* or in this chapter.

THE UINTAH RAILWAY COMPANY

YEARLY INCOME

Year Ended	Railway Operating Revenues	Railway Operating Expenses	Railway Tax Accruals	Net Railway Operating Income	Interest Charges	Net Income	Dividend Charges
June 30, 1905	$ 21,952	$ 33,546			pymts		
1906	165,569	110,244	$ 1,820	$ 53,504	$55,125	$ −1,621	
1907	239,053	113,826	4,559	125,227		94,698	
1908	229,450	118,644	5,602	86,966		87,534	
1909	243,758	142,096	6,323	71,511		74,604	$166,250
1910	300,547	166,301	8,411	111,808		114,676	
1911	372,909	214,067	15,800	116,021		123,380	61,250
1912	318,608	218,610	20,526	50,122		50,558	61,250
1913	369,911	194,905	22,781	115,076		116,845	
1914	229,762	171,892	14,649	8,236		10,049	
1915	275,012	224,193	13,791	37,011		40,123	
1916	421,588	252,270	13,226	156,090		158,918	
Dec. 31, 1916	407,724	292,374	16,905	98,306		100,829	135,000
1917	494,834	292,737	21,128	180,730		184,394	146,250
1918	452,256	301,650	34,873	115,711		120,264	151,875
1919	493,061	387,456	39,509	65,859	14	69,559	
1920	750,924	610,678	35,659	104,578	945	104,293	
1921	181,190	360,193	29,474	−208,720		−208,055	
1922	381,769	347,288	29,279	5,102	27,012	−21,555	
1923	431,373	390,951	29,420	10,988	15,717	13,869	
1924	436,048	412,513	28,231	−5,153	17,367	−22,623	
1925	453,342	397,571	31,705	23,872	20,922	2,277	
1926	445,267	377,794	30,730	36,688	21,505	14,024	
1927	437,020	404,935	29,311	2,774	21,755	−21,790	
1928	474,334	396,528	24,721	52,829	23,823	28,666	
1929	487,830	408,683	24,266	54,877	22,586	33,083	
1930	346,387	296,796	24,086	25,505	21,451	5,069	
1931	293,711	240,749	23,176	29,786	20,214	10,601	
1932	232,649	189,165	20,622	22,853	18,387	5,149	
1933	239,710	186,092	20,255	33,363	15,739	20,481	
1934	259,965	210,294	23,071	26,598	13,792	16,013	
1935	266,638	189,801	26,876	49,961	11,432	41,018	153,000
1936	232,119	181,528	27,364	23,227	8,889	16,425	
1937	271,195	205,486	34,377	31,332	6,336	27,163	39,375
1938	162,382	149,367	25,436	−12,421	6,322	−15,725	
1939	4,686	37,667	8,173	−41,154	2,307	−43,096	

It becomes apparent, upon examination of the preceding figures, that the "Net railway operating income" shown for the fiscal years 1907 through 1914 is not a true figure for the net *railway* operating income. A bit of sleight of hand seems to have been indulged in by the accountant. Somehow the income and expenses for the operations of The Uintah Toll Road Company were included. The following table, showing the net revenues of both the railway and the stage road operations, helps clear up the confusion as well as showing the persistent losses resulting from the stage road end of the business.

THE UINTAH RAILWAY COMPANY AND THE UINTAH TOLL ROAD COMPANY
YEARLY REVENUES AND EXPENSES

Year Ended	Operating Revenues— Rail Operations	Operating Expenses— Rail Operations	Net Revenue From Rail Operations	Outside Operations— Revenues	Outside Operations— Expenses	Net Revenue— Outside Operations	Total Net Revenue
June 30, 1907	$239,053	$113,826	$125,227			$−30,529	$ 94,698
1908	229,450	118,644	110,806	$ 73,000	$ 91,238	−18,238	92,568
1909	243,758	142,096	101,662	70,356	94,184	−23,828	77,834
1910	300,547	166,301	134,246	87,855	101,822	−14,027	120,219
1911	372,909	214,067	158,842	115,429	142,450	−27,021	131,821
1912	318,608	218,610	99,998	90,091	119,441	−29,350	70,648
1913	369,911	194,905	175,006	70,635	107,784	−37,149	137,857
1914	229,762	171,892	57,870	58,486	93,471	−34,985	22,885

YEARLY RAIL TRANSPORTATION REVENUES

Rail-line Transportation Revenues

Year Ending	Freight	Passenger	Mail	Express	Total
June 30, 1905	$ 21,925	$ 904			$ 22,829
1906	149,312	11,186	$ 1,561	$ 649	162,757
1907	217,291	12,119	3,543	860	233,949
1908	209,036	11,372	3,512	1,065	225,019
1909	225,433	11,644	3,490	1,000	241,626
1910	281,136	12,778	3,493	1,150	298,642
1911	347,000	17,298	3,963	1,607	369,976
1912	293,424	16,385	3,957	2,005	315,880
1913	346,313	15,027	3,963	1,718	367,141
1914	205,693	16,292	4,345	760	227,189
1915	183,787	15,055	8,054	1,107	208,071
1916	314,305	15,392	7,971	1,225	338,949
Dec. 31, 1916	296,150	14,603	7,971	1,360	320,136

The Interstate Commerce Commission did not report freight and passenger revenues for class II railway companies between 1917 and 1935 inclusive.

Dec. 31, 1936	223,232	1,061	3,538	149	227,980
1937	261,881	1,315	3,532	171	266,899
1938	155,989	840	2,948	145	159,922
May 17, 1939	3,006	241	555	63	3,865

1. For the years prior to 1917, discrepancies between the totals of the freight, passenger, mail, and express columns above, and the total revenue from rail transportation, are accounted for by "miscellaneous" passenger revenues, usually "Excess baggage revenue." This discrepancy never amounted to more than $120.

2. This information is provided by the U.S. Interstate Commerce Commission, *Annual Report on the Statistics of Railways in the United States,* for the year indicated.

Roster of Equipment

LOCOMOTIVES

No.	Type	Builder	C/N	Date	Cyls.	Drivers	Engine Weight	Weight on Drivers	Tractive Effort
1	Shay, 37-2	Lima	888	5-1904	10x12	29½	37 tons	---	15,625
2	Shay, 45-2	Lima	939	10-1904	11x12	32	50 tons	---	18,750
3	Shay, 45-2	Lima	1513	4-1905	11x12	32	50 tons	---	18,750
4	Shay, 45-2	Lima	1575	11-1905	11x12	32	50 tons	---	18,750
5	Shay, 45-2	Lima	1674	6-1906	11x12	32	50 tons	---	18,750
6	Shay, 50-2	Lima	3054	2-1920	11x12	32	54 tons	---	21,885
7	Shay, 50-2	Uintah Ry.	---	12-1933	11x12	33	59 tons	---	21,885
10	2-8-0	Baldwin	24271	5-1904	14x18	36	67,100	59,200	13,300
1st 11	2-8-0	Baldwin	5011	3-1880	15x18	36	56,000	---	12,450
2nd 11	2-8-0	Baldwin	36093	2-1911	14x18	36	67,100	59,200	13,300
12	2-8-0	Baldwin	14771	3-1896	16x20	37	70,800	62,500	17,700
20	0-6-2T	Baldwin	25896	6-1905	13x18	34	68,670	60,570	13,700
21	0-6-2T	Baldwin	25953	7-1905	13x18	34	68,670	60,570	13,700
30	2-8-2	Baldwin	36908	9-1911	19x22	40	149,000	120,000	30,300
40	2-8-2	Baldwin	40953	9-1913	17x22	42	119,400	86,400	23,160
50	2-6-6-2T	Baldwin	59261	6-1926	15x22	42	236,300	194,500	42,075
51	2-6-6-2T	Baldwin	60470	4-1928	15x22	42	246,000	202,000	42,075

NOTES ON LOCOMOTIVES

No. 1 Purchased new. Scrapped 6-30-1928.

No. 2 Purchased new. Scrapped in 1934, 1935 or 1936.

No. 3 Purchased new. Scrapped 10-1933.

No. 4 Originally Waldorf Mining & Milling Co. #2, Denver, Colo.; then Argentine Central Ry. Co. #2, Silver Plume, Colo. Purchased by Uintah Ry. in 1910. Scrapped 4-1928.

No. 5 Ex-Argentine Central Ry. Co. #3. Purchased by Uintah Ry. in 1910. Rebuilt in 1930 by the Uintah Ry. with a new boiler (Lima repair order R-24240, Nov., 1929). Scrapped after Uintah Ry. abandonment in 1939.

No. 6 Purchased new. Sold to Feather River Lumber Co. second #3, Delleker, Calif., in May, 1927. Scrapped by Hyman-Michaels Co., San Francisco, in 1938 or 1939.

No. 7 Boiler (#R-14298) from Lima; locomotive assembled at U. Ry. Atchee, Colorado, shops from spare parts. Scrapped after Uintah Ry. abandonment in 1939.

No. 10   Purchased new. Sold to Eureka-Nevada Ry. second #10 in 1927. Scrapped c. 1938.

1st
No. 11   Originally Denver & Rio Grande #55, named Tomichi. Leased to Silverton R.R. on 8-27-1891, returned 11-17-1891. Sold to Uintah Ry. #5 or #55 on 5-23-1904 for $3000, and renumbered 11 soon afterward (date unknown). Scrapped in 1911 prior to the arrival of second #11.

2nd
No. 11   Purchased new. Scrapped in 1927.

No. 12   Originally Florence & Cripple Creek R.R. #10, named Independence. Became Cripple Creek & Colorado Springs R.R. #36 in April, 1915. Sold to Uintah Ry. in 8-1917. Rebuilt with new boiler (Baldwin extra order #5209-1924) by Uintah Ry. Atchee shops in 1924. Sold to Eureka-Nevada Ry. second #12 in 1937, but was not relettered. After the 1938 abandonment of the E.-N. the engine sat derelict at Palisade, Nevada, until after World War II. Sold to Robert F. Caudill and moved to Las Vegas, Nevada, for display at Last Frontier Hotel Museum. Moved again about 1962 to display at "Fort Lucinda" along U.S. Highway #93-466 between Boulder City, Nevada, and Lake Mead. Now lettered Gold Strike Express No. 7-11.

No. 20   Purchased new. Scrapped after Uintah Ry. abandonment in 1939.

No. 21   Purchased new. Scrapped after Uintah Ry. abandonment in 1939.

No. 30   Purchased new. Scrapped in 1939 after Uintah Ry. abandonment.

No. 40   Ex-New York & Bermudez Co.'s R.R., Venezuela (G. & LaB.R.R.) #10, then #20. Acquired by Uintah Ry. in June, 1919. Scrapped after Uintah Ry. abandonment in 1939.

No. 50   Purchased new. Sold by scrappers to Sumpter Valley Ry. #250 in June, 1940. Converted to burn oil, with side tanks removed and tender added. Retired in 1947 and sold to Hyman-Michaels Co. Resold 7-1947 to International Rys. of Central America #250. Engine was derelict at Escuintla, Guatemala, after 1964.

No. 51   Purchased new. Sold by scrappers to Sumpter Valley Ry. #251 in June, 1940. Converted to burn oil, with side tanks removed and tender added. Retired in 1947 and sold to Hyman-Michaels Co. Resold 7-1947 to International Rys. of Central America #251. Retired c. 1963 to supply parts for #250, the engine sat derelict at Escuintla after that date.

No. 55   See first No. 11.

Engines #40, #50 and #51 were superheated, the former while it was on the Uintah Railway; all others on the roster were saturated steamers. Engines #30, #40, #50 and #51 were equipped with Walschaert valve gear, and all the other engines had Stephenson gear.

As is often the case with locomotive rosters, different values for some of the above dimensions are reported by different sources. Usually these differences are pretty small, and result from rebuildings and other changes in the particular locomotive involved. For instance, Uintah Railway records show that Consolidation No. 12 had a total engine weight of 68,000 lbs., weight on drivers of 60,000 lbs. and a tractive effort of 20,584 lbs. after she was rebuilt with the new boiler in 1924. Similar differences, although smaller in magnitude, were noted for Shay No. 5, Consolidation first No. 11 and Mikado No. 30.

Also, in keeping with the usual practice of their builder, class designations are given for the Shays. For example, a Shay of class 37-2 would be a 2-truck Shay with a nominal weight of 37 tons. The actual weight of Shay locomotives seldom corresponded with the class figure, though, and a 50-2 class might weigh anywhere from 45 to 60 tons in operating order, but it was still classed as a 50-2 Shay. This practice caused some confusion, as might be expected, and more than one Uintah Railway roster showed the weight of engines 2, 3 and 5 as 45 tons. Likewise, different figures can be found for the tractive effort of a given Shay. The values given in the roster for engines 1 through 5 are "stock" tractive efforts from Lima catalog #12, and are with "stock" gear ratios. The Uintah's own roster, as of 1931, indicates that Shays 2, 3 and 5 had tractive efforts (after rebuilding) of 19,150 lbs., 20,300 lbs. and 20,300 lbs. respectively.

Credit is due to many sources for helping compile this roster. The starting point was the Uintah Ry. roster which was published in *Locomotive Notes #5* (May, 1963) courtesy of Linwood W. Moody of Brooks, Maine, and compiled by the late H. S. Shafer, Master Mechanic of the Uintah. Other published sources include *Baldwin Locomotives*, V. 2, no. 1 (July, 1923), p. 22, and *Steam in the Rockies: A Steam Locomotive Roster of The Denver Rio Grande*, compiled and published by the Colorado Railroad Museum, Golden, in 1963. Additional data is from Charles E. Fisher, president of The Railway & Locomotive Historical Society; H. L. Goldsmith; Robert C. Gray of Orinda, Calif., Jack M. Holst of Portland, Oregon; Victor Koenigsberg, publisher of *U.S. Steam Locomotive Directory*; Robert A. LeMassena of Denver; P. E. Percy of Lima, Ohio; Gordon S. Ramsey; Ralph D. "Dan" Ranger, Jr. of Vallejo, Calif.; Doug S. Richter; The Uintah Railway "Engine Data" sheets in the collections of the Colorado Railroad Museum and the late E. Victor Earp; and Dr. S. R. Wood of Stillwater, Oklahoma. My thanks to all these men.

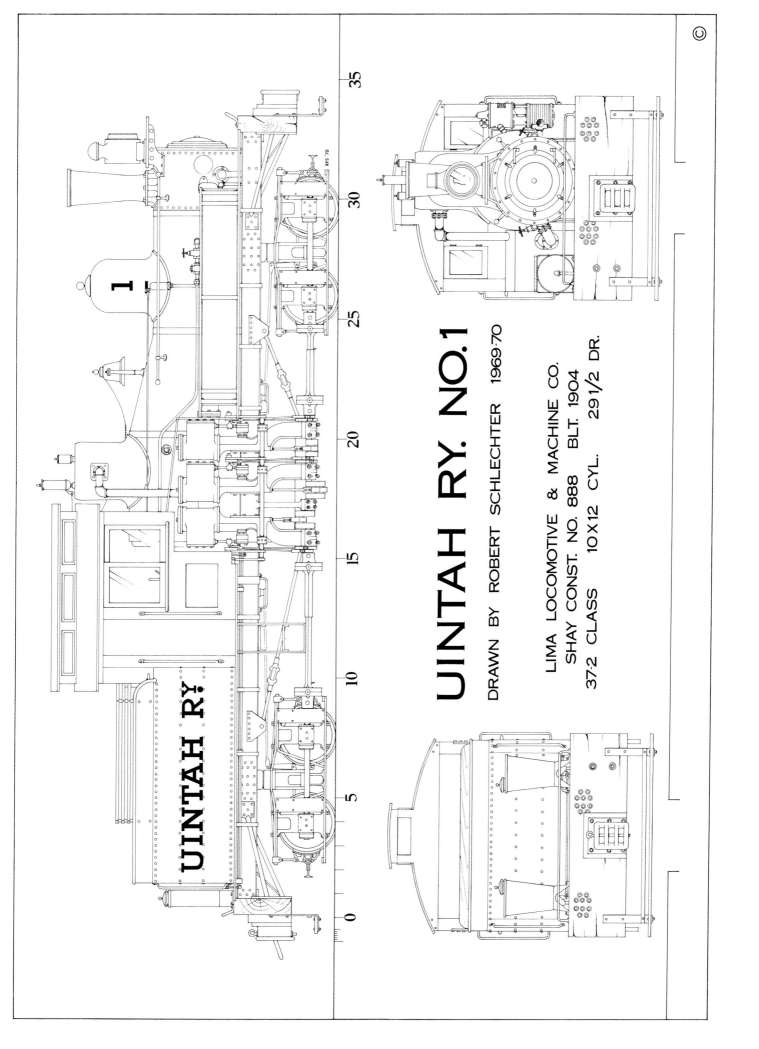

UINTAH RY. NO.1

DRAWN BY ROBERT SCHLECHTER 1969-70

LIMA LOCOMOTIVE & MACHINE CO.

SHAY CONST. NO. 888   BLT. 1904

37-2 CLASS   10X12 CYL.   29 1/2 DR.

UINTAH RY.

1

RFS 70

0   5   10   15   20   25   30   35

©

Five of the Uintah's seven Shays are shown here. Except for the Lima builder's photo of No. 6 (above) they are all at their home base — Atchee, Colorado. In fact Atchee-built No. 7 (below) never ventured more than a few miles from there at any time during her short six-year lifetime. The No. 5 (bottom, opposite page) is pictured with her new boiler. Turn back to page 89 to see what this same Shay looked like with her original boiler. Like No. 5, the No. 4 (left) came from the Argentine Central, and most likely that inexact UINTAH R.R. lettering was applied before she was shipped from Silver Plume to the Uintah. (*Left, upper two photos: Colorado Railroad Museum Collection; left below: L. W. Moody Collection, from E. L. DeGolyer, Jr.; above: Lima Locomotive Works, from P. E. Percy; below: Roy F. Blackburn photo*)

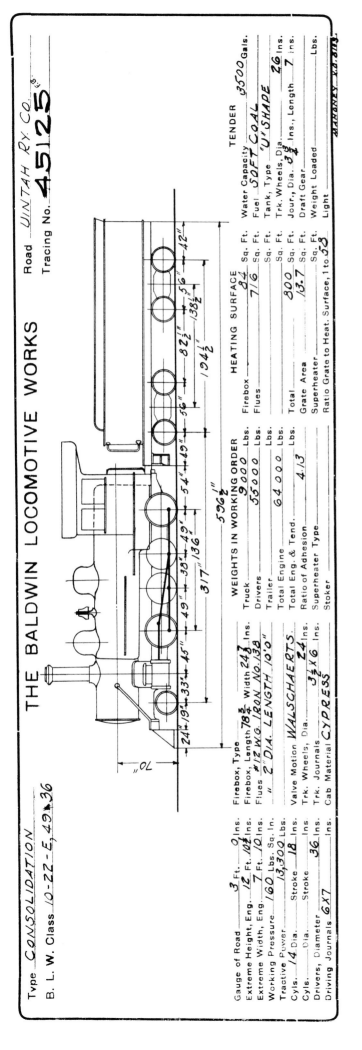

THE BALDWIN LOCOMOTIVE WORKS

Type CONSOLIDATION
B. L. W. Class 10-22-E, 49 36

Road UINTAH RY CO.
Tracing No. 4125

Gauge of Road 3 Ft. 0 Ins.
Extreme Height, Eng. 12 Ft. 10½ Ins.
Extreme Width, Eng. 7 Ft. 10 Ins.
Working Pressure 160 Lbs. Sq. In.
Tractive Power 13,300 Lbs.
Cyls. 14 Dia. Stroke 18 Ins.
Cyls. Dia. Stroke Ins.
Drivers, Diameter 36 Ins.
Driving Journals 6X7 Ins.

Firebox, Type
Firebox, Length 78¾ Width 24¾ Ins.
Flues #12 W.G. IRON No. 138
Flues " 2" DIA. LENGTH 10' 0"
Valve Motion WALSCHAERTS
Trk. Wheels, Dia. 24 Ins.
Trk. Journals 3½ x 6 Ins.
Cab Material CYPRESS

WEIGHTS IN WORKING ORDER
Truck 9000 Lbs.
Drivers 55000 Lbs.
Trailer Lbs.
Total Engine 64000 Lbs.
Total Eng. & Tend. Lbs.
Ratio of Adhesion 4.13
Superheater Type
Stoker

TENDER
Water Capacity 3500 Gals.
Fuel SOFT COAL
Tank, Type "U" SHAPE
Trk. Wheels, Dia. 26 Ins.
Jour., Dia. 3⅞ Ins., Length 7 Ins.
Draft Gear
Weight Loaded Lbs.
Light

HEATING SURFACE
Firebox 84 Sq. Ft.
Flues 716 Sq. Ft.
Sq. Ft.
Total 800 Sq. Ft.
Grate Area 13.7 Sq. Ft.
Superheater Sq. Ft.
Ratio Grate to Heat. Surface, 1 to 53

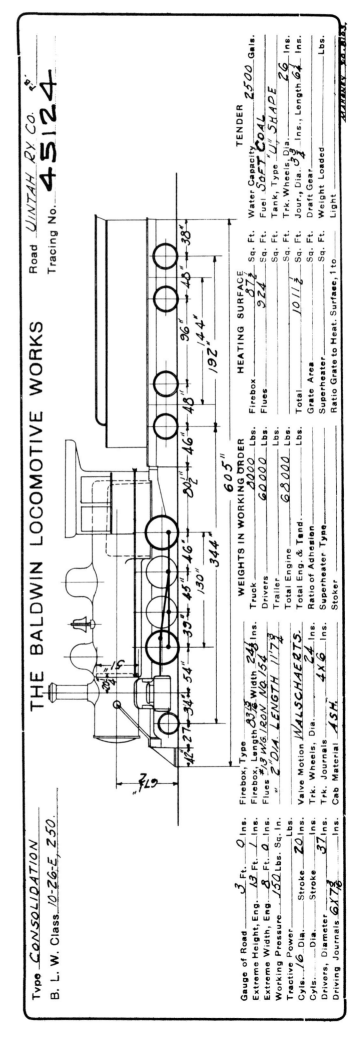

THE BALDWIN LOCOMOTIVE WORKS

Type CONSOLIDATION
B. L. W. Class 10-26-E, 250.

Road UINTAH RY CO.
Tracing No. 4124

Gauge of Road 3 Ft. 0 Ins.
Extreme Height, Eng. 13 Ft. 1 Ins.
Extreme Width, Eng. 8 Ft. 0 Ins.
Working Pressure 150 Lbs. Sq. In.
Tractive Power Lbs.
Cyls. 16 Dia. Stroke 20 Ins.
Cyls. Dia. Stroke Ins.
Drivers, Diameter 37 Ins.
Driving Journals 6X7½ Ins.

Firebox, Type
Firebox, Length 83¾ Width 24¾ Ins.
Flues #13 W.G. IRON No. 154
Flues " 2" DIA. LENGTH 11' 7½"
Valve Motion WALSCHAERTS
Trk. Wheels, Dia. 24 Ins.
Trk. Journals 4 X 6 Ins.
Cab Material A.S.H.

WEIGHTS IN WORKING ORDER
Truck 8000 Lbs.
Drivers 60000 Lbs.
Trailer Lbs.
Total Engine 68000 Lbs.
Total Eng. & Tend. Lbs.
Ratio of Adhesion
Superheater Type
Stoker

TENDER
Water Capacity 2500 Gals.
Fuel SOFT COAL
Tank, Type "U" SHAPE
Trk. Wheels, Dia. 26 Ins.
Jour., Dia. 3¾ Ins., Length 6¼ Ins.
Draft Gear
Weight Loaded
Light

HEATING SURFACE
Firebox 87½ Sq. Ft.
Flues 924 Sq. Ft.
Sq. Ft.
Total 1011½ Sq. Ft.
Grate Area Sq. Ft.
Superheater Sq. Ft.
Ratio Grate to Heat. Surface, 1 to

First No. 11 (top) photographed in front of the newly-built hotel in Mack about 1905 has the characteristic appearance of a D.&R.G. class 56 Consolidation — the Rio Grande headlight, diamond stack and wooden cab with four panels under the windows. Compare this with the photo of the same engine on page 26. The Uintah made a few changes. At the right is No. 12 at Mack just before being shipped to the Eureka-Nevada, and No. 20 at Baldwin ready to be shipped to the Uintah. *(Top: Frank A. Kennedy photo from Denver Public Library Western Collection; center: Gerald M. Best photo, Doug S. Richter Collection; bottom: H. L. Broadbelt Collection)*

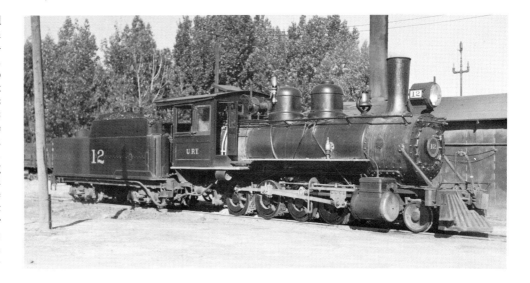

UINTAH RAILWAY No. 10 and second No. 11 (opposite, left). UINTAH RAILWAY No. 12 (opposite, right).

219

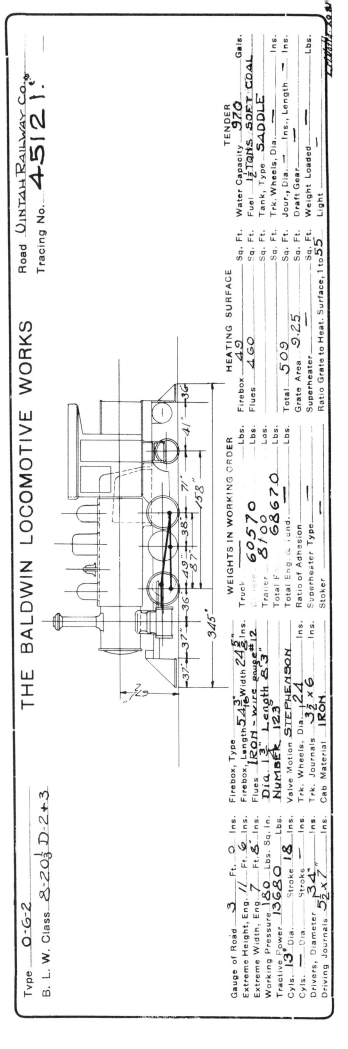

Type 0-6-2

B. L. W. Class 8-20⅓ D-2+3

THE BALDWIN LOCOMOTIVE WORKS

Road UINTAH RAILWAY CO.

Tracing No. 45121

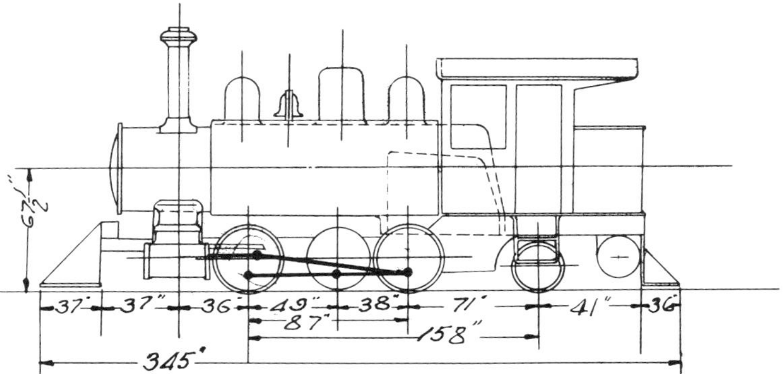

Gauge of Road 3 Ft. 0 Ins.
Extreme Height, Eng. 11 Ft. 6 Ins.
Extreme Width, Eng. 7 Ft. 8" Ins.
Working Pressure 180 Lbs. Sq. In.
Tractive Power 13680 Lbs.
Cyls. 13" Dia. Stroke 18 Ins.
Cyls. — Dia. Stroke — Ins.
Drivers, Diameter 34" Ins.
Driving Journals 5½ x 7" Ins.

Firebox, Type
Firebox, Length 54 3/16 Width 24 5/8 Ins.
Flues IRON - wire gauge #12
Dia. 1¾" Length 8'3"
NUMBER 123
Valve Motion STEPHENSON
Trk. Wheels, Dia. 24 Ins.
Trk. Journals 3½ x 6 Ins.
Cab Material IRON

WEIGHTS IN WORKING ORDER
Truck — Lbs.
Drivers 60570 Lbs.
Trailer 8100 Lbs.
Total Eng. 68670 Lbs.
Total Eng. & Tend. — Lbs.
Ratio of Adhesion
Superheater Type —
Stoker —

HEATING SURFACE
Firebox 49 Sq. Ft.
Flues 460 Sq. Ft.
Sq. Ft.
Sq. Ft.
Total 509 Sq. Ft.
Grate Area 9.25 Sq. Ft.
Superheater — Sq. Ft.
Ratio Grate to Heat. Surface, 1 to 55

TENDER
Water Capacity 970 Gals.
Fuel 1½ TONS SOFT COAL
Tank, Type SADDLE
Trk. Wheels, Dia. — Ins.
Jour., Dia. — Ins., Length — Ins.
Draft Gear —
Weight Loaded — Lbs.
Light —

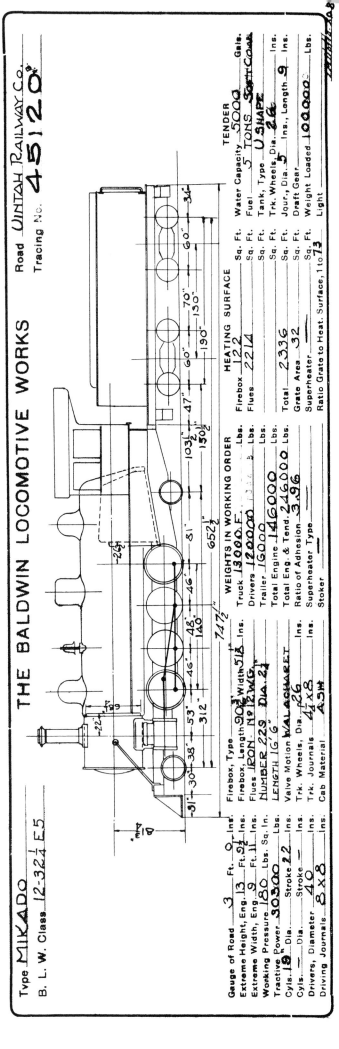

Type MIKADO

B. L. W. Class 12-32¼ E5

THE BALDWIN LOCOMOTIVE WORKS

Road UINTAH RAILWAY CO.

Tracing No. 45120

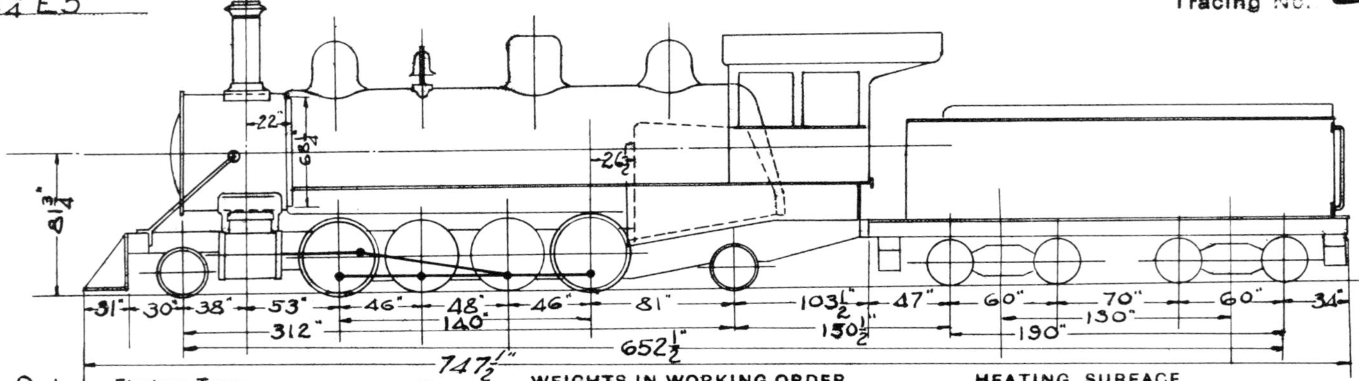

Gauge of Road 3 Ft. 0 Ins.
Extreme Height, Eng. 13 Ft. 9½ Ins.
Extreme Width, Eng. 9 Ft. 11 Ins.
Working Pressure 180 Lbs. Sq. In.
Tractive Power 30300 Lbs.
Cyls. 19" Dia. Stroke 22 Ins.
Cyls. — Dia. Stroke — Ins.
Drivers, Diameter 40 Ins.
Driving Journals 8 x 8 Ins.

Firebox, Type
Firebox, Length 90 3/16 Width 51 1/8 Ins.
Flues IRON No 12 WG.
NUMBER 229 DIA. 2¼"
LENGTH 16'6"
Valve Motion WALSCHAERT
Trk. Wheels, Dia. 26 Ins.
Trk. Journals 4¼ x 8 Ins.
Cab Material ASH

WEIGHTS IN WORKING ORDER
Truck 13000 F. Lbs.
Drivers 120000 Lbs.
Trailer 16000 Lbs.
Total Engine 146000 Lbs.
Total Eng. & Tend. 246000 Lbs.
Ratio of Adhesion 3.96
Superheater Type —
Stoker —

HEATING SURFACE
Firebox 122 Sq. Ft.
Flues 2214 Sq. Ft.
Sq. Ft.
Sq. Ft.
Total 2336 Sq. Ft.
Grate Area 32 Sq. Ft.
Superheater — Sq. Ft.
Ratio Grate to Heat. Surface, 1 to 73

TENDER
Water Capacity 5000 Gals.
Fuel 5 TONS SOFT COAL
Tank, Type U SHAPE
Trk. Wheels, Dia. 26 Ins.
Jour., Dia. 5 Ins., Length 9 Ins.
Draft Gear
Weight Loaded 100000 Lbs.
Light

Ready to leave for Baxter Pass and Dragon, tank engine No. 21 poses with her crew next to the coaling dock and water tank at Atchee on a winter afternoon. Combination car No. 1 behind her would be the mainstay of the Uintah's passenger service from the first to the last. Renumbered 50 in 1924 and then completely rebuilt and sheathed with steel in 1934, the car brought up the rear of the road's last train in 1939. Below, fresh from the erecting floor at Baldwin is Mikado No. 30 — one of the largest narrow-gauge engines in the world at the time. *(Above: Frank A. Kennedy photo from Denver Public Library Western Collection; below: Baldwin Locomotive Works, from H. L. Broadbelt Collection)*

UINTAH RAILWAY No. 20 and No. 21 (opposite, left). UINTAH RAILWAY No. 30 (opposite, right).

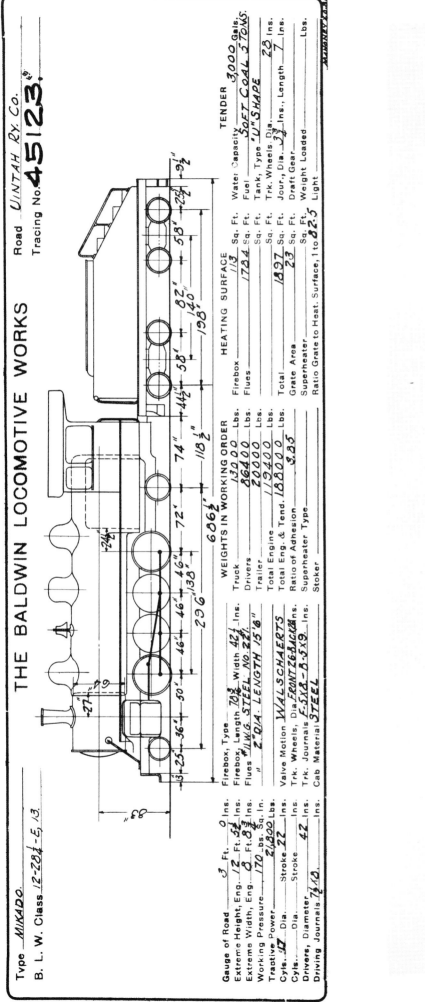

THE BALDWIN LOCOMOTIVE WORKS

Type _MIKADO._

B. L. W. Class _12-28¼-E, 13._

Road _UINTAH RY. CO._

Tracing No. **45123.**

Gauge of Road	_3_	Ft.	_0_	Ins.
Extreme Height, Eng.	_12_	Ft.	_5½_	Ins.
Extreme Width, Eng.	_8_	Ft.	_8⅜_	Ins.
Working Pressure			_170_	Lbs. Sq. In.
Tractive Power			_21,800_	Lbs.
Cyls. _17_ Dia.	Stroke	_22_		Ins.
Cyls. _____ Dia.	Stroke			Ins.
Drivers, Diameter			_42_	Ins.
Driving Journals _7⅛Dia._				Ins.

Firebox, Type		
Firebox, Length _70⅞_ Width _42¼_		Ins.
Flues _#_ _IW.G. STEEL NO. 221_		Ins.
_" _2" DIA. LENGTH 15'6"_		
Valve Motion _WALSCHAERTS_		
Trk. Wheels, Dia._FRONT26BACK28_		Ins.
Trk. Journals _F.5X8-B.5X9_		Ins.
Cab Material _STEEL_		

WEIGHTS IN WORKING ORDER

Truck	_13000_	Lbs.
Drivers	_86400_	Lbs.
Trailer	_20000_	Lbs.
Total Engine	_119400_	Lbs.
Total Eng. & Tend.	_188000_	Lbs.
Ratio of Adhesion	_3.85_	
Superheater Type		
Stoker		

HEATING SURFACE

Firebox	_113_	Sq. Ft.
Flues	_1784_	Sq. Ft.
		Sq. Ft.
		Sq. Ft.
Total	_1897_	Sq. Ft.
Grate Area	_23_	Sq. Ft.
Superheater		Sq. Ft.
Ratio Grate to Heat. Surface, 1 to _82.5_		

TENDER

Water Capacity	_3000_	Gals.
Fuel	_50FT COAL 5TONS._	
Tank, Type	_"U" SHAPE_	
Trk. Wheels, Dia.	_28_	Ins.
Jour., Dia. _3¾_ Ins., Length _7_		Ins.
Draft Gear		
Weight Loaded		Lbs.
Light		

N.Y.B.CO.G.& LA.B.R.R.

4798

Above is the No. 40 at Mack in 1938, and below, articulateds No. 50 and 51 at Baldwin's Eddystone plant when they were new. *(Above: Gerald M. Best photo; two below: H. L. Broadbelt Collection)*

UINTAH RAILWAY No. 40 (opposite page) built as New York & Bermudez Co. No. 10 *(Baldwin photo from E. V. Earp Collection)*

No.	Builder, Description and Remarks

50 Mack Brothers Motor Co., Allentown, Pa., 1905. Construction of this vehicle, the first rail motor car built by Mack, started in Brooklyn, N.Y. sometime during 1903 and was completed at the new Allentown plant early in 1905. It had a short chassis, a longitudinally placed six-cylinder gasoline engine, a four-wheel shaft driven rear propulsion truck. A seating capacity of ten was claimed although photos indicate that nine adults would have been a tight fit. This car was quite successful on the Uintah Ry. and was used extensively by General Manager Cooley and other officials. It was retired between 1921 and 1924.

31 Builder and date built unknown, but apparently built new for the Uintah sometime between 1904 and 1910. This was a steam motor, with a vertical boiler inside the body and gear and chain drive to the wheels. The body had a British or continental look, and had four doors and 11 or 12 windows on the right side alone. The car had 4 wheels, all powered, and pulled a very small 4-wheel trailing car. This vehicle apparently was a total failure, and was then converted into a self-propelled vehicle having another form of motive power (perhaps storage battery, or gasoline motor)

and different running gear. The latter was also unsuccessful and was apparently then converted into a caboose, which was also short-lived. This vehicle may also have been numbered 51, perhaps when it was re-powered.

number unknown (if any)
Buick, 1916 touring car. Rebuilt with flanged wheels for railway use in 1922. Used for about two years thereafter, mostly by the survey crew at first, then retired and destroyed by Master Mechanic Sharp.

52 Ford, Model "T" coupe, apparently of 1922 or later model year. Equipped with flanged wheels and additional tank for circulating radiator water at Atchee shops about 1934. This Model "T" was used mostly by Superintendent E. Victor Earp until the railroad was abandoned in 1939.

Credit for the data on Mack rail car No. 50 belongs to Randolph L. Kulp, editor, *History of Mack Rail Motor Cars and Locomotives* (Allentown, Pa.: Lehigh Valley Chapter, National Railway Historical Society, 1959). Information on the other vehicles is pretty sparse, and what there is comes from photographs and from two Uintah railroaders, Bruce Angus and E. V. Earp.

Mack rail car No. 50 (left) is at Mack. Also sitting next to the depot at Mack is the mysterious No. 31 (top) and at the same place on another day (center) a motor car with the same body but an entirely different running gear. Many years later No. 52 (right) was pictured at practically the same location. *(Left: Gerald M. Best Collection; top: F. A. Kennedy photo from D. H. Gerbaz Collection; center: Denver Public Library Western Collection; right: R. H. Kindig)*

Car Number	Type of car	Seating Capacity	Notes
1	Combination	22	Built for The Uintah Ry. by American Car & Foundry Co., St. Louis, Missouri, in 1904. Dropped from roster between 12-1923 and 4-1924. Apparently rebuilt in 1924 at Atchee into combination car No. 50.
25	Combination	22	Ex-Colorado & Southern Ry. No. 25. Appears on Uintah in 9-1924. (The C&S sold No. 25 on 2-25-1924 to A.T. Herr [Herr-Rubican Supply Co.]). It was a 1905 rebuild of a combine built by Bowers & Dure in 1875 as Denver, South Park & Pacific No. 125. Renumbered as C&S 25 in 1911 and on the Uintah Ry. roster until abandonment in 1939, this carbody was moved to Grand Junction, Colorado where it remained until it suffered fire damage and was scrapped c. 1959.
50	Private Coach	30	Ex-Pullman Co. sleeping car (see note below). Named *Columbine* and listed as Private Coach in the *Equipment Register*. Dropped from roster in early 1921 and used for parts in 1924 to build combination car 50.
50	Combination	22	Rebuilt from underframe of No. 1 and shortened carbody from No. 50 by 9-1924. As rebuilt, this car had both end platforms; the front platform was removed by 1929. In 1934 the car was rebuilt at the Atchee Shops with steel sheathing, new wood interior, etc. Used on the last regular train, 5-16-1939. Carbody sold and remained in the same yard in Grand Junction with bodies of 25 and B-8. All but one berth seating section was removed and sold. Carbody sold in 1979 to the Colorado Railroad Museum in Golden, arriving there 7-19-1979.
51	Coach-Sleeper	40	Ex-Pullman Co. sleeping car (see note). Listed as coach by 1922. Dropped from roster in 1926. This carbody was a home in Atchee until 1939, then a home in Mack, Colorado for at least 30 years. In 1976, Jake Smith bought the property and moved the carbody to a trailer park next to his Colorado Club in Mack. He used it first as a shop, then as a storage shed. In 1990, Mesa State College student Rodger Polley discovered the car and paid Smith $150 for it. In 1992, Polley donated it to the Rio Grande Chapter of the National Railway Historical Society and it was moved on May 6, 1992 to their display at Cross Orchards Living History Farm near Grand Junction.
52	Combination	32	Ex-Pullman Co. sleeping car (see note). Rebuilt to combination car c. 1905, probably by the Uintah Ry. Rebuilt with seating capacity reduced from 32 to 22 in 1921 or early 1922. Dropped from the roster between 8-1923 and 4-1924. Carbody apparently set out at Atchee as a residence until 1939, and presumably scrapped soon thereafter.
B-8	Business Car	22	Built in the early 1870s by D&RG Burnham Shops, Denver, as Denver & Rio Grande baggage car No. 4, later No. 100. Rebuilt as Business Car second K in April 1888. Renumbered B-8 in 1913. Purchased by The Uintah Ry. in 1927, retaining the number B-8. During 1923-25, this was the D&RG's Gunnison Division business car and it had both standard and narrow gauge trucks, which were changed at Montrose so the superintendent could use it between Grand Junction and his headquarters at Gunnison. When the division was abolished in 1925, the car became surplus and was sold to the Uintah within two years. After the Uintah was abandoned, the carbody sat in Grand Junction for 20 years. In 1959 it was purchased by the Colorado Railroad Museum, where it is on display atop trucks from Rio Grande Southern No. 0260.

Note: The last three narrow gauge Pullman sleeping cars used on the Denver & Rio Grande, on their Roster #38 of 10-15-1901, were the *Americano*, *Antonito* and *Toltec*. D&RG's contract with Pullman's Palace Car Company for maintenance and operation of sleeping cars was signed on December 26, 1879. *Americano* and *Toltec* were part of the original seven-car order built by Pullman's Palace Car Company at the Detroit Car Works in 1880 (Lot 76). *Antonito* was part of the next order (Lot 108), five cars received in 1881. All were built to Plan 73A. Fewer of these Pullmans, and 12 built in 1882-83, were needed after the Denver-Ogden line was standard gauged in 1890. During the 1890s they were used on night trains to Alamosa, Creede and Cripple Creek. The last known use of these cars on the D&RG was in the summer of 1902. The D&RG used them at times on standard gauge trucks.

Henry Schlacks was the D&RG's Superintendent of Motive Power & Car Department under President E.T. Jeffrey in 1901. When George Gould gained control of the D&RG that year, he replaced many of its officers with his own men; Schlacks was replaced by 1902. In 1904-06, Schlacks bought at least six unneeded sleeping cars from The Pullman Company (which was renamed Dec. 30, 1899 from Pullman's Palace Car Company) and resold them to three 3-foot-gauge railroads. He bought the *Americano*, *Antonito* and *Toltec* from Pullman in February 1905 and resold them to The Uintah Railway, where they became 50, 51 and 52. Which Pullman became which car on the Uintah is unknown. Evidence in No. 50 indicates that it was slightly different from the original order, and thus it was probably the *Antonito*.

Thanks to Edward Pritchard and Bob Richardson of the Colorado Railroad Museum for much of this passenger car data; to Jackson C. Thode for information on the Pullmans; and to Rodger Polley of Grand Junction for information about car 51, which he saved.

For more information on the 3-foot-gauge Pullman sleeping cars, see Henry E. Bender Jr., "Mahogany Splendor: The Narrow Gauge Pullman Cars," *Narrow Gauge and Short Line Gazette*, March/April 2001, pp. 18-25. Also Jackson C. Thode's *A Century of Passenger Trains: A Study of 100 Years of Passenger Service on the Denver & Rio Grande Railway, Its Heirs, Successors and Assigns* (Denver, Rocky Mountain Railroad Club 1972), pp. 101, 121, 126, 132, and 139. For an 1880 builder's photo of the *Toltec*, see Lucius Beebe and Charles Clegg's *Narrow Gauge in the Rockies* (Howell-North, 1958) p. 45, reprinted by Heimburger House Publishing Company in 1994, or George Hilton's *American Narrow Gauge Railroads* (Stanford University Press, 1990) p. 204.

FREIGHT CARS

FREIGHT EQUIPMENT

The freight cars of this Company are marked "The Uintah Railway", and numbered and classified as follows:

M.C.B. Designation	Kind of Cars Class	Numbers	Dimensions Inside Length ft. in.	Inside Width ft. in.	Inside Height ft. in.	Outside Length ft. in.	Width at Eaves or Platform ft. in.	Height from Rail To Eaves ft. in.	To Top of Platform or Run'g Board ft. in.	To over-all ft. in.	Doors Side Width ft. in.	Side Height ft. in.	End Width ft. in.	End Height ft. in.	Capacity Cubic Feet Level Full	Pounds or Gallons	No.
XM	Box	200 to 203	31 6	7 6	6	32	9	9 8	10 4	12 1	5 6	5 9	1 8	2 4	1417	30000 lb.	4
XM	Box	210 to 223	31	7 6	6	31 6	9	9 6	10 2	12 2	5 6	5 9	1 8	2 4	1395	40000 lb.	14
SM	Stock	400 to 405	31 6	7 6	6	32	9	9 8	10 4	12 1	5 6	5 9	1 8	2 4	1417	30000 lb.	6
SM	Stock	410 to 415	31	7 6	6	31 8	9	9 4	10 2	12 4	5 6	5 9	1 8	2 4	1395	40000 lb.	6
GS	Dump	300 to 320	25 6	7	4	26 6	8 4	6 9	3 5	7 8					714	30000 lb.	21
FM	Flat	100 to 107	32	8		32	8		3 2							30000 lb.	8
FM	Flat	110 to 139	32	8		32	8		3 2							40000 lb.	30
FM	Flat	140 to 172	32	9		32	9		3 2							50000 lb.	33
		Total															122

The Uintah Railway was originally equipped, in 1904 and 1905, with a total of 37 freight cars, built at American Car & Foundry Company's plant in St. Louis, Missouri. These consisted of eight boxcars, numbered 200 to 207; five stock cars, numbered from 400 to 404; twelve drop-bottom gondolas, 300 to 311; and twelve flat cars, numbered 100 to 111.

Between 1910 and 1912 another 42 cars were added, so that by September, 1912, there were 18 box cars, ten stock cars, 24 gondolas and 27 flat cars, for a total of 79. Wrecks, and occasional rebuilding and renumbering of cars, brought a few more changes and by the end of 1919 the roster included 16 box cars, 14 stock cars, 21 gondolas and 28 flats, still totalling 79 cars. Then, beginning in 1920 the railway started building more flat cars at their Atchee shops until, by December, 1921, there were 71 flat cars in service. Thus the 1924 roster above reflects the maximum size of the Uintah's fleet — changes after that date were negligible, with only one box and one stock car disappearing in the next fourteen years (and that box car became a tool car).

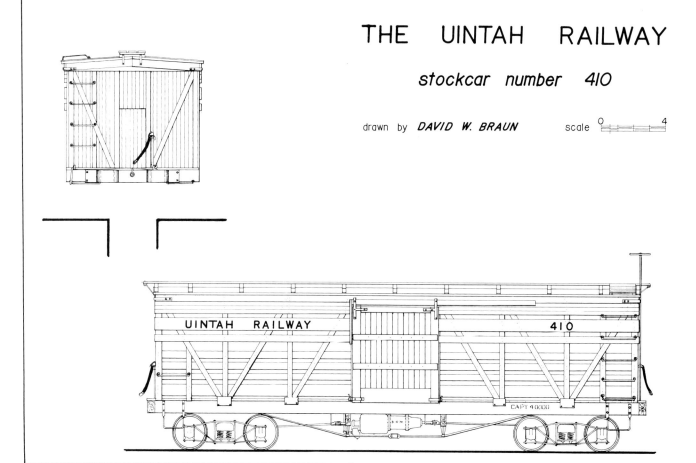

THE UINTAH RAILWAY

stockcar number 410

drawn by **DAVID W. BRAUN**   scale 0 4

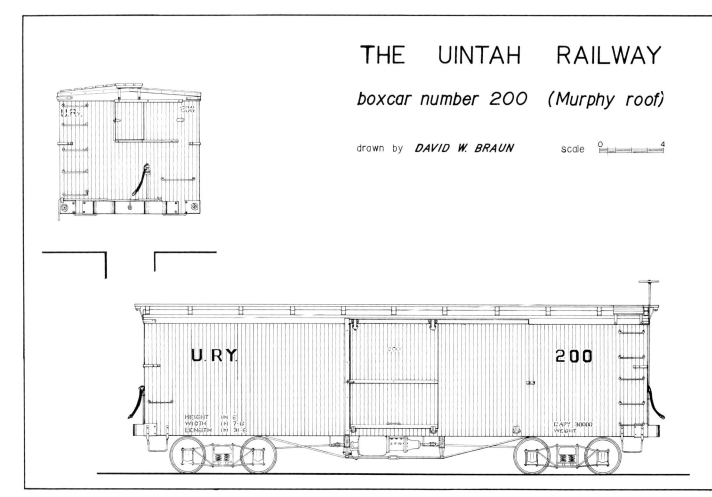

THE UINTAH RAILWAY

boxcar number 200 (Murphy roof)

drawn by **DAVID W. BRAUN**   scale 0 4

Flat cars and boxcars were the most versatile, and most of the Uintah's revenue traffic moved in sacks stacked on flats (top photo). By the time No. 150 was photographed on November 7, 1938, there would be very few more carloads of gilsonite moving from the mines down to Mack. Boxcar No. 212 was photographed a year later during the scrapping of the line. The only unusual feature of the Uintah Railway's freight cars was the buffer and air hose arrangement above the coupler at each end (right). *(Three photos: Roy F. Blackburn)*

229

Type of Cars	Numbers	Remarks
Water Cars	106, 117, 118, 122, 132	These were flat cars mounted with three, or occasionally two, cylindrical wooden water tanks. They were converted back to ordinary flat cars about 1916 when the steel water cars were built.
Water Cars	020 to 024	Rectangular steel water cars built at the Atchee shops in late 1915 or early 1916. Within about two years water car 022 was apparently renumbered 018.
Water Cars	017, 019	Rectangular steel water cars built at Atchee in 1928 or early 1929, bringing the total number of these cars up to 7. In 1939 the G. & H. Supply Co., scrapping the Uintah, offered six of these for sale: numbers 017-021 and 023. The D.&R.G.W. in May, 1940, bought all six, renumbering them (in order) from 0465 to 0470. At least three of these, 0465, 0469 and 0470, were still on the Rio Grande's narrow gauge late in the 1960s.
Cabooses	01 to 03	Photographs show more than two varieties of 4-wheel cabooses on the Uintah. It seems likely that cabooses 01 and 02 were rebuilt, probably more than once. In later years both had cupolas. Caboose No. 03 was an 8-wheel crummy used on the less severe portion of the line south of Atchee. All three were scrapped after abandonment.
Tool Cars	011, 012 (later 001, 011, 0112)	One tool car was added to the roster, and another renumbered, in 1917 or 1918. Then in 1921 the three cars were renumbered B1, B2 and T12. The prefix "B" indicated a car in "Bridge and Building" service, while the T12 was in "Wrecker" service.
Tool Car	B3	Another "Bridge and Building" car, converted from a boxcar in 1928 or early 1929.
Snow Plows	1, 2	Wedge or Bucker plows. One was retired and the other renumbered to K1 in 1921.
Pile Driver	001	Renumbered P1 in 1921.
Ditcher	D1	Purchased new from American Hoist & Derrick Co., St. Paul, Minn., in 1924.

No one ever bothered to take a close-up of one of the old wooden water cars, but they can be spotted in a few photos such as the one of Atchee. *(Frank A. Kennedy photo from V. L. McCoy Collection)*

The center photo shows two of the more modern steel water cars built at the Atchee shops about 1916. Note the hose draining the precious liquid into the pipe at the lower left, for pumping into the tall water tank at Mack. Four-wheel caboose No. 01 at Atchee (right) served as a base of operations for the survey crew when this photo was snapped in 1922. *(Above: L. W. Moody Collection, from Everett L. DeGolyer, Jr.; right: A. T. S. Stoney photo)*

By the late 1930s these were the three cabooses remaining on the Uintah Railway — four-wheelers No. 1 (above) and No. 02 (right) and eight-wheel No. 3 (below). All three were pictured at Atchee on the same August day in 1937. *(Three photos: R. B. Jackson, from Gerald M. Best Collection)*

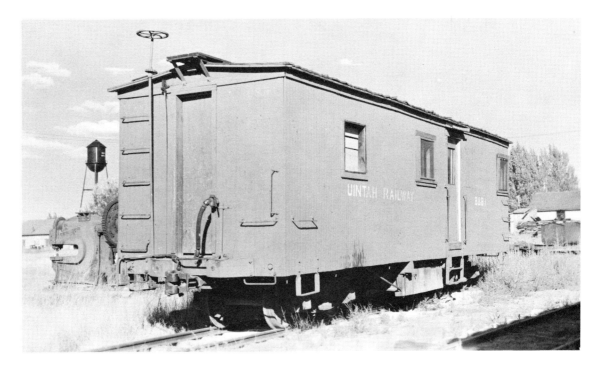

The bridge and building gang car, B&B 1 (above) was rebuilt from an old box-car — a usual source for work cars on many railroads. The wing-type snow spreader at the left was also a modification of one of regular freight cars — gondola No. 320, obviously. But the wedge plow (below) was designed and built entirely by the men at Atchee. Rotary snowplows were never seriously considered for the Uintah because of the extreme sharpness of many curves on the line. *(Top: Gerald M. Best photo; center: L. W. Moody Collection, from E. L. DeGolyer, Jr.; below: Everett L. DeGolyer, Jr. photo)*

The Uintah's American ditcher sat in the weeds at Atchee (top) in August, 1939 — no longer needed. Some of the Gilsonite Route equipment did see further service, though. In the center picture are five of the steel water cars and the tender from Mikado No. 30 atop standard-gauge flat cars at Minturn, Colorado, en route to Salida and the Rio Grande's 3-foot gauge. The date is April 21, 1940. Uintah water cars 017-021 and 023 became D.&R.G.W. 0465-0470, and No. 30's tender became D.&R.G.W. W-499 and was assigned to Rotary **OM** at Chama, New Mexico, in 1962. Rio Grande No. 0469 (below) was at Durango in 1966.(*Top: Everett L. DeGolyer, Jr. photo; center: R. H. Kindig; bottom: Ernest W. Robart*)

Index

237

West Salt Wash, 20†, 24, 33, 35°, 53, 119, 196°
West Tavaputs Plateau, 127
Western Pacific Ry., 43
Western Shale Co., 134
White, Forest, 169
White River, 12, 15, 23, 29, 37, 52†-54, 60°, 61, 67, 81, 93, 95, 109, 111, 133-134, 137, 171, 174, 200°

White River bridge, 59, 109, 111, 171, 174°
White River plateau, 37
White trucks, 163
Whiterocks Indian Agency, 13, 14, 16
Whiterocks, Utah, 11, 12, 52†
Whitney, Oregon, 192
Wilcox Academy, 109
Willow Creek, 15

Wilson, Robert H., 170°
Wilson-Snyder Manufacturing Co., Braddock, Pa., 201
Wimmer, Harvey J., 89
Winder, George C. (laborer), 151
Windy Point, 40°-41°-42†, 47
Woodward, L. H., 14
wool and sheep, 58°, 59, 109, 111, 137, 165, 167, 185
World War I, 123-124, 153

wrecks and accidents, 65, 67, 69, 83, 85, 89, 91, 96, 103, 106°-107, 109, 114°-115, 124, 129, 137, 139-140°, 147, 151
Wyoming, 10†, 15

— Y —
Young, Brigham, 12
Yount, Jessie (conductor), 88°

— Z —
Zellers, Joe, 170°

WESTBOUND / EASTBOUND

elephone Calls	Telegraph Calls	No. 19 Second Class Leave Daily Except Sunday	No. 1 First Class Leave Triweekly Mon., Wed. and Fri.	Miles From Mack	STATIONS AND SIDINGS	Miles From Watson	No. 2 First Class Arrive Triweekly Tues., Thur. and Sat.	No. 20 Second Class Arrive Daily Except Sunday	Car Capacity of Sidings, Location of Water, Fuel and Turning Stations
— —	A		11.30 a	0	MACK D	62.8	3:15 p		45 Y W C
					—4.2—				
			F 11:40	4.2	CLARKTON	58.6	F 2:20		7
					—7.3—				
			F 12:01 p	11.5	SPRAGUE	51.3	F 2:05		20
					—6.0—				
			12:15	17.5	COOLEY	45.3	1:50		10
					—2.6—				
— — — —			F 12:30	20.1	CARBONERA	42.7	F 1:45		24 C
					—8.2—				
— — —		6.01 a	S 1:15 / 1:45	28.3	ATCHEE	34.5	S 1:25 / • 12:55	11.01 a	74 Y W C
					—1.8—				
		6.20	1:55	30.1	MORO CASTLE	32.7	12:30	10.45	
					—2.1—				
		6.40	2:15	32.2	SHALE	30.6	12:20	10.25	10
					—2.0—				
— — —		7.20	S 2:40	34.2	BAXTER PASS	28.6	S 12:05 p	10.01	17 Y
					—1.9—				
		7.35	2:50	36.1	DEER RUN	26.7	11:45	9.30	6
					—1.3—				
		7.45	F 3:00	37.4	COLUMBINE	25.4	F 11:35	9.15	8 W
					—2.5—				
— — —		8.05	F 3:15	39.9	McANDREWS	22.9	F 11:12	8.45	9
					—1.0—				
		8.20 a	S 3:20 / 3:40	40.9	WENDELLA	21.9	S 11:05	8.30 a	22 Y W C
					—1.2—				
			3:42	42.1	SEWALL	20.7	10:45		7
					—4.5—				
			3:55	46.6	EAST VAC	16.2	10:25		9
					—1.4—				
			3:57	48.0	URADO	14.8	10:15		2
					—5.3—				
— — — —	DN		4:20 / 4:40	53.3	DRAGON D	9.5	10:05 / 9:45		36 Y W C
					—1.3—				
			4:42	54.6	COUNTRY BOY	8.2	9:37		7
					—1.1—				
			4:47	55.7	RECTOR	7.1	9.35		7
					—2.9—				
			4:50	58.6	UTE	4.2	9:25		6
					—3.5—				
			5:05	62.1	RAINBOW JUNCTION	0.7	9:17		Y W
					—0.7—				
—	WN		5:30 p	62.8	WATSON D	0	9:15 a		29
		Arrive Daily Except Sunday	Arrive Triweekly Mon., Wed. and Fri.				Leave Triweekly Tues., Thur. and Sat.	Leave Daily Except Sunday	

(*From* THE UINTAH RAILWAY COMPANY, EMPLOYEES' TIME TABLE NO. 25, TO TAKE EFFECT SUNDAY, AUGUST 23, 1931, AT 12:01 A.M., *in D. H. Gerbaz Collection*)

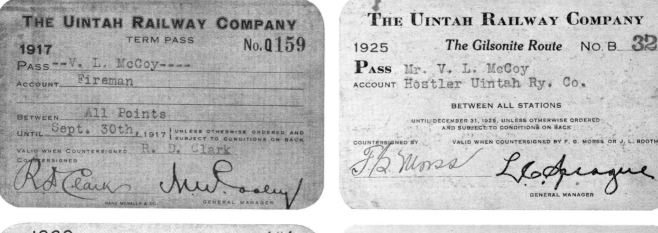

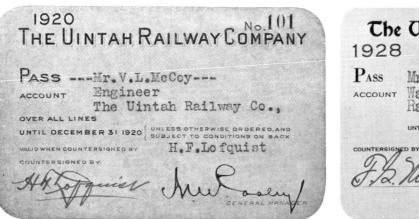

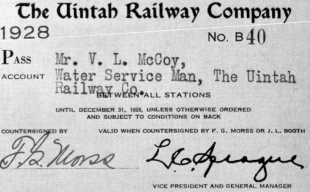

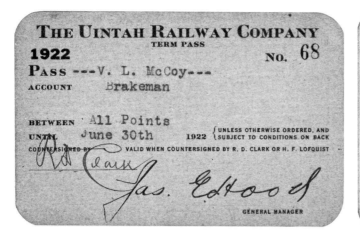

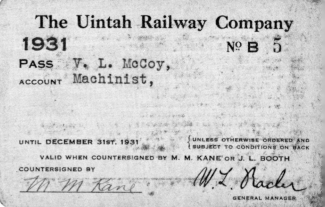

V. L. "Roy" McCoy held a number of positions during his career with the Uintah, as illustrated by these annual passes from his collection.

ADDENDA AND ERRATA FOR
THE UINTAH RAILWAY:
The Gilsonite Route
By Henry Bender Jr.

The following are errors found in *Uintah Railway*, as well as new information:

Page 5: the hyphenated word at the bottom of column 1 should be "substance."

Page 21: insert the superscript numeral 1 at the end of the second paragraph.

Page 31, column 2: delete the last two sentences in the second paragraph. Although The Uintah Railway did purchase the very first Mack rail motor car in 1905 (the one shown on pages 32 and 224), there were two men named John M. Mack. Their companies were not related. John M. Mack, the president of General Asphalt Company and its subsidiaries, the Barber Asphalt Paving Company and The Uintah Railway Company (and others), was a Philadelphia financier active in both the contracting and traction fields. He helped reorganize the original Barber Asphalt empire shortly after its crash in about 1901. He died in 1915 and his obituary was published on page 9 of the *New York Times* of January 27, 1915. It began, "John M. Mack, the contractor and financier and the leading figure in the asphalt war several years ago, died at his home today after a brief illness, in his sixty-third year."

John M. Mack, the motor truck pioneer, was the first president of the Mack Brothers Motor Car Company in 1905. In 1901 he was the head of a small Brooklyn, New York wagon firm established by three brothers, which was incorporated in 1901 and went into motor vehicle repair and construction work by 1902. After Mack Brothers Motor Car Company was sold in 1911 to a financial syndicate, then John M. Mack left to found the Maccarr Company in Allentown, Pennsylvania in 1912. This company soon failed and was reorganized as the Maccar Truck Company, which then moved to Scranton, Pennsylvania where it operated until 1935. John Mack died in 1924 when he drove his Chandler coupe in front of a line car of the Lehigh Valley Transit Company at a grade crossing. His obituary was published in the *Allentown Morning Call* March 15, 1924, on pages 5 and 7. He was 60 when he died.

Page 33, column 2: the 10th line of text, change the word "other" to "near." The saloon was across the tracks but not across West Salt Wash from the main part of Atchee.

Page 61, column 2: delete everything after the superscript number 13 in the second line of text, until the next paragraph. Editor Dan Hillman was not referring to any machine built by the Mack Brothers. He was writing about an Iroquois motor stage, built in or shortly before 1905 by the Iroquois Iron Works of Buffalo, New York. The Iroquois Iron Works is believed to have been a subsidiary of the Barber Asphalt Paving Company, which also had its operating headquarters in Buffalo. The Iroquois company built the machinery necessary for the heating and spreading of asphalt and also apparently built a few automobiles and self-propelled rail cars. An article titled "Iroquois Motor Stages" in the *Cycle and Automobile Trade Journal*, Volume 10, No.7 (January 1, 1906) includes two photographs. One of these, captioned "The Iroquois Bus in Utah and the stage which it has supplanted," is the same photograph published in a booklet that The Uintah Railway published about 1905.

The following is quoted from that January 1, 1906 *Cycle and Automobile Trade Journal*, pages 219 and 220:

The Iroquois Iron Works, 178 Walden Ave., Buffalo, N.Y., have completed a 60 hp stage, which they have put through the hardest and most exacting of road tests. The company has endeavored to design a wagon that would meet the transportation problem from one town to another in districts where electric railroads are impractical and for hotels and resort places for sight-seeing parties, etc. The one aim being to build the machine good enough to travel over any kind of roads and with power enough to go anywhere that four horses would pull a wagon. Their first car was shipped to Utah, where it was tested out and taken over roads that were almost impassable for horses and wagon. This car was run over the Price trail between Vernal and Fort Du Chesne [sic], Utah, a distance of 28 miles, through the canyons, over the mountains and across the desert. The car was in charge of Mr. W.G. King, Gen'l Mgr. of the Iroquois Iron Works, and a party of six others. They carried an extra 50 gallon tank of gasoline, and had a surveyor's level and barometer along, and all grades were accurately computed. This trail is about 6,000 feet above sea level. In many places grades exceeded 22%, and for five miles in one stretch sand nine inches deep was encountered, and in other places ruts were so deep that the front axle dragged the ground. On arrival at Fort Du Chesne, the Quartermaster Sergeant could not believe that the car had come safely over the Price trail as he said he never brought an army wagon over without something being broken. The only thing that went wrong on the car after being subjected to as hard a test as ever given a motor car, was that the right hand front mud guard was broken. This wagon is now in operation daily between Dragon and Bonanza, Utah, a distance of 24 miles, and makes the trip in two hours. It formerly required four hours to make the trip with a four horse stage which the motor bus has now supplanted. This car when geared for passenger work has a speed of 18 miles per hour on direct drive, and will seat 15 people comfortably. The cushions are very deep and have springs placed very close together and the car rides very comfortably, almost as easy in fact as when pneumatic tires are used. The Iroquois Iron Works invites correspondence from parties interested in this type of vehicle.

Page 62: delete "The year is 1906" from the caption. The photo of the "Manhattan" omnibus was most likely taken around 1910. It was taken before October, 1911 when The Uintah Railway was extended to Watson. (Note on page 91 that a new 12-passenger Mack auto arrived in December, 1910.) The "Manhattan" was one of four used by The Uintah Railway. A retouched photo of one, named *Wahnagh* and lettered with The Uintah Railway Company and the Mack names, was published in 1913 in a bus catalog by International Motor Company. The photo is captioned "Mack 'Western Greyhound' Combination Mail and Passenger Stage."

Thanks to Mack truck historian John B. Montville for his research correcting pages 31, 61 and 62 of *Uintah Railway*.

Page 64: "know" should be "known."

Pages 72, 92, 112, 126 and 178: the photos taken by D&RG company photographer George Beam were quite likely taken the week of August 12-16, 1912 when Beam toured The Uintah Railway and the Uintah Basin with F.A. Wadleigh of the D&RG. They were escorted by Capt. Cooley as far as Watson, and by W.D. Halpin while driving through the Basin. Thanks to Jackson C. Thode for this added information.

Page 90: add to the caption of the center photo that it shows Shay No. 7 climbing the 7.5% grade above Shale approaching the top of Baxter Pass on May 9, 1939 one week before the Uintah ran its last scheduled train. The top photo on page 90 shows, behind the two engines, the ex-Colorado & Southern combination car No. 25, which the Uintah purchased in 1924.

Page 106: "the morning after" should be "the next afternoon." An interesting sidelight about the wreck of Consolidation No. 10 at Bridge 2A (described on pages 103, 106 and 107 of *Uintah Railway*) has been published in a book titled *The Rocks Begin to Speak* by LaVan Martineau (Las Vegas, Nevada: KC Publications, 1973). Its author found an account of the wreck chiseled in rock on the old Uintah and Ouray Ute Reservation, in the pictographic language known to many tribes. Martineau shows a photograph of the rock writing and gives his translation of it in considerable detail. The writing, he says, is unique in that it records an incident in the history of white men and not the Ute tribe of which the unknown author was a member. He also shows a previously unpublished photo of the wreck itself and refers to *Uintah Railway* to substantiate his translation.

Page 136: the upper left corner of the photo at the top is missing; what appears to be sky in that photo isn't sky.

Page 149: in the first paragraph, correct the chief engineer's name to A.O. Ridgway. His full name was Arthur Osbourne Ridgway. Make the same correction in the index, page 238.

Page 199-204: Chapter 10, "Gilsonite Up To Date," was out of date within four years after *Uintah Railway* was first published in 1970. Chapter 10 is from the American Gilsonite Company's *Gilsonite Guidebook*, written by Paul S. Rattle, now retired from American Gilsonite; he lives in Grand Junction.

By the early 1970s, producing petroleum products from Gilsonite became uneconomical. In 1974, American Gilsonite Company sold the refinery and pipeline when it became clear that Gilsonite was more valuable for other uses than as a refinery feedstock. The refinery was converted to refine crude oil and the pipeline was sold to Texaco for carrying crude from the Rangely Oil Field. Both are now idle (October, 1995). The refinery was resold two or three times and then went into default, owing Mesa County $1 to $1.5 million in back taxes. The refinery equipment is being sold off.

Gilsonite is used in more than 160 products, primarily printing inks, paints and protective coatings, oil well drilling muds and cements, asphalt modifiers for road paving, foundry sand additives, and building materials. Gilsonite inks for high-speed newspaper and magazine presses have low rub-off. In asphaltic paints and varnishes, Gilsonite enhances hardness, gloss, weather and chemical resistance. Addition of Gilsonite to oil-well drilling fluids helps minimize hole washout by stabilizing shales and sealing off highly permeable sands while reducing torque and drag. The first asphalt roofing shingles and floor tiles contained Gilsonite and were so good that they established those products' market positions.

An American Gilsonite Company mine can produce as much as 25 to 30 tons of Gilsonite per shift with a two-person mining team. Shafts are sunk along the Gilsonite vein, 1,000 feet apart. A headframe sits atop each shaft, supporting the man-cage that carries miners down the shaft and the pipe that carries the Gilsonite up. Drifts are cut horizontally from the shaft, and mining starts on either side. Miners work on 45-degree slopes using hand-held air-driven chipping hammers. The broken pieces fall to the bottom of the slope, where a vacuum system sucks the Gilsonite in a 14-inch diameter air-lift pipe up to the surface and into elevated bins for truck loading. Gilsonite is mined by hand to minimize contamination from the surrounding rock. Careful hand-mining eliminates the need for more expensive processing later.

Commercial quantities of Gilsonite are found only in the Uintah Basin. Vertical veins range up to 1,500 feet in depth, from a few inches to 22 feet wide, and up to 12 miles long. Mining is now down to the 1,100- and 1,200-foot levels on the Bonanza vein, where it is six feet wide. ACG also mines other veins in the area.

Trucks haul the Gilsonite the short distance to Bonanza, Utah (about 47 miles southeast of Vernal), where American Gilsonite Company invested $8 million in an automated processing plant with a capacity of 120,000 tons per year. Here the Gilsonite is sorted by grade, dried, screened to classify it by particle size, stored in silos, and packaged as needed for customers. Some of it is fed to a pulverizer. Some grades are compounded with other materials for specific customers. It is loaded in bulk into containers or bagged in one-ton bulk bags or in 50-pound and 25-kilogram triple-walled paper and plastic bags—all color-coded according to Gilsonite grade.

American Gilsonite Company is the largest exporter, by volume, of container shipments from the state of Utah and one of the largest exporters of ocean-going containers from West Coast ports. Over half of its Gilsonite is sold to foreign markets through an extensive foreign distributor network. Nevertheless, the business is smaller today than it was in 1970. The company had about 75 employees in 1995, down from 250 to 175 in the 1960s. Production of Gilsonite then was approximately 400,000 tons going to the refinery, plus 110,000 tons to the base business. In 1994 and 1995, production totaled approximately 40,000 tons per year.

The Gilsonite Manufacturing Company was formed in 1888 by Samuel H. Gilson and a partner to acquire as many gilsonite claims as possible and to market the varnish Gilson had invented. A successor firm (see *Uintah Railway*, pp. 17-19) later became part of Barber Asphalt Paving Company, which became Barber Oil Corporation. In 1946, American Gilsonite Company was formed when Standard Oil Company of California (Chevron) joined Barber Oil as joint owner. In 1981, Standard's successor, Chevron Corporation, purchased Barber Oil Company's remaining 50% interest and became the sole owner of AGC. In 1983, AGC became an operating division of Chevron Resources Company, a division of Chevron Industries, Inc. Based in San Ramon, California, Chevron Resources explores for and develops minerals and nonpetroleum energy sources worldwide.

In 1991, AGC was acquired by Stratford Enterprises Company. The companies were then merged and operate under the name American Gilsonite Company.
(This information is from Roy E. Nelson, Chairman and CEO of American Gilsonite Company, interviewed October 9, 1995 in his Salt Lake City office, and from the firm's eight-page brochure, *Gilsonite*, printed circa 1991. Gilsonite, with a capital G, is a registered trademark of American Gilsonite Company.)

Page 213: in the notes for Shay No. 4, change "then Argentine Central" to "for Argentine Central."

Page 213: Shay No. 6 was owned by the Feather River Lumber Co. until 3-1945 when it was sold to scrap dealer Hyman-Michaels, according to Michael Koch, *The Shay Locomotive*, page 452.

Page 214: in the notes for No. 10, change "scrapped c. 1938" to "scrapped in 1938."

Page 214: add that No. 12, after sitting derelict at Palisade, Nevada, was moved in 1947 to a field three miles west of Elko, Nevada by a man

who planned to build a tourist railroad there. Nothing ever came of these plans and, in due time, the engine was sold to Robert F. Caudill and moved to Las Vegas, Nevada.

Page 221: delete the information about passenger car No. 1 being renumbered and lasting until 1939.

Page 224: the Mack rail car apparently was retired in 1924; at least the listing for it vanished from *The Official Railway Equipment Register* between April and September, 1924.

Page 224: rail car No. 52 was originally a Ford Model T Roadster, not a coupe. The same correction is needed to the caption on page 173.

Pages 224 and 225: that mysterious rail car with all the windows is still a mystery. However, examining the pictures, it appears that its original configuration is the one in the center photo on page 225. The top photo, then, shows it after it was rebuilt into a steam motor—with a vertical boiler inside and a smokestack and small whistle above the roof. The original car had a number ending in 0. The steam motor was Number 31. It seems likely that this car was built (and perhaps rebuilt?) by the Iroquois Iron Works of Buffalo (the same firm that built the motor stage that the Uintah tested in 1905). An Iroquois advertisement in *Cycle and Automobile Trade Journal* of January 1, 1906, says. "We manufacture also automobiles for railroad use, built along the lines of locomotives for construction and strength with capacity for from 30 to 50 passengers."

Page 224: add motor car Number 51 with seating capacity of 8 which appears in a 1912 listing in *The Official Railway Equipment Register*. Nothing else is known about this car except that it was gone from the *Register* by April, 1917.

A half century after The Uintah Railway was torn up, the Rio Grande Chapter of the National Railway Historical Society located and acquired six Uintah cars, and displays them at Cross Orchards Living History Farm, 3073 F Road, Grand Junction, Colorado, along with a wooden pile trestle that once spanned Whiskey Creek between Wendella and Dragon, Utah. They have restored box cars 200 and 221, stock car 412, and bridge and building workcar B&B #1. In May, 1992, passenger car 51 was moved from Mack to join the display. Caboose 3 is there, too, being restored during 2000-2003. Business car B-8 and steel-sheathed combination car 50 are at the Colorado Railroad Museum in Golden. Scale drawings by Gary Caviglia of Uintah Railway locomotives and cars are published in the following issues of *Narrow Gauge and Short Line Gazette*:

Uintah Ry. Mack rail motor car 50, July/August 1990 p. 71.
Uintah Ry. 4-wheel cabooses, Nov./Dec. 1993, pp. 24-25.
Uintah Ry. 0-6-2T 20 and 21, March/April 1994, pp. 60-61.
Uintah Ry. passenger cars 1, 50, 51 and 52, May/June 1994, pp. 46-47.
Uintah Ry. 8-wheel caboose 3, July/August 1994, p. 25.

A scale drawing by Rodger Polley of Uintah Railway 2-8-2 No. 40 was published in *Narrow Gauge and Short Line Gazette*, Jan./Feb. 1992, p. 35. The Jan./Feb. 1990 *Gazette*, in "Along the Uintah" by Charlie Getz (pp. 20-22) cites other articles about The Uintah Railway.

Add one more car to The Uintah Railway roster. On June 13, 1995, the body of a caboose and passenger car Number 01, previously unknown to me, was trucked from a farm at 999 Road 25 near Grand Junction to the Cross Orchards Living History Farm. It had apparently been at 999 Road 25 since the Uintah was torn up in 1939. It was used since 1990 by Estra Reasoner to store feed for her chicken and goats. The Reasoners had lived there 42 years.

The car was built at an unknown date, probably at Atchee, from a flat car. The stake pockets still show near the bottom of the siding. It is box car-shaped, with a short platform and end door on one end. A Cross Orchards volunteer carman said it was built for use on the north end of The Uintah Railway, north of Wendella, where it accommodated occasional passengers. Quite likely it was built in 1911 when The Uintah Railway extended its track to Watson and Rainbow, perhaps to carry miners from their homes in Dragon to the new mines at Rainbow. The car has benches lengthwise along the inside walls, and the number "01" nailed above the end door. ("Rare caboose added to railway exhibit" by Patrick Cleary, *Grand Junction Daily Sentinel*, June 14, 1995.)

For an essay that ranks the Uintah as the world's second crookedest railroad, see Ted Wurm, "'Crookedest Railroad in the World'—Who Says So" in *Railroad History* 160 (Spring 1989), pp. 22-49.